COMING ON STRONG

COMING
ON
STRONG

Gay politics and culture

edited by

SIMON SHEPHERD & MICK WALLIS

London
UNWIN HYMAN
BOSTON   SYDNEY   WELLINGTON

Published by the Academic divison of
Unwin Hyman Ltd
15/17 Broadwick Street, London W1V 1FP, UK

Unwin Hyman Inc.,
8 Winchester Place, Winchester, Mass. 01890, USA

Allen & Unwin (Australia) Ltd,
8 Napier Street, North Sydney, NSW 2060, Australia

Allen & Unwin (New Zealand) Ltd in association with the
Port Nicholson Press Ltd,
Compusales Building, 75 Ghuznee Street, Wellington 1, New Zealand

First published in 1989

British Library Cataloguing in Publication Data

Coming on strong: gay politics and culture
1. Male homosexuality
I. Shepherd, Simon. II. Wallis, Mick.
306.7'662

ISBN 0-04-445351-5
0-04-445352-3 pbk

Library of Congress Cataloging in Publication Data

Coming on strong / edited by Simon Shepherd and Mick Wallis.
    p.   cm
Bibliography: p.
Includes index.
ISBN 0-04-445351-5 – ISBN 0-04-445352-3 (pbk.)
1. Homosexuality – Political aspects – Great Britain.
2. Gays – Great Britain – Social conditions.
3. Gay liberation movement – Great Britain.
I. Shepherd, Simon. II. Wallis, Mick.
HQ76.3.G7C66   1989
306.76'62'0941–dc20   89-5756
                                                          CIP

Typeset in 11 on 13 point Sabon by Computape (Pickering) Ltd,
and printed in Great Britain by Billing and Sons,
London and Worcester

Contents

Biographical Notes

Joseph Bristow studied at the Universities of London, Stirling and Southampton. He currently teaches English at Sheffield City Polytechnic where he is also a member of the Centre for Popular Culture. His publications include *The Victorian Poet: Poetics and Persona* (Croom Helm, 1987) and *Empire Boys: Adventures in a Man's World* (in preparation), as well as articles on Victorian poetry, Oscar Wilde and homosexuality. He is a volunteer on the Sheffield AIDS Education Project.

Richard Dyer lectures in Film Studies at the University of Warwick. He edited *Gays and Film* (BFI, 1977) and is the author of *Stars* (BFI, 1979) and *Heavenly Bodies* (Macmillan, 1987). He has nearly finished a book on films by, for and about lesbians and gay men.

Sue Ellis is a postgraduate research student at University College, Swansea, and is co-ordinator and co-founder of Principal Parts.

Mark Finch co-programmed Channel 4's first lesbian and gay cinema season, *In the Pink*, and has written on film for *City Limits, Gay Times, Screen* and *Square Peg*, as well as for the second edition of Richard Dyer's *Gays and Film* (New York: Zoetrope, 1985). He now works with the Programming Unit of the British Film Institute.

John Fletcher teaches at Warwick University. He has edited a special issue of *Screen* on 'Melodrama and Transgression' (1988), and contributed an essay on 'Poetry, gender and primal fantasy' to *Formations of Fantasy* (Methuen, 1986). He is co-editing a collection of essays on Julia Kristeva, due out late 1989.

Jamie Gough has been active in the gay movement and the socialist movement since the early 1970s. He has lectured in Town Planning, worked as an economist at the GLC, and is now carrying out research on local economies. With Mike MacNair he is co-author of *Gay Liberation in the Eighties* (Pluto Press, 1985).

Sunil Gupta is an 'independent' photographer, writer and occasional lecturer. He is a Canadian citizen, born in India, now living in London. A graduate of the Royal College of Art, he has been a member of the Photography Advisory Group of the Arts Council since 1986.

Paul Heritage is a lecturer in Drama at the University of Manchester and is co-founder of Principal Parts.

Andrew Lumsden, b. 1941. National newspaperman 1963–72 (*Daily Telegraph, The Times*) specializing in business and finance. Specialist writer on Pacific Rim economies 1974–7. Co-founder *Gay News* 1971, editor *Gay News*, 1982–3. Commissioning editor *New Statesman* 1984–7. Co-author with Gillian E. Hanscombe of *Title Fight*, an account of *Gay News*'s last years (Brilliance Books, 1983).

Mike Macnair lectures in Law at the University of Leeds and is co-author, with Jamie Gough, of *Gay Liberation in the Eighties* (Pluto Press, 1985).

Bill Marshall was born in Newcastle in 1957. He is currently lecturer in French at Southampton University. He has published on various aspects of culture and politics in France in the twentieth century, and has been active in gay student groups and switchboards.

Les Moran lectures in Law at Liverpool Polytechnic. He is a member of the Critical Legal Conference.

Ben Perks left care at 16 (1985) and became development officer for NAYPIC. At 17 he became the youngest person ever to serve on a local authority, Lambeth, in December 1985. In July 1986 he began writing a book on his own life in care with Jill Preece, former editor of *Woman* magazine; also helped various media projects, for example, *Forty Minutes* on child prostitution. In December 1986 he set up a parliamentary monitoring/media consultancy business, trying to create a positive image of young people in media and trades unions as well as Parliament. He has no formal qualifications and was expelled from several schools. He was 18 when he wrote this essay.

Tom Robinson became known as an out-gay singer-songwriter with the Tom Robinson Band's successes from 1977 onwards. After that he worked briefly with Sector 27, before developing a solo career as composer and cabaret performer as well as singer-songwriter.

Terry Sanderson is media correspondent for *Gay Times* and is author of *How to be a Happy Homosexual – a guide for gay men* (The Other Way Press, 1986). He has been active in gay politics for fifteen years and lives in London.

Simon Watney was until recently senior lecturer in Communications at the Polytechnic of Central London. He is currently working on the Teaching About AIDS project at Bristol Polytechnic. He has lectured and written widely on the subject of AIDS in Britain and the United States, and is chair of the Policy Group of the Terrence Higgins Trust. He is the author of *Policing Desire: Pornography, AIDS and the Media* (Methuen, 1987).

Simon Shepherd and **Mick Wallis** have been living together for fifteen years and have sex when and where they can get it. They are ordinary rate-payers. They do not pretend to a family relationship, though many of their friends and relations (and their children) tend to regard them as having one.

Acknowledgements

For their advice, comments and conversations at so many different stages, the editors would like to thank Jonathan Dollimore, Elaine Hobby, John Lucas, Alan Sinfield, Christine White.

Introduction

This is a book that the commissioning publisher didn't dare to print.

We had best begin by telling the story of the book's origins, for that story will indicate something of the politics and paranoia surrounding gays in Britain in the 1980s.

The MUP story

In 1985 we were asked by a commissioning editor at Manchester University Press to write a book on gay issues. The book was to be political rather than academic; indeed we had been asked to do it because we tended to be involved in gay political activism rather than gay academic research. Such a book, we felt, would have to involve and represent more people than ourselves: an initial range of topics was drawn up through discussions within a short-lived (but jolly) gay theory group, called Queory. That list of contents was then further developed through discussion with our commissioning editor. The overall view of the book was that it should be up-to-the-moment and polemical in tone.

Keeping in close contact with our editor in the ensuing months, we wrote a formal proposal for the book in summer 1987. This proposal was sent by the Press to three referees, all of whom made suggestions and all of whom recommended the project go ahead. This 'package' was then put to the editorial board of MUP in June 1987. It was discussed and approved. We delivered the first draft of the typescript early in 1988.

This first draft was sent out to two referees (two of those who had seen the original proposal). They both recommended publication of the book; one of them had serious reservations about two of the essays and his suggestions were incorporated in some of the major re-working that went into the final draft. It was proposed at this stage to put the book into MUP's 'Cultural Politics' series, which had been invented in the months since our book was first thought of. This meant that the series editors both read the book and both recommended publication. So when the final draft was delivered in April 1988, publication had been recommended by four academic referees, all appointed by the Press.

Later in April, we were told that there might be some problem in getting the editorial board of the Press to approve the book. There had already been talk of fears about Section 28 of the Local Government Act. We attempted to allay these fears by pointing out to the Chief Executive and the Editorial Board that Section 28 did not affect universities or publishing houses. Despite this, talk about Section 28 persisted. The editorial board of the Press decided to call in yet another 'referee'.

A third 'reader's report', together with reports from inside MUP, suggested that the book was not sufficiently academic, and that it had been badly edited. Worries were expressed about what the tabloid press would say if it learned that a university press was publishing this book, worries that the book addressed a committed and left-wing audience. The academic grounds which were listed as barriers to publication were that the 'level' was uneven, that it had a 'narrow focus' and that it had been written 'for a particular kind of gay audience'. It is interesting, however, that the Cultural Politics series specifically aimed to reach beyond narrowly defined 'academic' writing, to *perform* 'cultural politics' by giving a voice to different sorts of experience and language. Although we refuted most of these academic objections – to the satisfaction of the series editors – MUP continued to repeat them; and, despite being asked, they never offered any explanation of why the original readers' reports were rejected.

In response to what they saw as the politically-motivated refusal to publish, the Cultural Politics series editors resigned from their positions. At about this time the story went public: five publishers expressed interest in the book (one, indeed, finding it too 'academic'), and within a week we had agreed terms with its current publisher.

On being a non-academic book

Our view, and that of many other people, is that MUP's rejection of this book was based on political rather than academic grounds. But let's now take seriously their 'academic' reasons and analyse them more closely. They claimed, in brief, that the book was some sort of homosexual conspiracy, that it had a limited range of topics which sought only to address a gay male audience; that it was too whingeing or polemical in tone. These 'academic' accusations are speaking a familiar language, which is that of a liberal heterosexual response to gay lifestyle and culture. In effect it rejects our language and anger, by claiming the complaints are over the top and baseless. It won't take seriously any language or argument that it has not itself invented, since it expects everybody to employ its own terms of reference. It expects always to be the main audience addressed, and resents discovering it is not so. It is apt to categorize as 'conspiracy' any cultural formation that does not explicitly address liberal heterosexuality.

Culture – and we'll return to this point – is not merely artworks: it is a way of making sense of lives, and also simply of surviving. It is meeting-places, helplines, jokes and leaflets. Our concern with gay culture is not a concern

with gay sensibility and the genius of Marlowe and Michel-
angelo. It is a concern with the everyday process of survival
in an oppressive heterosexual world. That process of survival is not, however, merely defensive: it is positive and
creative. It *makes* the conditions of our unity, resilience and
pleasure. Any opposition to this culture must of course be
political. Those selfsame 'academic' arguments used by
MUP were, even if taken at face-value, political.

Gay culture does not only look outwards, fearfully; it
also looks inwards and finds in itself various sets of
relationships, divisions as well as unity. Looking in, it finds
debate as well as celebration. Gays know they are not the
coherent, as it were uniform, minority that a heterosexual
world wants to see. Furthermore, we consciously speak of
our diversity in order to solve our differences. We seek to
create alliance among ourselves on the basis of positive
reciprocation; we reject an alliance formed on the basis of
default, namely that of us all belonging to a category
defined and policed by straights. The concept of gay culture
in this book comprises more than heterosexuals might
want: more various, more divided and more politicized
(which partly comes from the process of working out how
to live together, to articulate and then to resolve differences). A concept of 'gay culture' that is an autonomous
thing, inhabited by a mystical 'gay sensibility', is one that
merely fulfils a heterosexual category.

The essays in this book speak for diversity. They are a set
of different voices, not simply arguing together but using
different terms of reference, different theories and assumptions about the world. The book makes life difficult for a
reader by *not* offering a position of final resolution, and
instead offers diversity. It offers positions with which to
identify, and then positions which criticize. Living within
gay culture is a matter of continual self-identification, then
debate, then modification, then redefinition. The deliberately different styles of the essays range from angry experiences to carefully camp, 'distanced' prose. They are styles

of anger and irony, styles produced by and in turn responding to heterosexual culture.

In 'academic' terms, we hear, the style of the book is 'uneven'. This is deliberate and we think valuable: activists, journalists and academics speak their own languages. It was imperative to the aims of the book that it reached out beyond the confines of the academy. That it did not reach any further than it does is a cause for regret, though we have to remember that for many activists at the present time the act of writing an article for a book comes pretty low on the political agenda. Furthermore, this is still a society in which many people feel alienated and mistrustful about writing, or are just simply too busy to do it. For a variety of reasons, and to our regret, there is nothing from an older gay man, or from a gay youth; the Afro-Caribbean gays we approached were all too busy, though supportive of the project; none of the disabled gay groups we approached felt they could provide an article. Being white and able-bodied, we are very conscious that our editorship has not enabled some of the usual institutional silences to be broken.

The essays speak from different positions and at the same time they overlap with one another; they refuse to fit into neat categories, and to sectionalize them would be to misrepresent and unnecessarily limit them. So they are in an order which can be dipped into or read consecutively. That ordering is *loosely* arranged into the following sequence: the impact of AIDS (given opening position not only as the greatest crisis affecting the gay community, but also one which has produced so many diverse modes of creative response); the relationship of gay sexuality outwards – to heterosexuality and heterosexual masculinity; the relationship of the gay community inwards – to the arguments and demands of minority and other groupings; gays and the dominant order part 1: law, moralism and gay sexual identity; gays and the dominant order part 2: gays within the history of state and society; gays and opposition: three essays on gays and the Left. Of course, these groupings will dissolve as soon as you begin any of the essays. And as to what library catalogue cards will do with it, well ... we'll see you on the shelf.

Political debates: gender

In what follows we shall attempt to describe the context in which this book comes to be published; and in doing so we hope to clarify the framework of political struggles and theoretical debates within which the individual essays are written. Some readers may want to skip this and dive into the middle of the book; this is some context for those as want it. Before we begin we should stress that our account represents only our position as editors; we don't speak here for the rest of the contributors, and indeed a number of them would probably want to contest what we say.

This book was originally designed to be part of a pair: we felt that it had to have a lesbian companion. Significantly, the first publisher was much slower about pursuing a contract for the lesbian half of the pairing, and in the event that publisher printed neither book. Each book sought a home where it could find one. But the principle behind our original insistence still needs speaking about. While the significance and implications of the pairing of lesbian and gay books may be obvious to most lesbians, heterosexual feminists and gay men, they are less so to many others. Consequently, what is at issue here is almost entirely unregarded in our general culture.

Most simply put, the issue is that, while lesbians and gay men may be apparently linked in that they have – or perceive – a common enemy, they are also divided – by the fact of men's domination over women in the very structure of our social system. From the first moments of 'Gay Liberation' in the late 1960s, lesbians found it necessary to organize separately and sometimes *against* gay men in order to fight the supposedly common object of attack: patriarchy.

The basic situation is that of a simultaneous *identity* and (perceived or actual) *antagonism* of interests between lesbians and gay men. Such a state of tension has continued to produce a range of political positions and arguments within and between the two groupings in the intervening years. At the present time the feminist anti-pornography lobby in the United States is felt by many gay men to be a major threat to their interests and lifestyle; the extent to which some lesbians are seen to be a part of that lobby is a mark of a potential and actual distance between lesbians and gay men. On the other hand, many women feel directly threatened by a culture which celebrates masculinity and cultivates 'impersonal' and casual sex; there is, perhaps, an unbroken line of oppression which links drag to direct rape. Such a *clear* antagonism of interests seems to be becoming less marked currently in Britain, particularly since the formation of alliances to fight Section 28 (of which more later – see p. 16 onwards).

We want to suggest straight away that finding solutions to this antagonism is in the main a problem for men rather than women. Women organize against the oppression which they face from men. The tactical inclusion of men in such organization – through new forms or within existing parties or campaigns – always runs the danger of accommodating to oppressive norms. Men are not merely structurally placed in dominance over women in our culture (as in employment, legal rights, etc.); they are culturally produced as oppressor, conditioned into dominance from infancy. This is not at all to suggest that gender oppression is fundamentally personal. It is to suggest that men's support of women's rights can only finally be concrete if it includes a readiness to relinquish power. A clear parallel is the involvement of middle-class radicals in the class struggle.

Lesbians are oppressed differently from gay men. They face a specific set of problems. Many would argue that as women they are automatically more oppressed than are gay men: on an abstract scale of oppression lesbians are some-times said to be structurally 'especially oppressed'. We are not concerned with setting up a hierarchy of oppressions – it produces little other than a rhetoric of righteousness. But if there are to be solidarities between lesbians and gay men, it is clearly necessary for gay men to accommodate to the conditions of women's struggle.

For lesbians, in the absence of a workable and concrete solution, the option seems clear: political separatism. If gay men fail properly to address the collective and structural oppression of all women by all men, they not only collude in that domination: they lose their allies in struggle. And indeed they create a situation in which some lesbians may prefer to enter into an alliance with Moral Majority 'femin-ism', which is itself based on beliefs that in the long term would destroy all homosexuals.

Some of the essays in this book reflect the urgency of dealing with this problem as *men*.

Without denying the reality of women's oppression in all its forms, we want to stress that the politics of the women's movement, the theory and practice of feminism, does not exist as a seamless whole. Within the logic of common oppression, resistance and sisterhood, there are not only differences of class, race and sexuality: there are also deep *political* differences. The range within feminism of analyses of women's oppression, and the political programmes drawn from them, demands, at the least, that we speak of *feminisms* in the plural. At the moment, within Britain and the United States these differences are strikingly apparent around pornography and lesbian SM: socialist feminists are clearly engaged in a struggle with 'radical' separatists.

Our insistence, as gay men, that we speak of feminisms comes from our own political position. We acknowledge that it is common for men to concern themselves with women's 'divisions', and that in thus focusing attention away from themselves they avoid questioning their own complacent outlook. But for us this debate within feminisms is personally urgent: its implications go deep into our own political and social practices. In brief, our position is opposed to and rejects all 'essentialisms', which is to say all beliefs founded on a concept of predetermined and permanent human characteristics which remain untouched and unchanged by the movement of history, the development of cultures and societies.

We identify essentialist feminism as that which insists on a true and unitary Feminism based on a female principle or essence which remains immutable, eternal, unmarked by historical changes; the abstract principle of Woman. This concept works to hide all real differences between women; it conceals those divisions which occur along the lines of race, class and sexuality. It also conceals the fact that gender roles are socially constructed, a fact which it is necessary to recognize as a first step towards fighting against them. On the one hand, it can fail to ask just how much Anita Bryant and Jill Knight can possibly share in common with Black or Latin women or socialist feminists. There were some in Britain who viewed the accession to power of a woman Prime Minister as something preferable to a Labour Party male. On the other hand, it can all too easily establish pecking orders of oppression, creating categories of the 'especially oppressed' arranged in a permanent, moralized hierarchy and spoken of in the language of righteousness.

The idea of an essential Womanhood denies the existence of a variety of contending feminisms; but it insists on the difference between the essentially 'feminine' and the mistaken realities of 'unwomanly' women. For *us* this is not merely political and intellectual nonsense, in that it obscures the fact of historical change and the reality of social inequality – other than through gender. It also, straightforwardly, threatens us as gay men: we do not conceive that we are slaves to our biology – any more than we believe that our not being heterosexual men *automatically* disarms us as potential threats to all women. None the

less, our daily experience of the hostility of heterosexual
men is too real to be erased by the notion that we are
necessarily and inescapably all linked because we're men.

We have talked of 'essentialism' and of 'political separatism'. We ought, at this stage, to make clear what we see as
the difference between the two. We see feminist separatism
as a political tactic made necessary by the fact of men's
power over women in our social system: women make
space for themselves, to develop their own solidarity and
strength, in order to turn against their collective oppressors, men. From this, we distinguish essentialism as a
political idea and practice that insists on the biological and
indeed eternal antagonism between men and women. From
the essentialist perspective it is necessary that women
separate themselves from all areas of political activity
which involve coalitions with men, since all such alliances
are distracting and illusory. The separatist, by contrast, will
be sceptical of alliances with men, but will not always
oppose them on principle. For gay men, the consequence of
essentialism is that the reality of our oppression is denied.
No distinction is made between gay and straight, since we
are all biologically male, irrespective of our differing social
positions; the queer-basher and the gay corpse both have
willies. We refuse to see separatism and essentialism as
equivalent principles, whether such a claim comes from
essentialist feminists *or* from female and male anti-
feminists.

When we agreed to edit this collection of essays principally by gay men, we understood that the project would
necessarily involve looking at our links with socialist lesbians and other anti-essentialist feminists. It is, as we've
said, a question for *men* to explore how they may best
relate to women's struggle for liberation. This position does
not expect women to approach us for alliances. The one
woman represented in this book is there precisely because
of a joint work: the man's work is only possible through
alliance with the woman; if it wasn't joint it wouldn't exist.

To explore positive and progressive alliances also means, however, refuting that which is regressive and reactionary. We need to define a radical gay politics *against* the reactionary, essentialist, strands of feminism.

Political debates: class

We have tried above to trace aspects of the relationship between gay men and lesbians on the basis of their gender difference. But there is another set of differences which relate to, impinge on, interact with those of gender. We are thinking of differences of class. Gender difference and class difference – and the ways in which they are struggled over – mutually affect one another. The relationship between the gay movement and the women's movement is shaped by the relationship between both the politics of sexuality and the politics of class. It has only been within the last couple of decades in the West – since a brief period post 1917 of Bolshevism – that the organizations and parties of the Left have ceased uniformly to regard sexual political issues as 'bourgeois deviationism'.

More recent developments have taken two forms. On one hand, Marxist-orientated work has attempted to demonstrate the historical complexity of the relationship between class and gender (and hence sexuality); it sees both class and gender difference in terms of labour and relations of production. On the other hand, the 'fragments' of the Left have attempted to address the actual areas in which there is at present resistance to oppression.

Many rank-and-file lesbians and gays see this as somewhat cynical, resulting from the fact that the groupings of the Left have conspicuously lost a 'vanguard' position in the class struggle: in these situations lesbians and gays see themselves, resentfully, as fodder. Lesbians and gays who often do not belong to any leftist grouping have made many political initiatives through self-organized, autonomous groupings. Such initiatives have consciously followed the model of other 'rainbow' alliances. The United States has seen the formation of 'rainbow' alliances of groups of the oppressed, which have little place for, or tradition of, organized Left leadership. The campaign a few years ago against the Briggs amendment and the backlash against homosexuals in the education system showed the power of lesbians and gays organized autonomously as lesbians and gays; and by campaigning lesbians and gays become more politicized and are strengthened in their struggle. This is perhaps evident not so much in the activities to get Harvey Milk elected as in the reaction to the judiciary's connivance at his murder. Such autonomous organization and increased politicization are also evident in Britain,with the campaign against Section 28 of the Local Government Act (which attempts to ban what it vaguely terms as the 'promotion' of homosexuality). One of the significant features of the campaign against Section 28 was the often tense relations between activists who were motivated as lesbians and gays and those who represented organized 'parties'.

But the *problem* with autonomous organization, the problem of the gut idealism which resented Left cynicism, is that it effaces differences of class. It is significant that we have seen the widespread evaporation of the anti-Section 28 organizations: for where there is no basis in a worked out class position both the analysis and the opposition vanish when the urgency of the specific issue which brought them into being also vanishes. Rainbows, like their pots of gold, are indeed illusions.

For some on the Left, the project of campaigning around sexual politics remains a retreat from class politics – where 'class politics' is understood as the sole perspective for the conduct and achievement of all liberation struggles. For others, although such a possible retreat is there to be guarded against, it is nevertheless a risk worth taking or indeed one that *has* to be taken. Then there are those others for whom the activity of 'class' politics has become ossified: it is merely a verbal formula, an abstraction. This abstraction is itself 'essentialist': it is based on a sociological concept of class which concentrates on traditionally-defined 'communities' rather than on real positions within industrial and social production.

Some of the essays in this book bear directly on these questions: we would suggest that all, in that they come from an active engagement in gay politics, are situated somewhere within them.

When our original publisher blocked this book, we were accused – wrongly – of putting together a collection of essays which all came from a male gay Marxist position. This accusation was, of course, wilfully blind to the range of political positions represented in the book and also ignorant of the fact that there is no such 'coherent' position. The arguments around sexual–political and class analyses of society are not resolved. An analysis of oppression is only useful for as long as it assists those who are oppressed. Thus over the years the concerns of Marxist analyses have been changed, modified, added to. The demands of women (and anti-sexist men) forced changes to the current understanding and practice of Marxist theory. The debates continue as to how oppression may best be analysed, and therefore ended. But these debates are also creative in that they have challenged the assumptions on which previously dominant theory has rested. Two contributions to this book make the demand for a change in dominant Marxist theory; many others are written within a consciousness of the debates and demands.

Working with our differences

MUP's alarm at finding that the book they had commissioned turned out to be 'gay' and 'Marxist' (categories they could only understand in very simple and negative terms) was not only theoretically blind. It was also completely unaware of the realities of political activity. In actual *practice* the problem of organizing around such issues as, for example, Section 28 or the Helms amendment is shaped by the differences we have outlined above: gender differences, class differences, the tendency towards autonomy versus affiliation to the organized Left. These differences produce a real problem area: campaigns abort, many activists burn out or fade into cynical despondency. But these deep and active divisions can also be seen as an area of growth: new forms and bases of organization are being wrought. No one knows what the new forms of political struggle are going to be; but we're happy to bet that they're not going to be the programmes of the British Labour Party or of Democrat liberalism, nor those of orthodox Stalinism or Trotskyism. In Britain we have seen depressing examples of stand-off in the Organization of Lesbian and Gay Action, with arguments between, for example, the hard-line Left, essentialist lesbians and 'common-sense' middle-of-the-road unity campaigners. But at the same time, the urgency and purpose to have out these arguments and seek to construct necessary alliances (or develop new vanguards) form a positive point of growth.

Our effort as editors of this collection of essays was twofold. The first, of course, was to produce analyses and anger directed against an oppressive heterosexual status quo. But second, we attempted to put together essays which spoke from differing positions of oppression, and hence spoke with different languages, different analyses, different agendas for action. Some contributors call into question the fundamental assumptions of others. We hope that the interplay of analyses forces a rethinking of easy orthodoxies. Yet we also hope that we've not produced that complacent and delightful academic commodity of the 1980s, a celebration of 'pluralities'. There may be a plurality of positions, but those positions are angry and urgent. The rethinking at a theoretical level is necessary because the demands at a practical level are real and pressing. Linking the various voices and divergent analyses there is the rage against the dominant.

Such a questioning of orthodoxies cannot be reduced to nor adequately represented by an *academic* notion of 'theory'. In practical terms – and especially within some areas of socialist feminist and socialist lesbian practice – recorded or traditional theory is regularly outstripped. The inexorable movement through the 1970s towards taking up woman-defined positions perhaps happened culturally before it was analysed theoretically. And now, Joan Nestle's work on butch-femme roles in the context of older women coming back into the movement, and work on race by numerous Black women (including, of course, Alice Walker) are challenging essentialist elements of feminist theory.

The ideas and arguments that count are those that define and determine immediate practice. It is here – in practice – that new forms and alliances of organization, new forms of struggle and of theory emerge, albeit on the basis of the old. For example, in gay men's responses to the AIDS crisis in the United States a new positive attitude to the disease was accompanied by, and was part of, a new upsurge of gay direct action; a new refusal to accept the passive category of 'victim' and the assertion of collective rights to health care provision and benefits. And this is no 'spontaneous' outburst, but carefully directed anger and theory becoming action, action building theory.

For the most part, this book concerns itself with the politics of gay culture and with gay critiques of dominant culture. We said at the start that we understand culture to consist of all the activities by which we make sense of and direct our lives in modern society. Our lives, being shaped by class as well as race and sexuality, are various, so our culture is varied. Thus we refuse the monolithic notion of a 'gay culture' which is so beloved of the tourists – whether they are naff couples who like to spend the occasional

Saturday in a gay disco or whether they are style-conscious readers of up-to-the-moment mags. Gay culture is not a commodity, even though it includes commodities, and may be critically prone to commercialization in Western urban centres. 'Gay culture' is nothing less than a set of ways of living. These ways of living always involve choice, struggles, engagements, and the very *possibilities* of living. 'Gay culture' is therefore also deeply political, though it cannot be reduced to one political position.

Books about 'culture and politics' are trendy at present. Like many others, this book faces being swallowed up into what might be called the politics of 'culturalism'. 'Culturalism' is the assumption that cultural struggles are the really important ones. It shares with the belief in autonomous organization an idea that self-definition by political or cultural minorities takes precedence over all other considerations (such as class affiliation), and it very often makes no reference to the concrete necessity for organizing. 'Culturalism' is a politics of lifestyles, a form of new liberalism which is not dissimilar to old-fashioned armchair radicalism. The practices of, say, 'radical' literary criticism are content to borrow the language of revolution and tour the venues of struggle, happy to describe the world but inclined to take a raincheck on changing it.

Promoting homophobia

Even as we were making this cultural product, this book, the realities of political struggle were forced upon our attention. Indeed, they helped to shape the publication history of this book. For in Britain in December 1987 the general backlash against lesbians and gays received new blessing and impetus from the Thatcher government in the form of Clause (now Section) 28. Inserted into a Local Government Bill designed severely to limit the activities of locally-elected representative bodies, the infamous Clause sought to prohibit local authorities from 'promoting' homosexuality. In the debate on the Clause in the House of Commons, the Tory MP Elaine Kellett-Bowman was reported to express her approval of a fire-bomb attack on the offices of *Capital Gay*. (She later became a Dame in the 1988 New Year's Honours List.) The wording of the Clause was taken from similar initiatives in the United States, the most recent, in November 1987, being Senator Jesse Helms's successful attempt to ban all federal funding for Safer Sex education (the North Atlantic alliance has given Britain more than cruise missiles). Helms and his supporters depict sodomy as the sole cause of the spread of AIDS, and they require AIDS education to emphasize 'abstinence outside a sexually monogamous marriage'. The Helms amendment, even more nakedly than Section 28, not only assaults the lifestyle of gays but also engineers the likelihood of their deaths.

The Section 28/Helms wording is intentionally vague enough to allow plenty of space for extremely vicious and bigoted interpretations. In Britain this wording alone furthered the effect of the Clause in that it promoted self-censorship, even before the Clause became law (as in the case of MUP). It precisely encouraged the implementation of and submission to attitudes moulded by the venomous hostility of the tabloid press, which also furnishes and enshrines the language spoken by queer-bashers as they carve up the faces of lesbians and gays with sharpened screwdrivers. (If heterosexual readers find such images oversensational, it is because their presses do not report the attacks, which are regular, organized, and on the increase.)

During our weeks of quarrelling with Manchester University Press, with the Helms amendment awaiting presidential approval and Clause 28 about to enter into law, our attention was next taken by news of the anti-gay brutality so openly displayed at the Republican Party convention, and by the Democrat candidate's backtracking on gay rights. (We omit the weekly fare of rehearsed police arrests and spontaneous queer-bashings.)

But we want perversely (and we claim a right to be perverse) to put a more positive case. The Helms amendment and Section 28 express the strength of the backlash, but they also speak a fear and loathing of what has been already achieved. In the case of Helms it is the scale and efficiency of gay self-organization in response to a health crisis, but reaching much further than that. Section 28 is directed at councils as legislative bodies, where lesbians and gay men have shown that they can win popular support and be elected as recognized homosexuals. Open lesbian and gay campaigning has, in Britain, constructed firm alliances with the Labour Left and the trades union movement. Leftist Labour councils now recognize that lesbian and gay issues belong firmly on their agenda. Section 28 is also directed at community projects such as resource centres, video projects, community theatre groups, lesbian and gay youth groups, lesbian and gay Black groups, lesbian and gay trades union sections: groups which form links between various sectors of the oppressed. Furthermore, their activity offers a form of social relationship that is not structured by the family, while their cultural products question the centrality and supposed naturalness of the family. In both respects they question an ideal which the Thatcher government, like the Reagan presidency, exploits in order to promote its own authority.

The apparent 'spread' of homosexuality is thus evidence of something acutely more dangerous to government than gay rights. It is a sign and symptom of the critical instability of the Western nuclear family, itself a key structure for the reproduction of patriarchal capitalism's consenting subjects. It is also a spread of solidarity with homosexuals, and a realization among homosexuals of the logic which links their situation to that of other groups. In other words, it is a conscious linking-up of various groups of so-called minorities. They unite in an analysis which shows that, despite very real differences of experience, there is common ground in facing an enemy which seeks to divide groups of the oppressed from one another.

The initiatives which have led to lesbian and gay policies and patronage on a very few local councils show something new has happened to the homosexual minority. The clear-cut division between a commercial 'scene' and 'political gays' is fading. Initial ghetto building in the metropolitan centres at first produced an illusion. From both inside and outside the ghetto it was sometimes possible to imagine a grouping both essentially unified in itself and separate from the rest of 'politics'. But the practice of 'gay politics' over a generation has revealed and begun to build the potential and necessary links with wider struggles, just as the politics of race, class, disability, youth – and gender – have radically transformed the possible basis of any future gay politics. A point of celebration is that to state this is, for most of the current generation of young lesbian and gay activists – including a new wave brought rapidly into being by the creation of Clause 28 (how's *that* for promotion?) – simply to reiterate so much history.

A place in the Sun

The current generation has not known the years of illegality, nor the 'hedonism' of a Gay Liberation Front explosion. Whereas GLF politics adopted the stance of a romantic Big Refusal, the new generation is marked by an angry and radical/revolutionary desire for change. GLF burst forth in a period of relative economic stability and social and political liberalism: present struggles grapple within a period of intense political reaction. The current generation of young activists stands upon the ground so eccentrically prepared by a predominantly libertarian politics with an anger and resolve which have been built through their *practice* as lesbians and gays, whose right to self-definition they regard as unquestionable.

Radical politics are currently marked by the importance of campaigns – especially single issue campaigns. There are, of course, arguments as to why; and if the revolutionary Left increasingly seeks to organize itself around and through such issues (or to put it the way the revolutionary groups do, seeks to organize the campaigns) it does so with a great measure of uncertainty. A successor to (and improvement on, to our minds) a sectarian group that subscribed to the 'bourgeois deviationism' theory a decade and a half ago recently published a leaflet proclaiming that 'Now the Gays are Getting Angry'. At last they have noticed ... But such a change is a measure and symptom of a major redefinition of analyses and forms of struggle that is continuing – and continues to be fraught.

Now, more obviously than ever before, it seems that there is not a single shared gay 'identity', no single thing summarized as 'being homosexual'. This is not any longer simply a matter of styles within, say, a gay pub whereby the punters indicate the wide variety of ways in which they see themselves placed within society. It is clear in a con-crete sense, in that the gay pub is no longer itself the only focal point for being gay in. The division of 'scene' and 'non-scene' no longer approximates to being 'out' or 'closeted'. It is possible to be out in a variety of scenes and venues. The gay pub or bar no longer necessarily has a central status. This status was anyway highly ambiguous, since the bar not only provided a public gathering place but also the conditions which fostered lesbian and gay alcoholism. And so too there are many gays, especially younger ones, who cannot afford the 'pleasures' of the commercial scene. Gay public identity has had to be developed outside, and sometimes in opposition to, the world of the gay bar or club. The singleness of 'identity' has been replaced perhaps by a set of links and alliances. A ghetto political consciousness exists, but it is no longer the dominant consciousness among self-defining gays.

To describe such a generational shift might suggest that the commercial ghetto is a bastion of reaction. It is of course not: it is a bastion of recreation (with all the possible difficulties and contradictions that idea involves). The self-styled apolitical pubs and clubs have hitherto appeared to be the areas always slowest to mobilize in a crisis. But our pubs and clubs, and now our cinemas and centres, our newspapers and magazines, are areas of cultural resource and social definition that we need and value. And just as the gays came raging out of the Stonewall bar on Christopher Street in 1969, sickened by yet another raid by queer-bashing cops, Section 28 has been so blatant in its assault as to have produced a renewed wave of militancy from a previously 'unpoliticized' sector of all generations. It is a measure of the current political crisis and of the widening, developing and maturing of our institutions that this 'bar-room' militancy is quickly attuned to a sense of shared interest, shared struggle.

Gays are (if we can borrow a slogan from our sisters) Everywhere. This delightful truth is regularly drawn to our attention by the *Sun* which, in its constant campaign to discover yet another famous gay, keeps on demonstrating how many and how talented we are. When this book first began it aimed to reflect the diversity of gay culture. The intention was to produce neither a new gay history (a valuable one has appeared in 1988 from Routledge: *Radical Records*, eds Bob Cant and Susan Hemmings) nor a new work of theory, but to collect reports and thoughts about aspects of gay life in the 1980s. We firmly intend to carry on discussing our differences, celebrating our diversity, being here, coming on strong, so that we can enjoy a very gay 1990s.

Have a good read, and above all have a bona time.

CHAPTER ONE

Psychoanalysis, sexuality and AIDS

Simon Watney

At a recent talk at the Institute of Contemporary Arts in London, Robert Young described psychoanalysis as 'a theory of unhappy relationships', including those with other disciplines and bodies of theory (In conversation, 18 March 1987). The relation of gay men and lesbians to the *institution* of psychoanalysis is undoubtedly unhappy in the extreme. For neo-Freudian analysts, our sexuality is still widely regarded as a result of 'hidden but incapacitating fears of the opposite sex' (Bieber *et al.*, 1962, p. 203), while openly gay men and lesbians are still categorically excluded from the very possibilities of training as analysts ourselves by all the leading centres of psychoanalytic training in Britain and Western Europe. This is not, however, to conclude that we have nothing to learn from the larger project of psychoanalysis as envisaged and developed by Freud. In this essay I want to consider some of the ways in which Freud's work illuminates many aspects of the general 'sleep of reason' surrounding AIDS, including the assumption that we can ever be entirely rational about sex.

Psychoanalysis and 'family' values

In his recent history of the medical profession in Nazi Germany, Robert Lifton traces the centrality of doctors in the theory and practice of 'medicalised killing' (1986, p. 4). Doctors devised and supervised every stage of the elaborate surgical technology which ensured the death of millions of Jews, gypsies, anti-fascists, and those regarded as 'degenerate' in the light of Nazi science, including lesbians and gay men. For these Nazi doctors, such killing was regarded as a *therapeutic* imperative. As one pointed out: 'I am a doctor and I want to preserve life . . . out of respect for human life I would remove a gangrenous appendix from a diseased body. The Jew is the gangrenous appendix in the body of mankind' (p. 16). Then as now, most doctors accepted the dominant common sense of state authority. Hence the radical diagnosis which followed Hitler's prescription in *Mein Kampf* in the mid-1920s that: 'anyone who wants to cure this era, which is inwardly sick and rotten, must first of all summon up the courage to make clear the causes of this disease.' This is *precisely* the tone of countless contemporary commentators who claim to 'make clear' the cause of AIDS in the lives of the supposedly 'inwardly sick and rotten' who reveal its symptoms. Then as now, medicalized metaphors of contagion and plague informed both medical practice, and the social policy which it served, often defined by institutions which cannot simply be equated with the state.

For the Nazi doctors psychoanalysis represented a particular threat, in so far as Freud's work and influence were officially regarded as a major instrument of sexual degeneration, 'a breakdown of the family, and loss of all that is decent' (Lifton, 1986, p. 42). It is one of the larger ironies of *our* times that this same grim and essentially vulgar rhetoric continues to dominate both 'popular' and supposedly 'scientific' attitudes towards the immediate and inescapable fact of human sexual diversity. One of the most

moving aspects of Freud's career concerns his own struggle
to come to terms with the direct consequences of his own
theoretical discoveries about the organization of sexuality.
In a supplementary note from 1915 to his seminal 1905
Essays on Sexuality he noted that:

> Psychoanalytic research is most decidedly opposed to
> any attempt at separating off homosexuals from the rest
> of mankind as a group of a special character ... From the
> point of view of psychoanalysis the exclusive sexual
> interest felt by men for women is also a problem that
> needs elucidating, and is not a self-evident fact. (Freud,
> 1977, p. 56)

For Freud the study of sexuality begins with the concept of
desire – that which precedes both actual sexual behaviour
and sexual identities. Desire may be for almost any object,
and the central organization of sexuality is thus structured
around what he describes as 'object-choice', whether it is
directed towards the same or the opposite sex, or both. For
psychoanalysis it is the stability and *fixity* of any object-
choice which requires explanation, not the object itself.
Sexual desire is not grounded in a simple biological drive or
urge, but in instincts which seek pleasures which cannot be
'adequately explained in terms of the satisfaction of a basic
physiological need' (Laplanche and Pontalis, 1983, p. 418).
   Psychoanalysis thus offers a fundamentally anti-
naturalistic explanation of sexuality. As a method of
psychological inquiry it sets out to recover repressed
mental materials – fantasies, wishes, and so on, over which
we exercise no conscious control, and to which we therefore
have no direct access. Yet psychoanalysts have only rarely
turned their attention to the massive repression which the
institution of modern psychoanalytic theory and practice
exhibits in relation to its own most basic insights. On the
one hand, Freud offers us a complex picture of human
sexual diversity understood as the very essence of our being

as a species; on the other, he strenuously attempts to confine this perception within the narrowest and most orthodox model of supposedly 'normal' psychosexual development, with heterosexual intercourse as its 'natural' goal. It is at just this point that we may introduce Freud's own concept of 'resistance' in order to begin to explain the conflict at work in his writings between his commitment to a theory of sexuality grounded in what people actually want, enjoy and *do* sexually, and the cultural priorities of Judaeo-Christian tradition.

There is little evidence of any such conflict in the modern institution of psychoanalysis, which serves principally to police and reinforce a moral and cultural agenda which would have profoundly shocked Freud. Indeed, it is particularly regrettable that psychoanalysts should so frequently be found lining up with the most reactionary social forces in contemporary Britain, regarding homosexuality as a dangerous and intrinsically pathological condition, rather than an intrinsically unremarkable and even commonplace fact of sexual life. This leads analysts to abuse the honourable concept of therapy, and to impose punitive and sadistic 'therapies' on people whose lives they refuse to accept as fully and ordinarily human. Lesbians and gay men are the human sacrifice which today's analysts offer up to the shrine of an imaginary ideal of heterosexuality which Freud exposed before the First World War. It is thus both salutary and chilling to compare the insultingly oversimplified rhetoric of 'family life' and 'family values' so beloved of contemporary psychoanalysts, and the identical clichés of the Nazi doctors as they stood up on the ramp at Auschwitz, directing millions to the ultimate 'therapy' of the ovens. Whenever analysts speak casually of homosexuality as a 'personality disorder' on the explicit assumption that 'heterosexuality is the biologic norm and that unless interfered with all individuals are heterosexual' (Bieber *et al.*, 1962, p. 319) we may all be sure that we are listening historically down-wind from the death camps.

'Civilized' sexual morality and modern nervous illness

In 1908 Freud wrote a paper which is effectively a sup-
plement to his far more celebrated *Essays on Sexuality*,
written three years earlier. *'Civilized' Sexual Morality and
Modern Nervous Illness* is perhaps the most devastating
critique ever launched against the institution and the values
of heterosexual marriage, with its double-standards of
morality for women and men, which are bound 'to induce
in its members concealment of the truth, false optimism,
self-deception and deception of others' (Freud, 1985).
Generally speaking, he writes, 'our civilization is built up
on the suppression of instincts'. However, the sexual
instinct is not a simple phenomenon, but is 'made up of
many constituents or component instincts' which are more
constant and strongly developed in man because our sexuality 'has almost entirely overcome the periodicity to which
it is tied in animals'. Yet 'civilized' sexual morality proceeds
exactly as if this were not the case, and women and men
alike come into and out of oestrus. The result is that anyone
living outside its terms and values will be regarded as a
form of criminal or 'outlaw'. Freud then makes one of his
boldest theoretical assertions: 'in man the sexual instinct
does not originally serve the purpose of reproduction at all,
but has as its aim the gaining of particular kinds of
pleasures'.

   This diversity of aims and objects and pleasure is
however only 'serviceable' to the cultural values of 'civilization' through normalizing strategies which reduce sexuality to a single goal, with the 'aim of uniting the genitals'.
This leaves two major exceptions: first, 'perverts', in whom
'an infantile fixation to a preliminary sexual aim has
prevented the primacy of the reproductive function from
being established', and second, 'inverts', in whom 'in a
manner that is not yet quite understood, the sexual aim has
been deflected away from the opposite sex'. By this time the
ground has already been well prepared for the kind of

neo-Freudian reading of homosexuality as a pathological aversion to the opposite sex, which completely flies in the face of Freud's earlier point about the diversity of sexual object-choice, and the essentially non-reproductive character of human sexuality. For the picture of homosexual desire as a form of 'deflection' clearly presupposes a 'natural' heterosexual aim to sex. The full extent of Freud's own culturally normative values emerges in his observation that 'the constitution of people suffering from inversion – the homosexuals – is, indeed, often distinguished by their sexual instinct's possessing a special aptitude for cultural sublimation.' Here we witness the constitutive moment of what will become a commonplace of later twentieth-century psychoanalytic thought, extending out through the social sciences as far afield as sociobiology – the emergence of the homosexual as aesthete, his sensibilities sanctioned by his sexual object-choice.

At the same time we should notice that his sympathy is precisely *with* those who find themselves marginalized by the values and institutions of modern 'civilized' sexual morality. In his vocabulary, the terms 'invert' and 'pervert' were not judgemental. While we may fairly detect an unresolvable problem in Freud's attempt to make sense of the diversity of sexuality in the 'scientific' terminology of his day, we should not blame him retrospectively for the fact that the category of 'the perverse' has not subsequently shed its dismal cargo of negative social connotations. Thus, when he writes that:

more pronounced forms of the perversions and homo-sexuality, especially if they are exclusive, do, it is true, make those subject to them socially useless and unhappy, so that it must be recognised that the cultural requirements ... are a course of suffering for a certain proportion of mankind,

it is crucial to recognize that Freud is attributing the

suffering of gay men to the 'problems' of their host culture. Indeed, it speaks a very great deal for Freud that he was fully aware by 1908 of the specific damage which even pre-modern forms of sexual morality impose on those who are 'harmful' only to the purposes of a repressive sexual culture (of which he profoundly disapproved).

Thus, he notes:

> it is one of the obvious social injustices that the standard of civilization should demand from everyone the same conduct of sexual life – conduct which can be followed without any difficulty by some people, thanks to their organisation, but which imposes the heaviest psychical sacrifices on others.

Though, he continues, 'this injustice is as a rule wiped out by disobedience to the injunctions of morality'.

Here Freud stands unambiguously on the side of sexual and cultural dissidents and disobedience to patriarchal authority. In his view, everyone is damaged by a culture rooted in the ideal of total sexual abstinence before and independent of marriage: 'Anyone who is able to penetrate the determinants of nervous illness will soon become convinced that its increase in our society arises from the intensification of sexual restraints.' Thus marriage emerges as an institution which guarantees its own failure, with the emergence of

> the 'double' sexual morality which is valid for men in our society [which] is the plainest admission that society itself does not believe in the possibility of enforcing the precepts which it itself has laid down.

While he regards women as

> only endowed in a small measure with the gift of subli-mating their instincts ... experience shows, I repeat, that

women, when they are subjected to the disillusionment of marriage, fall ill of severe neuroses which permanently darken their lives.

A culture which aims at 'the retardation of sexual development and sexual activity' emerges as a royal road to general misery, and all but universal sexual neurosis (except for those sexual dissidents who have taken Freud's advice and refused both its values and its practices). It is precisely this implication which leads Freud ultimately back in line with patriarchal authority, in his conclusion that one of the 'harms' of the cultural aggravation of sexual behaviour:

> is to be found in the spread of homosexual satisfaction; in addition to all those who are homosexuals in virtue of their organisation, or who become so in childhood, there must be reckoned the great number of those in whom, in their maturer years, a blocking of the main stream of their libido has caused a widening in the side-channel of homosexuality.

The very strangeness of this metaphor suggests something of the threat Freud seems to feel himself, in this particular fantasy, concerning the possibility of homosexuality as a *voluntary* option in adult sexual life, albeit conditioned by the constraints of an over-civilized sexual morality. Hence the extremely 'troubled' tone of this entire text, its unusual lack of resolution, and its telling internal conflicts. For at the very point at which he articulates, and not without difficulty as we have seen, a moving description of the plight of women and gay men under patriarchy, he contradicts his more frequent tendency to hold women directly responsible and to blame for male homosexuality. Here, more clearly even than is to be found in the earlier *Essays on Sexuality*, Freud refuses what Craig Owens has described as 'the myth of homosexual gynophobia' as an 'explanation' of homosexual desire.

This myth informs the entire belief-system of neo-Freudian 'therapy' together, as Owens points out, with a substantial current in modern psychoanalytically-oriented feminist theory (Owens, 1987, p. 219). He argues that this myth 'remains perhaps the most powerful obstacle to a political alliance of feminists and gay men', because it obscures 'the profound link between misogyny and homophobia in our culture'. It thus becomes critically important to return to those moments in Freud's work when he himself most frankly contradicts and challenges those who continue to sanction their profoundly uncivilized morality in his name. Hence the lasting political significance of his picture of the pathological family, visiting its miseries on the children it produces, in a pattern of cultural reproduction which can only be actively challenged in the assertion of female and non-reproductive sexuality. It is precisely this same combination of misogyny and homophobia which underpins recent parliamentary moves in Britain to enact a legally binding distinction between 'real' and 'pretend' families in Clause 28 of the 1987 Local Government Bill – the furthest move that 'civilized' sexual morality has attempted in the direction of imposing its own miserably impoverished vision of 'family' life on the actual complex network of British social life.

Psychoanalysis and AIDS

One of the most striking aspects of contemporary debates concerning the future of the HIV pandemic focuses on the vexed question of heterosexual transmission. While some voices suggest that HIV is an immediate threat to *all* heterosexuals who are sexually active, others deny that it poses any risk at all. Three medical factors seem to be important at this point. First, we need to recognize with Professor Michael Adler that 'the commonest mode of transmission throughout the world is by sexual intercourse.

Whether this is anal or vaginal is unimportant' (Adler, 1987, p. 1). However, this knowledge is frequently undermined by the widely prevalent epidemiological concept of 'high-risk groups', which implies that some groups are intrinsically more vulnerable to HIV than others. This in turn is powerfully reinforced by the deeply misleading notion of 'homosexual acts', held to be primarily responsible for the transmission of the virus.

Second, we need to understand the delay between HIV infection, and the onset of subsequent illness resulting from damage to the body's immunological defences or its central nervous system. This means that the number of AIDS patients at any given time is a reflection of sexual behaviour five to ten years previously. Third, we need to understand the modes of transmission of HIV, which is not a contagious condition which may be 'caught' via casual contact, but a virus with distinct and well-known modes of infection. Unfortunately, little of the above seems widely appreciated, and a public discourse which talks repeatedly of the so-called 'AIDS virus' and 'AIDS carriers' only serves to confuse and obscure these relatively simple facts (see Watney, 1987a). The result has been a great deal of conflicting information about HIV disease, and consequent uncertainty and confusion in many minds.

Thus, for example, the *Daily Express* warned its readers 'AIDS peril ignored' on 3 February 1988, while less than two weeks later the same paper claimed that there is almost no risk at all of contracting HIV from heterosexual intercourse (Clare, 1988; Hill, 1988). The latter report speaks of catching AIDS, as if a syndrome of over forty distinct conditions could be 'caught'. Such language reveals the widespread ignorance concerning almost every aspect of HIV disease which is sadly so typical of mass media commentary, in Britain and elsewhere (see Watney, 1987b). AIDS is still widely regarded as a direct result of so-called promiscuity, and a moralistic agenda continues to undermine health education materials which emphasize that it is not one's sexual identity or number of sexual partners *per se* which put one at risk, but the nature of one's sexual behaviour – whether with one person of either sex, or fifty of each. Sexual intercourse, whether anal or vaginal, without the use of a condom, permits the transmission of HIV. This risk is obviously increased in those social groups affected by the virus for over a decade before its very existence was known. But this is no reason for complacency for other people.

One recent survey of the sexual partners of American heterosexuals with AIDS demonstrates clearly that

the overall incidence of HIV antibody among spouses of patients in this study was 58%. The seroconversion rate for male spouses (42%) was similar to that of female spouses (38%). These findings suggest that HIV may be transmitted in either direction with similar frequency. (Heiss, 1987)

Yet the writer of a lengthy article in *The Times* can still ask why it is that he does 'not know anybody *who knows anybody* who has contracted AIDS or been tested positive' (Lyndon, 1988). Besides the fact that you can't 'contract AIDS', this merely reveals a sadly typical ignorance of the epidemiology of HIV. It also suggests something else which is equally significant, namely, the cultural divisions in British society between gay and heterosexual men. In these circumstances it is impossible not to relate the widespread denial of the imminent danger of an HIV epidemic among British heterosexuals to the grotesque homophobia of British society (see Watney, 1987c).

The sheer scale and obstinacy of this denial would be remarkable if HIV were no more serious than measles or the common cold: in relation to an incurable condition it is frankly astonishing. For it is a denial which not only regards the possible deaths of tens and hundreds of thousands of gay men with complete indifference, but places those who are themselves so shockingly indifferent to the fate of others at real risk. Psychoanalysis proves helpful at just this point, because it argues that the forces of *repression*, which make gay men seem less than human, are identical with those at work in *resistance*. Furthermore, Freud argues that these same forces are also at work in the process of *transference*, whereby unconscious wishes are projected on to other people (see Laplanche and Pontalis, 1983). These three terms help us to understand the psychological mechanisms which inform so much public (i.e., heterosexual) commentary on the subject of HIV disease. They also help us to work our way to what exactly it is that such commentary goes to such elaborate lengths to protect its readers from acknowledging.

HIV has affected different communities in different parts of the world, according to the ways in which it spread before its existence was known. In Britain, it has primarily affected gay men until now, unlike the situations in Spain or Italy, for example, where it has most frequently affected heterosexuals who are injecting drug users, and their sexual partners. It has therefore become associated in Britain with homosexuality *as such*, and this is abundantly clear from countless TV documentaries and newspaper stories. We should, however, recognize that there is no *intrinsic* connection between HIV and gay men or their sexual behaviour. In this respect the continued homosexualization of HIV disease in the face of all the worldwide evidence concerning the diversity of social groups already affected strongly implies that the notion of HIV as a 'gay plague' in fact protects heterosexuals from facing up to something which they find even more frightening than AIDS – namely, the diversity of sexual desire.

For the irrationality which affects attitudes towards people with HIV or AIDS is not confined to gay men. As Cindy Patton points out,

We should understand that the idea of 'heterosexual

AIDS' is *another* social construction, which distances
heterosexuals with AIDS from the rest of the population
... AIDS has such power as a supposedly 'gay disease'
that *anyone* who gets it becomes 'queer' by association –
even haemophiliacs. This came up in a really simple way
for me. One lesbian asked me, 'Well, do you actually
know any lesbians who are having Safer Sex?', and I
replied that *I* do. She immediately gave me this look
which implied, 'what disgusting things have you done
that put you at risk?' So I became a queer lesbian in her
eyes, simply by identifying with the need for Safer Sex.
(Patton, 1988)

Yet the notion of 'heterosexual AIDS' is not simply a *social*
construction, as Patton's own argument demonstrates. It is
the displaced anxiety concerning 'perverse' sexualities
which fuels and reinforces such conscious attitudes.

Almost any amount of homophobic and racist 'explanations' of HIV among gay men or Black Africans and
Americans seem currently preferable to acknowledging
that HIV can be transmitted by *any* kind of unprotected
penetrative intercourse, and that heterosexuality is no
automatic 'natural' defence for European or American
whites. While we should, of course, be highly sceptical
about unproven assertions concerning the alleged origins of
HIV in Central Africa, this should not lead us to think of
AIDS in Africa as just another myth. Certainly 'African
AIDS' is yet another cultural construction which serves to
protect the illusion that sex between white people is
somehow intrinsically different (and 'safer') than between
Blacks. But it is a very strange anti-racist position which
moves from criticizing the undoubted racism of most
Western coverage of AIDS in Africa, to denying that AIDS
is really a serious problem in Africa at all. As with the
notion of 'heterosexual AIDS', HIV disease is either seen
totally to saturate an entire population, or else to be a total
fiction. A cursory glance at the latest World Health Organi-

sation statistics on AIDS in Tanzania and Uganda makes very grim reading indeed, and demonstrate that AIDS in Africa is certainly not simply a white racist myth, no matter how racist the cultural construction of 'African AIDS' might be in the West.

In these circumstances it is crucial to be able to criticize the structure of the argument which holds that the source of *any* viral infection is somehow its *cause*. If the geographical origin of HIV ever does emerge, we should not hold the population of that region to be somehow personally responsible. In this way we can challenge both racist and homophobic arguments, though it is clear that such positions are never rational. We need only compare depictions of Black African sexuality as an infernal domain of blood sacrifice, scarification and cannibalism, to similar depictions of gay male sexuality, to understand the immensely powerful force of repression and fantasy at work in both sets of images. Psychoanalysis will suggest that we consider this obsessive concentration on supposedly *excessive* Black and gay sexuality as a projection which reveals much about what exactly is repressed in white heterosexual Western societies. The hysterical defence of childhood 'innocence' undoubtedly suggests much about the difficulties our culture faces concerning children's sexuality. Here once more, psychoanalysis has much to teach us.

Conclusion

Deep psychological anxieties concerning the diversity and mobility of sexual desire are evidently at work throughout public commentary on AIDS. A widespread and highly significant inability to acknowledge that nobody *chooses* to get sick implies the existence of powerful resistance to the fact that HIV is, after all is said and done, a virus with known and therefore preventable modes of transmission. The logic of this resistance *requires* that AIDS should continue to be taken for granted as a 'gay plague'. This is not an accidental description, but protects and strengthens a fantasy of supposedly 'natural' heterosexuality, attacked on all sides by sinister perverts. In this respect we should recognize that the cultural picture of 'sick' homosexuality derives historically from Victorian notions of homosexual desire which were rooted in the metaphors of contemporary germ theory. The precise degree of psychological damage which this involves for individual 'self-confessed' heterosexuals remains to be calculated. In the meantime we should note that from the very beginnings of the HIV pandemic all Safer Sex information for heterosexuals has been produced and distributed by lesbians and gay men. It is profoundly ironic that the very forces which continue to marginalize and oppress us have resulted in strong levels of collective awareness which have underpinned the astonishingly successful containment of HIV among gay men in particular, via Safer Sex education and practices in our communities.

AIDS has taught lesbians and gay men a tremendous amount about the institutions and psychology of heterosexuality, and it is difficult for us not to regard the posturings and pretences of our straight friends without a complicated sense of plain astonishment, pity and concern. Sadly, it seems that they still stubbornly refuse to accept that they have anything to learn from us. Perhaps what is needed is a policy of compulsory quarantine for all *heterosexuals*, accompanied by a massive national therapy campaign conducted by lesbians and gay men, which might help them to become a little less frightened of their own sexual desires. For they have so much more than us to learn about the workings of repression, and they are tragically far less well prepared to accept the unconditional and absolute necessity for Safer Sex.

It is also difficult for lesbians and gay men not to note the terrible isolation in which so many heterosexual women and men feel obliged to live their lives, and the shocking psychological violence that the competitive cults of mach-ismo and 'femininity' do in their lives. For centuries homo-phobia has hurt and wounded and even killed *us*. Now it seems that it is turning back on heterosexuals themselves, in their refusal and inability to acknowledge the reality of HIV disease. At this moment in time there seems little to prevent a major HIV epidemic among heterosexuals, unless they can identify and overcome their own self-destructive homo-phobia. That is the underlying tragedy of AIDS today, a tragedy which most heterosexuals seem totally unable to comprehend.

References

Adler, M. (1987) *The A.B.C. of AIDS* (London:BMJ).

Bieber, I. *et al.* (1962), *Homosexuality: A Psychoanalytic Study of Male Homosexuals* (New York: Basic Books).

Dover, C. (1988), 'AIDS peril ignored' (*Daily Express*, 3 February), p. 24.

Freud, S. (1905), *Three Essays on the Theory of Sexuality*, in A. Richards (ed.), The Pelican Freud Library (PFL), Vol. 7 (Harmondsworth: Penguin, 1977).

Freud, S. (1908), '"Civilized" Sexual Morality and Modern Nervous Illness', in A. Dickson (ed.), PFL, Vol. 12 (Harmondsworth: Penguin, 1985).

Hill, D. (1988), 'Spreading the false message of AIDS' (*Daily Express*, 19 February), p. 8.

Laplanche, J. and Pontalis, J-B. (1983), *The Language of Psychoanalysis* (London: Hogarth Press).

Lifton, R. J. (1986), *The Nazi Doctors: Medical killing and the psychology of genocide* (New York: Basic Books).

Lyndon, N. (1988), 'Has anyone here got AIDS?' (*The Times*, 25 January), p. 11.

Mess, T., MD (1987), 'Selected annotated references', *AIDSFILE*, vol. 2, no. 2 (San Franscisco General Hospital Medical Center, June).

Owens, C. (1987), 'Outlaws: Gay men in feminism', in Alice Jardine and Paul Smith (eds), *Men In Feminism* (London: Methuen).

Patton, C. (1988), 'Safer sex and lesbians: becoming queer. Cindy Patton talks to Simon Watney', *The Pink Paper*, No. 14 (25 February).

Watney, S. (1987a), 'The subject of AIDS', *Copyright*, vol.1, no. 1 (Harvard).
Watney, S. (1987b), 'AIDS U.S.A.' *Square Peg*, vol. 17.
Watney, S. (1987c), *Policing Desire: Pornography, AIDS and the media* (London: Methuen).

CHAPTER TWO

AIDS and the cultural response: *The Normal Heart* and *We All Fall Down*

Sue Ellis and Paul Heritage

It seems difficult now to identify the time when AIDS ceased to be a distant 'gay cancer' and became a disease that deeply affects each of our social and personal lives. For some the change was immediate and acute – others have only just begun to negotiate the profound impact AIDS has made.

'The impact of AIDS' – it is a phrase that crops up again and again; it conjures up visions of some kind of viral hit-and-run accident, which leaves devastation and a sense of tragic waste trailing in its wake. Indeed, one of the first things to emerge from the AIDS crisis is a new terminology that has its own set of coded meanings and metaphors, by which we try to assess and understand what is happening. Certain cultural images have risen to prominence or have been given new currency in the world of AIDS-speak – images of infiltration and betrayal no longer carry the thrilling potency of a 1950s style scare about red queers in MI5. Instead they operate at an infinitely more localized level – the 'screening' of the body itself. Gay men are compared quite regularly to walking time-bombs waiting to explode, and the language of sickness and sexuality, disease and deviance, have become inextricably inter-twined.

On this level, AIDS ceases to be a virus and becomes culturally contagious – it also becomes far more deadly. Dependent upon the exploitation of guilt and fear, this panic systematically isolates and encloses the individual with its relentless focusing of the attention inwards. Collective political action becomes extremely difficult; energies are sponged away, its potential diffused in what we have come to recognize as a well-rehearsed formula of repression.

Mainstream theatre makes ample use of this process of cultural osmosis, with its almost imperceptible construction of myths, images and ideas. It may gather together hundreds of people in one place, but they certainly haven't come to talk to each other – indeed such interaction is positively discouraged, as anyone who has tried to offer the crisps round will know. Each faces front, involved in her or his own private communication with the stage world, passively consuming whatever it has to offer. It is a theatre of affirmation, not inquiry, where the individual consciousness is adjusted to what already pre-exists. The audience goes to have its various 'anti-social' tendencies enacted and exorcised. The erring woman either returns to hearth, home and husband, or she kills herself. The king expiates his 'crimes' against his parents by blinding himself, and the city is saved. The heroine in doublet and hose usually ends up in a dress for her wedding – she must, because order is always restored.

There is, however, an alternative discourse that is active in presenting a rather different reality. The individual, far from being adapted to her or his daily life, is encouraged, prodded or provoked into challenging the assumptions on which that daily life depends. In this oppositional theatre, the audience is asked 'expressly to discover that what happens all the time is not natural' (Brecht, 1977, p. 37), and it is at this point that intervention can begin.

This has already been started in the gay community, which is no longer simply being 'hit' by AIDS – it is fighting back. Gay people have been and are active in seeking to redefine their situation in what is now a two-way process. In simple language terms, the shift from 'AIDS victim' to 'person with AIDS' represents an attempt to change negative attitudes, while on a larger stage important statements are being made, such as torchlight gatherings in Trafalgar Square, giving a positive response to counteract the plague mentality. As the gay community affirms its own position, the whole perspective shifts.

The theatre also, as an important site of social organization, is capable of reinforcing an existing social structure or questioning its very preconceptions, and it is a place where that battle for meaning — and power — is fought out and rendered visible.

This essay deals with cultural responses at both ends of the M4 motorway. Swansea and London may be linked by a motorway, a high-speed train and a rapide coach, but it will be a long time before attitudes commute as freely as human travellers. Hence London reviewers could greet Larry Kramer's *The Normal Heart* — the capital's most famous AIDS play — with the 'raviest reviews in town' (*City Limits*, 29 May 1986) while the mere announcement of *We All Fall Down* — Swansea's most notorious AIDS play — led the *South Wales Evening Post* to scream 'AIDS PLAY SHOCK!' on its front page. Billboards promised pictures to accompany this lurid story, which must have been a disappointment to a sensation-hungry readership, when all that was shown was the Dylan Thomas Theatre where this dangerous play was to be performed. *The Normal Heart* played to standing ovations from its London audience and the written equivalent in the review pages of the national press. The tears of both audience and critics soaked all the reviews as each of the reviewers tried to convey just how s/he was moved, upset, enlightened or 'knocked out' by this 'white hot blast' of a play. The Swansea media's response was no less emotional: shock gave way to 'AIDS PLAY ANGER' as the local press and radio followed the troubled progress of the play through to its first night. While *The Normal Heart* took its place 'amongst the most glorious chapters in The Royal Court's history' (*The Listener*, 3 April 1986), the management of the Dylan Thomas Theatre tried to ban *We All Fall Down* on the basis that it was a 'homosexual exercise' which would unnecessarily alarm the public. In the best traditions of censorship they decided they had a duty to protect citizens from 'crude propaganda'. As the story progressed over the weeks prior to performance the banner headlines continued, while local councillors joined the fray, warning of serious public disorders if the play were staged. 'Concerned Christians' expressed their concern but scant Christian love in the letters' pages of the same newspaper which had only recently featured a story on its front page calling for the formation of local vigilante groups to attack gay people. The cast of *The Normal Heart* received universal acclaim from a bedazzled press who applauded 'the courage of all concerned for publicly and honestly confronting the taboo of AIDS' (*Sunday Today*, 6 April 1986). Meanwhile, one could read in the Swansea press how the cast of *We All Fall Down* – 'pro-gay activists' according to the Chairman of the Christian Research Institute – were the real menace to our society.

Principal Parts devised *We All Fall Down* with fine intentions of fighting ignorance and prejudice, but as the pressure from various 'moral' groups escalated – pickets, petitions, threatened funding withdrawal, and an attempt to stop the performance with a court injunction – the play ended up contributing, however unconsciously, to the very hysteria it had set out to combat. It became another AIDS story and, as such, it sold newspapers. The company were unable to prevent this simple, if not terribly skilful, manipulation of their work, and ultimately the play was viewed by the general public in the way in which the media chose to represent it. Revenge could be sought in the play itself, which was able to comment on its own treatment, but this seemed a sniper's shot in a battle that had already been lost. No one was interested in the meaning of the play, no one bothered to read a script or to ask what it was about before trying to ban it. It was the fact of the play itself, the actuality of performance, which produced the greatest shock, and implicitly posed the most serious threat. Up until this time in Swansea, any public discussion of AIDS was controlled very much by tabloid journalism and right-wing strategies – Principal Parts was outside of this territory and therein lay its challenge.

Principal Parts is a group of young performers already associated in the public's mind in Swansea with radical new writing, especially in the field of sexuality. This concentration in their work has aroused much controversy in the community, which would like to be able to accord a university company the respectability worthy of such a venerable institution. The productions tackled by the group are more than just plays – they are viewed as part of Swansea itself. Indeed, the *South Wales Evening Post* announced the successful fight against the ban of *We All Fall Down* as 'Curtain will rise on city AIDS play', thus locating it very precisely as the product of that specific community. At the same time the local media continued to identify it as something undesirable, something which should be resisted.

At the other end of the M4, *The Normal Heart* was hailed as a welcome addition to London theatre-land; it took place, after all, at an established venue which was part of a clearly defined metropolitan culture. The Royal Court, with its tradition of performing radical texts, has a recognizable voice which has shouted at audiences for over thirty years. One does begin to wonder, though, how much political potential there is in shouting, be it John Osborne or Larry Kramer – especially when it happens inside such a prestigious and commercial culture-factory as The Royal Court. But the play is constrained by much more than the place where it was performed.

Set in New York between 1981 and 1984, it follows the struggles of one man (Larry Kramer himself, thinly disguised as the character Ned Weeks), a wealthy and hotheaded gay writer who becomes politicised as his friends begin to die of AIDS. He provides the driving force behind the setting-up of one of the first AIDS support groups, GMHC, and begins an intense series of onslaughts on such targets as the influential *New York Times*, for ignoring the AIDS problem; on the indifferent officialdom of Mayor Koch and City Hall; and, on a more personal level, on his own brother, who represents a straight society whose 'single-minded determination to see us as sick helps keep us sick.'

But Weeks' main opposition comes from within the gay community itself, as the need for up-front campaigning and publicity becomes increasingly compromised by a very real nervousness for the jobs and incomes of those involved. As his lover is dying, Ned's mission to 'tell gay men to stop having sex' is abruptly curtailed with his expulsion from the organisation he helped to found. The play closes with an extraordinary deathbed marriage ceremony between Ned and Felix, presided over by their medical champion, the polio-crippled Dr Brookner, and Ned's brother.

The Normal Heart sought to release pressure on a minority group at a time when the panic about AIDS was intense. In fact it does precisely the opposite. The self-conscious fatalism of 'We must love one another or die' (W. H. Auden, 'September 1939', quoted in the Royal Court's programme of *The Normal Heart*) does little to obscure Kramer's central thesis that 'promiscuity' among gay men reduces them all to the level of murderers, and that in order to find true happiness – and prove that they really do have 'normal hearts' – they all ought to get married.

These are the ideas of the text; whether an audience is able to perceive them for what they are is a wholly different matter, because the play makes its ideological conclusion through its narrative, its 'story'. As the creation of an individual playwright, *The Normal Heart* is a complete and finished product: actors and director can do no more than 'interpret' what is already there. Even then they have little room to manoeuvre, because Kramer's voice – that of the angry gay activist – manifests itself almost exclusively through one immensely sympathetic character. Without Ned Weeks, the play simply falls apart, because he is its emotional barometer. He bangs off another piece of show-stopping (and evasive) rhetoric, and we reel in admiration. Or he is presented at a moment of excruciating pain – the curtain comes down with a crescendo that makes Ibsen look amateur, and we are left in tears. In order for the story to make sense, the audience has to invest heavily in what is ultimately, a fictional character, substituting his experience for their own, and worse, accepting his ideas as their own. Kramer knows only too well that the plot is the soul of the play, and leaves his audience no time to question or disengage, hurtling them along from one tense confront-ation to another so that in the end, they can only see at the level the playwright dictates.

John Gill, writing in *Time Out*, has a telling response to the play; he says it is 'heartrendingly engaging stuff' that has the 'power to shock, move and change'. Yet almost in the same sentence he recommends that the 'socio-political quibbles should be put aside'. Quite how it is supposed to effect change in our lives through gut-reaction alone is not entirely clear. But the response is, nevertheless, an impor-tant one, as it implies that *The Normal Heart* is somehow able to transcend its own political location by inducing an emotional overload in its audience. Herein lies its greatest danger – not only is it a text that contains inaccurate and, in the continuing crisis of AIDS, downright repressive informa-tion, it seems to have acquired a life of its own, divorced from the historical, political and cultural forces that pro-duced it. It has become, if you like, universal in its appeal. Already the play is a firm favourite on the British repertory circuit: many gay people feel that they are performing a service to their community by putting it on, and so it continues on its way, self-propagating, its irresistible reputation proving more important that its actual content. In August 1987, Focus Theatre Company mounted a production of *The Normal Heart* for the Edinburgh Festival Fringe, with the approval and blessing of the Scottish AIDS Monitor. Duly harrowed audiences emerged sniffling to face the collecting-box in the foyer. Donating gave people the opportunity to respond to the play's insistent appeal for funding, and at the same time, they could prove that they really did 'value' the lives of gay men. It is deeply alarming if this play, the first major cultural artefact to emerge from the AIDS crisis, can leave its audience with no more concrete solution that the furtive stuffing of 50p in a tin.

In conventional theatre, where the division of labour has always operated according to a rigid hierarchy, each individual worker carries out a predetermined function and stays within the realm of her or his expertise. Designers, performers and technicians may work very closely together as a production team, but they are in the end communicating ideas that have been structured by somebody else – in the 1980s that somebody is usually the director or playwright. Any ideological differences these workers may have are either deemed unimportant or become absorbed into a framework that will only admit a unified and coherent vision of the world. This can be seen in Claire Bloom's comments to an interviewer about her role in Central Television's *Intimate Contact*. Alison Peachey, writing in the *Express* found Bloom's detachment from her character (that of a golf-playing woman whose husband contracted AIDS from a prostitute) rather alarming: 'You might think that any actor [sic] who takes on a major role in a harrowing drama about AIDS would see themselves in a campaigning position ... "There's no point in pretending that I took the part in the hope that more people will learn about the disease," snaps Claire. "When I read the script I just knew that it was a tremendously good part."' Her co-star, Daniel Massey, found thinking about the controversy equally irrelevant – 'It's the quality of the writing that counts.' They cannot be blamed for their indifference – perhaps it was all part of Central's extremely careful marketing of such a 'sensitive' series; what is certain is that as performers, Bloom's and Massey's response was limited within strictly 'artistic' concerns, and nothing more was required of them.

For Principal Parts, as for most oppositional groups, this working method was unacceptable; it was only through exploring the insecurities and prejudices people have about sexuality, death and disease that the company were able to take control of their material – it was never something outside of their own lives and experiences. As each member of the group discovered more about AIDS, the information was filtered through an individual perspective; yet because the group was learning together – instructing one another – they developed a common view of the situation. The disagreements as well as the agreements were important to this process: the issue of penetrative intercourse, for example, remained a constant sticking point, but there was a unified understanding of how the government was responsible in conspiring to cause the deaths of gay men.

It came as something of a surprise for the media to learn that the group was comprised of gays and straights, females and males (just as it might appear anomalous for a female author to be contributing to a book on gay men's politics and culture). Those who asserted a visible gay profile were pushed into prominence by the press, who delighted in musing on their 'links' with a project about AIDS. This strategy was, in the end, double-edged. By making the play a hot news item, the press were required to report its progress, and had difficulty sometimes in deciding whether to champion the underdog or join the chorus of disapproval. As the play emerged victorious from its various battles this ambivalence between support and suppression grew less striking, but none the less ironic.

But the group's composition played a far more vital role than merely nonplussing would-be homophobes. One of the fundamental objectives of the play was to unsettle fixed notions of sexuality and to open up an active discourse on the assumptions we have about what is 'right' or 'true' for whom. The collaboration between female and male, gay and straight, was not merely a tactical alliance – it was an attempt to find a collective language through which the diversity itself could be accepted and celebrated. It is this rationale that lies behind what you are reading now.

The pluralist approach that informed *We All Fall Down* ensured that it operated on a variety of levels; it did not simply take its audience by the nose and lead it through the psychological trials and tribulations of a single protagonist. When the content centres around AIDS, this kind of narrative structure has little option but to finish with copious tears at the side of a hospital bed, where it necessarily becomes a closed agenda. And because they had made a personal and political commitment to examining how we all live with AIDS, rather than how some people die of it, Principal Parts found it imperative to seek out new forms.

Originally conceived in structure as a string quartet, *We All Fall Down* is divided into four distinct movements. The first explores the history of the gay community's response to AIDS through dance, and is anchored throughout by a series of commentaries varying from a homophobic comic's routine to a young man trying to get through to a help-line. The sequence culminates in a new sureness of physicality, and the dancers' growing sense of articulacy and solidarity.

The second movement takes the form of four separate accounts: a health educationalist, talking about her daily battles with media panics; a conflict between workers and management over an AIDS issue; a doctor about to perform the antibodies test; and a woman who has developed AIDS. Although highly individualised, each case-study moves beyond the immediately personal to ask insistent questions about the meaning of 'normality', about health and illness, and about exploitation.

Movement Three is a frenetic 'whodunnit' farce revolving around the dead body in the drawing room. Having established the cause of death as AIDS, the enigmatic Inspector Dick begins his investigations into all possible modes of transmission, clearing up a few of the myths in the process, and unravelling a hot-bed of sexual activity. One by one, the prime suspects are eliminated by virtue of their all having practised safer sex, which leaves only a grotesque portrait of Margaret Thatcher with nothing to say for herself. The movement returns chillingly to reality, with a detailed analysis charting this present government's action (or rather, inaction) since AIDS was formally recognised as a new disease in 1981.

There is no conclusive ending to the show: the final sequence, comprising a traditional protest song, can offer no answers, but places the arguments in the real world of the audience, where AIDS is an issue to be confronted in their own lives, and one which demands their action.

In abandoning the conventional 'plot' and introducing a structure that was deliberately fragmentary and open-ended, the company were able to negotiate a new kind of relationship with the audience, one that involved them in the same kind of debates and arguments that had triggered off the project itself. Performers crossed that sacred divide between stage and audience so that the pictorial illusion framed by the proscenium arch was constantly being broken up. Twenty minutes after the play began, it stopped abruptly while the cast interviewed members of the audience about what they had just seen. Using video cameras and radio microphones, the words and images of the audience were actively presented on the stage itself through a monitor, thus inverting the normal process of theatre. This was not the only point in the play where the audience were given a platform from which they could express their views on the action. The play had always been conceived as being incomplete without a discussion of the issues raised – they were not resolved within a theatrical fiction, because they exist in our material world and, as such, can be dismantled, examined and changed.

Perhaps one of the most important aspects of the project was that at no point did it ever stand still as a self-contained work of 'art'. The text underwent revisions virtually from day to day, as new theories and statistics emerged about the AIDS crisis; this was crucial to the piece as educational theatre, for it must be remembered that its performance predated the official government campaign. This fluid state was to change, however, when the play was transferred to an altogether different medium – that of video film.

We All Fall Down on video was compromised by much more than being inside a television box. Principal Parts could not control how it would be used in a specific situation, and, of course, this altered its meaning considerably. When it is used in schools, for example, teachers exert their own form of censorship by showing selections rather than the whole piece. The fragmentary nature of the text actually facilitates this process, so that the video can be seen to be supporting the assumptions and prejudices of those controlling its viewing. Those are hard lessons, for the temptation to use video as a means of promoting AIDS education is enormous. It has an immediate advantage over theatre in that, if it can be successfully marketed, it has an accessibility denied the usual fringe theatre performance. Quite simply, it can reach a lot of people, and will do so in surroundings that are safe and familiar. Video tempts further when one realizes the advantages of working within a medium that is recognizable, that has a known vocabulary, whereas theatre is increasingly alien and elite.

We All Fall Down was sponsored by the University of Swansea without interference. This is a rare luxury as video costs are extremely high and the involvement of funding bodies invariably means a loss of independence. This is shown by the more recent videos commissioned from

Principal Parts by organizations anxious to provide AIDS information for people with learning difficulties. Those who hold the purse strings will always seek to control the messages and images constructed. For example, the script for *Sign of the Times*[1] has been forced to use 'proper' language as opposed to the vernacular – characters in that video have to masturbate, because they're not allowed to wank. This is vaguely irrelevant anyway, as the major form of communication used is British Sign Language, which does not observe such polite absurdities. More significant, perhaps, is that the attempt to politicize the social implications of AIDS, and how it affects the individual, is sharply curtailed.

The original play had attempted to open up the AIDS debate at a time when its parameters were defined by those with vested interests to preserve. This process is being extended in important ways by a variety of projects with the profoundly deaf, the mentally handicapped and NACRO (National Association for the Care and Resettlement of Offenders). On a primary level it provides access to information for those who are either marginalized or simply ignored. By involving the people at whom the videos are aimed at all the levels of production, it is intended that they themselves find the voice to reach their own community. In exactly the same way as gay people have felt the need to take control of their lives in relation to AIDS, to produce their own cultural images, so too should this be possible with the mentally, physically and socially disabled. For anyone concerned about the control of sexuality, this video work has a significance highlighted by AIDS yet going well beyond it. To take one example: by promoting the principle that mentally handicapped people should be informed about safer sex, one challenges basic myths surrounding how their sexuality is perceived. Such myths are often contradictory but none the less powerful, as society is willing to believe, on the one hand, that mentally handicapped people are sexually irresponsible and promiscuous, and, on the other, that their sexuality corresponds to a so-called 'mental age' and is therefore non-existent. Invariably, 'deviant sexual responses' (which are taken to include masturbation and homosexuality) in the mentally handicapped arise simply because there is a refusal to accept that they experience the same needs and feelings as everyone else, and that they have the right to the appropriate education and information to understand and express themselves sexually.

This ideology parallels the way in which lesbians and gay men have been treated within our culture for centuries. For too long gay people have passively received the images constructed for them, images which have, in the last few years, become increasingly dangerous. In early 1988 Clause 28 of the Local Government Bill was being debated in Parliament. Its introduction indicated the Thatcher government's recognition and fear of the power of positive images; government is moving swiftly to eliminate all such 'promotion.' When we first drafted this essay, we ended with a plea to all those working as cultural practitioners to take up responsibility for challenging acquiescent oppression. When Clause 28 entered the legislation of this country, we were all forced to defend the very basis of our work: the right to express ourselves without censorship or intervention from a state whose main aim is the preservation of all that perpetuates its economic and ideological supremacy.

Notes

1 *Sign of the Times*, AIDS education video for the profoundly deaf, commissioned by Wales Council for the Deaf and funded by the Welsh AIDS campaign.
2 *The Normal Heart* will probably be appearing at a repertory theatre near you in the near future.
3 *We All Fall Down* is available from Albany Video, the Albany, Douglas Way, London SE8 4AG. Tel. 01 692 6322.

References

Brecht, B. (1977), *The Exception and the Rule*, trs. Ralph Manheim (London: Eyre Methuen), p. 37.

Boal, A. (1979), *Theatre of the Oppressed*, trs. Charles A. and Maria-Odilia Leal McBride (London: Pluto Press), p. 113.

Acknowledgement

The authors are deeply indebted to the cast of *We All Fall Down* and to Principal Parts.

CHAPTER THREE

Homophobia/misogyny: Sexual fears, sexual definitions

Joseph Bristow

It was in the fourth form of my repressive (and no doubt repressed) all-boys school that I first sorted out the distinction between homosexuality and misogyny. For some time I'd been making a silly mistake. My kind and rather nice-looking English teacher (whom we all reckoned was a poof) took some trouble to put me right. 'Homosexuality', he said, 'defines men loving other men. Misogyny, by contrast, means men hating women.' Many years later – and with an educational experience that has led me to write an essay like this one – some of the books I read and some of the voices I hear seem to contradict him. What I thought was a passing phase (my homosexual feelings and my confusion about homosexuality) has, it seems, refused to go away. Indeed, the misperception that I held when I was struggling to work out why I fancied some of the boys in my class turns up these days in even the most 'radical' places – and that includes some feminist writings.

Over the past decade, I've come to find out that the world of sexual politics can be just as violent and full of contest as the world (the patriarchal, heterosexual world) it criticizes, largely because the terms with which it deals lie at the centre of the greatest anxieties we experience in our everyday lives. How my sexuality exists in relation to the family, to work, to race, and to women now seems just as problematic as it did when I was in school uniform. The word 'gay' and the process of 'coming out' have resolved little in the way of understanding what male homosexuality actually means, why it takes certain forms of representation (on the gay 'scene', in particular), and why, above all, it preoccupies the minds of so many people, especially those who live in fear of it. With a raised consciousness there has come for me an intensified awareness of the sexual divisions that govern our society. Are sexual relations, I continually ask myself, really changing *that* much? Does the representation (a still very limited representation) of lesbians and gay men on popular television, for example, have any radical impact on our culture? At least in the classroom I had my English teacher to rely on. But, then, I'm now involved in a lifestyle that is still regarded as controversial in school (just think of the attacks on the Inner London Education Authority and their willingness to support the children's book, *Jenny Lives with Eric and Martin*, which tells the story of a young girl and her relationship with her father and his male lover). Certainly, positive images of gay life and gay loving could not have been brought up in one of my English lessons in the 1970s.

Half way through my higher education (in the early 1980s), I discovered the vital distinction between being classified as 'homosexual' and transforming that category by becoming 'gay'. 'Homosexual', I began to understand, was (and, to some extent, still *is*) a clinical definition derived from the researches of late nineteenth-century medicine and the more specialized discipline of sexology. 'Gay', by contrast, was a politically chosen term established after Stonewall (1969) that stood for pride, opposition and liberation, and was grounded (so I thought) in socialism. Then, a bit later, a newly-coined word entered my vocabulary – 'homophobia' – which described an irrational fear of homosexuals, the kind of fear that reached alarming pro-

portions with the press coverage of AIDS in 1983–4.
(Homophobia is a word that notably didn't get into the
press.) As time goes by, these words (as words will) have
come to mean slightly different things. Moreover, their
meanings change what can loosely be referred to as dominant ideology (that is, the myths we live by and are
subject to) neutralizes the political resistance of so-called
'deviant' groups. At the same time, we (lesbians, gay men,
feminists, socialists) attempt to forge a more precise range
of terms to analyse our sexual lives and the pressures
people place on us. What is more – and this is where we
truly glimpse a truly revolutionary future – oppressed
groups are now creating alliances (at times ridiculed as
'rainbow alliances') to challenge, in greater numbers and
with greater understanding between ourselves, the dominant ideology that weighs the power of the state against
us.

This essay takes a brief look at how men are defined as
'gay' within the popular (namely, gutter) press, within the
broad field of sexual politics and by gay subculture itself,
and how particular fears circulate around those (not altogether precise) definitions. Homophobia is, needless to say,
the social problem that keeps misidentifying (scapegoating,
mystifying, sensationalizing) lesbians and gay men as
corrupt, as diseased and, at times, as evil.

Since the demise of the Gay Liberation Front in the mid
1970s, the word 'gay' has been increasingly used in the
predominantly Tory press as an apolitical and covertly
pathological term. As the clinical overtones of 'homosexual' diminish to some extent, the word 'homophobia'
has emerged in the gay press to define the various kinds of
hatred directed against those of us who desire the same sex.
Homophobia is a word currently associated with radical
politics. By that, I mean that the Left (in the broadest sense)
has begun to understand what it means. 'Homophobia'
stands out as an authoritative term, in that it makes
heterosexuality seem as diseased as homosexuality was

once (and, frequently, still is) claimed to be. That said, 'homophobia' remains a rather awkward construction. 'Homophobia' gives the impression that there is a particular cause for hating both lesbians and gay men. But anti-lesbianism and anti-gay-maleness (equally clumsy, yet more specific) are, of course, distinct. Sexual fears about lesbians and gay men manifest themselves differently. Lesbians, for example, are at the receiving end of misogyny, which can come into operation to enable men to control a situation whether at home, at work, or in the street. Gay men can indeed be the agents of this kind of appalling sexual hatred. Furthermore, 'homophobia' is not a precise analytic tool when discussing kinds of anti-gayness that surface now and again in feminist writings, particularly those written from a radical lesbian–feminist perspective. Feminist *fears* of *gay men* may not be altogether unrelated to general fears of gay men. However, feminist *objections* to aspects of *gay culture* derive from a politics which some gay men would claim to share.

Finally – and I promise this will be the last in this series of dictionary definitions – there is a word that turns up regularly in sexual politics and has been at the centre of a number of trades union initiatives (supposedly) to protect lesbian and gay workers. This is, namely, 'heterosexism'. It is a cover-all term for the variety of anti-lesbian and anti-gay practices that can occur at work. Equal opportunities rhetoric has occasionally responded to charges against heterosexism by including protection clauses regarding sexual orientation in appointment procedures. There has been in a few (not many) cities in Britain an increased understanding of heterosexism in local government and social services (particularly in connection with housing policy). Again, like the term 'homophobia', 'heterosexism' wrongly lumps together lesbians and gay men as the same object of sexual discrimination. This focus on the perils of heterosexism has come at a time when lesbians and gay men have learnt the necessity of organizing *separately* from one another. No matter which terms we reach out for to work to our advantage, it seems, someone, somewhere is going to misrepresent us – and that includes ourselves whoever 'we' are.

Lesbian culture and gay culture are separated from each other at the point where those two terms of sexual fear and hatred – homophobia and misogyny – overlap. Since lesbians and gay men experience extraordinary forms of sexual loathing from the world at large, our sense of each other's cultural difference from straight society is fraught with exceptional anxieties. As the 1970s wore on, lesbians saw that the word 'gay' failed to define their struggles. Now, well into the 1980s, no longer are we talking exclusively of 'gay rights' but of 'lesbian and gay rights'. The current labour campaign (Labour Campaign for Lesbian and Gay Rights) and the corresponding legislation campaign (Organization for Lesbian and Gay Action) unite men and women on the issue of equal rights for those of us expressing same-sex desire. But where there is unity on that broad definition, there are substantial differences between us which relate to gender and sexuality. It is surely misrepresentative these days to refer (and I sometimes still hear it said) to lesbians as 'gay women'. Have we ever felt it entirely appropriate to talk of 'gay mothers'? And yet, there are further contradictions here since there are some women involved in same-sex relationships who refuse to associate with lesbian culture and lesbian politics. The word 'gay' now almost exclusively means men-loving-men. *Any* man (not a specific clinical or physical type) – married or single, butch or effeminate – has the option of having sex with other men.

If in the popular press the word 'gay' is used to denote men having sex with each other, in sexual politics it is – or at least used to be – associated with a more specific kind of lifestyle. This lifestyle is frequently a source of outrage and contempt, particularly to political reactionaries and some radical feminists. To be 'gay' in the larger urban centres of

Britain means going to gay pubs and clubs, places whose commercialism has increased a great deal in the 1980s. Gay culture is founded in these places, and, on the whole, what we call the 'scene' marks out those spaces where something close to a 'gay community' can be enjoyed. In even the most provincial gay pub, there are types of men who signal their sexuality through dress codes. In our bars, we encounter leathermen, drag queens, and, of course, clones (who, with their check shirts and moustaches, still seem to be in the majority). However, there are many men who don't conform to these clearly defined stereotypes. If one thing strikes me about the gay pubs in my own city, Sheffield, it is the *ordinariness* of many of the clientele – they could be drinking and smoking almost anywhere. The scene, of course, varies from town to town. Sometimes lesbians and gay men occupy the same pub (the women are usually fewer in number). Sometimes the managerial policy will be to exclude women altogether. Outside London (where a much more diversified scene exists), specifically lesbian spaces are hard to locate. My experiences in the 'regions' (and I've lived in the South, the Midlands, and now the North) tells me that the gay scene tolerates lesbians as long as they don't interfere with the cruising that goes on between the men.

Gay men want territories where they can rendezvous for sex (which can sometimes occur on the premises). We also require not just sexual contacts but somewhere to talk, drink, smoke – *socialize*. The gay scene is one of the few places where we can manage to be together without inhibitions. This can mean taking pleasure in casual sex, frequent partners and uncomplicated (because impersonal) relationships. When specific dress codes come into play, erotic identities can be quickly interpreted. Obviously, this subcultural activity runs wholly against received ideas of what it means to be a man and what it means to be 'respectable'. On the scene, sex is often non-monogamous, based on a principle of pleasure, and doesn't, to right-wing moralists at least, appear to be based on humanistic values

of truth, honesty, and personal commitment. In a gay club
or pub, there is – *conspicuously* – much loving, mutual
support, physical closeness and friendship among ourselves. Yet, it is the unusual and therefore shocking crui-
siness of the scene that can cause alarm in even the most
liberal people's minds. On the scene, dominant definitions
of love, friendship and sex are blurred, or to put it more
precisely, *realigned*. To be a friend, to be a lover, to want
sex are part of a continuum on the scene that heterosexuality (as an institution) cannot comprehend because of the
careful barriers that surround heterosexual categorizations
– such as the couple, the family and, of course, the defined
roles ascribed to man and woman within the gender
hierarchies that support heterosexuality. To heterosexuals
especially, the scene can appear decadent and hedonistic,
degenerate in a way that has always been attached to
accounts of same-sex love. All that has been said so far does
not aim to utopianize the 'scene', which can hold within its
closed doors the racism, sexism and ageism to be found in
any straight pub or club. Yet no matter how dreadful we
may find our places of social life, we always need to bear in
mind that we are *excluded* from expressing what we feel
from practically everywhere else.

What is more, gay men have in recent years expressed –
and, in that, participated in the construction of – what has
been an always potential interest in SM. The SM industry –
with its mail-order merchandise of bondage and domination: harnesses, handcuffs and nipple-clamps – has become
more visible than before. There are, perhaps, two reasons
for this. First, within popular culture, a powerful and highly
eroticized form of masculinity has emerged – for example,
in the individualistic law of the jungle survivor, Rambo,
whose body speaks of a hardened resistance to the most
brutal forms of 'natural' violence. This ultra-masculine
image is found particularly in cinema. Second, and not
unrelated to this, the advent of 'safer sex' to prevent the
transmission of HIV has encouraged us to concentrate our

erotic interests on non-genital sex – on fetishes, for instance. To outsiders, the erotic code of SM can look politically suspect because it plays with materials that connote masculine violence. It needs to be stressed that to participate in the gay scene – whether in a small regional pub, a denim club, or a leather bar – hardly requires a right-on political conscience. Being a part of gay culture is not about whether your desire is 'correct' or 'incorrect', innocent or guilt-ridden. It is, instead, simply about wanting certain kinds of sex – and, importantly, sex without shame. In some sections of gay subculture, this desire for SM is ever quickening its demands for more immediate and risk-taking eroticism as the scene becomes more machoized, glorifying images of male potency. And yet I'm not frightened by these macho-looking men. When I'm in a gay pub sitting, for instance, next to a skinhead, I'm sure he is unlikely to abuse me. The gay scene is – lest those who criticize our love of maleness forget it – one of the few places where men gather together to relate to each other sexually, and not with the hardened aggression and brutality that men exert upon each other in families, workplaces and all-male institutions like the army. The macho image present here is not the one that intimidates me on the streets – and yet this image is necessarily defined against the myth of masculinity which discourages sexual relations between men. There is something in the fear that kinds of hard and potent masculinity can generate that heightens the eroticism of these butch types. On the scene, such fear has a space in which it can become an expressed desire.

Analysing the 'butch shift' that has occurred on the scene, Martin Humphries (1985, p. 84) points to the political problems such ultra-masculinity raises:

> By creating amongst ourselves apparently masculine men who desire other men we are refuting the idea that we are really feminine souls in male bodies. Gay men can be diverse models of sexual desirability and it is for us to

explore and expand that diversity. What we need to be aware of is that the creation of masculine images, whilst subverting heterosexism, is not a radical redefinition of masculinity or a radical attack on the mores of patriarchy. It does hack away at the monolithic façade of patriarchal culture but it cannot end there.

To reiterate: gay men are out to show that we are not 'pansies', 'poofs', 'faggots', 'queers' – all those effeminizing and, implicitly, misogynistic insults first heard at school and which remain with us for the rest of our lives. But in mimicking 'real men', in fact taking masculinity to its most extreme in terms of representation (but not execution), it is questionable whether our pleasures in eroticizing the male body (even if to the point of parody) are subverting anything at all. Subversion, obviously, has to engage with (maybe even collude with) structures of dominance. The general political effect of the macho look adopted by some gay men is to answer back those who despise us. We are telling our haters that we are indeed men, and we can indeed appear really masculine, and yet we do what men are not supposed to do – fuck each other. Since some of us have made a decision to look very masculine, does that mean our femininity (our nancy-boy image) has been dispensed with? In leathers, or check shirts, or construction-worker hats, are we *really* men? These questions emerge from the way in which gay culture swerves between images that are ultra-masculine and ultra-feminine – we talk, after all, about leather *queens*. The non-gay world finds our manipulation of their images – which we are both accepting *and* rejecting – impossible to tolerate. Why hate gay men? Because we take heterosexual images to *extremes*. Because, it might be presumed, we indulge in acts that many 'straight' men would like to perform, and yet, for the sake of their power – at home, at work, on the streets – they *dare* not. Homophobia comes out of a confusion about the *lie* upon which heterosexuality subsists – that men are *naturally* more powerful than women, and that men *naturally* dominate women, physically, sexually, economically.

Recently, homophobia has received a considerable amount of theoretical attention, notably in relation to psychoanalysis. There is a thread running through Freud's work that claims that male heterosexuality is based (albeit precariously) on repressed homosexuality. I certainly don't accept the Freudian argument. It has, for one thing, contentious political implications. If taken on board – as it has been by some feminist and right-wing theorists[1] – this line of thinking suggests that the violent practices of patriarchy (most of which are misogynistic and homophobic) are at root homosexual. Take, for example, Kate Millett's discussion of Nazi ideology in her well-known, much-admired but now out of date book, *Sexual Politics* (1969, 1977, p. 167):

> Homosexuality [under the Third Reich] was vigorously denounced, and there were frequent homosexual purges in the military, despite the continued presence of Captain Roehm, a well-known homosexual, as leader of the stormtroopers. The virility cult of Nazi male culture, its emphasis upon 'leaders' and male community, lent the entire Nazi era a curious tone of repressed homosexuality, neurotically anti-social and sadistic in character. The men's house culture of the Nazi *Männerbünde* constituted something very like an instance of state-instituted deviance.

Millett's cultural analysis makes it seem as if anti-social neuroses and sadism are obvious manifestations of same-sex desire among men. Moreover, Millett implies, paradoxically, that homosexuality is all the more socially *obvious* ('state-instituted') because it is *repressed*. The logic of all this is, to say the least, hard to follow. In a received and reduced version of Freud such as Millett's, it must be inferred that repressed homosexual desire is the *cause* of the misogyny and homophobia that keep 'straight' men in power and women out of it. In other words, a fanatical patriarchy which relegates women to positions of subser- vience is *enabled* by a concealed yet supporting homo- sexuality that binds men together (*Männerbünde*). Such an argument gives the impression that gay men are the culprits of the sexual inequalities – between homosexual and heterosexual, man and woman – we have to struggle against. This glaring contradiction – that homosexual desire creates the oppression of homosexuality – appears over and over again in sociology, literary theory and varieties of feminist criticism. What Millett fails to see is that it is a fundamental feature of *heterosexuality* that fosters the Nazi fraternity.

An American feminist writer, Eve Kosofsky Sedgwick, has written a book about male bonding (as represented in a series of canonical works of English literature) which switches around the terms of this Freudian piece of think- ing. Sedgwick uses the word 'homosocial' – another newly- coined term – to analyse the non-sexual relationships between men that keep them in power. Homosocial rela- tions, Sedgwick states, enable men to be close together – in teams, hierarchies, institutions – while, at the same time, keeping them sexually apart. That is, men can work closely together *homosocially* as long as they operate *homo- phobically*. Homosocial relations are, therefore, based on homophobia. The key problem for heterosexual men, claims Sedgwick, is that they find it hard to ensure that homosocial and homosexual are maintained as opposites of one another. The line between the two, it seems, is preca- riously thin: 'For a man to be a man's man is separated only by an invisible, carefully blurred, always-already-crossed line from being "interested in men"' (Sedgwick, 1985, p. 89). Homophobia encourages homosocial relations which, in turn, must never be interpreted as homosexual. If Sedgwick is to be believed, and if moral panics arise because the line between homosocial and homosexual is exceptionally fine (and thus susceptible to being transgressed), then it follows that gay men are just as much men as our hetero-sexual counterparts. We belong, gay and straight, to a spectrum or continuum of *masculinities* that homosocial relations attempt to deny. We are, then, similar in that we men *desire* each other, sometimes genitally, sometimes not. Homophobia serves the purpose of telling us all how *unalike* gay and straight men are from one another. Sedg-wick's theory, therefore, explodes the myth that hetero-sexual men are repressed homosexuals, and stresses that, significantly, homophobia is a *heterosexual* problem.

Feminist writings sometimes point to the similarity between straight and gay men without bearing in mind how homophobia serves the interests of one kind of man and not the other. In their provocative study of sexual harassment in everyday life, *Georgie Porgie*, Sue Wise and Liz Stanley (1987, pp. 92–3) have an important point to make when they demonstrate that the problems men present to women in different situations relate not just to sex but to power. To prove this point, Wise and Stanley state that gay men (designated by the authors as their relished '*pièce de résistance*') are just as sexist as other men, even though we may not be aiming to make passes at women:

> Gay men are in no way sexually interested in women; but that doesn't stop them from using and abusing, patronising and ripping off women wherever and whenever possible. Certainly the history of lesbians' involvement with gay men in this country, both recently and historically, is characterised by gay men's contempt for women's needs, rights and worth, but presented within a rhetoric which proclaims our common oppres-sion. The techniques that they use to put women down may not involve the use of sexual behaviours but, cur-iously enough, they are often of a 'sexual nature' in a different way: 'oh I could never have sex with a *woman*,

it'd be like putting my cock in a can full of worms', as one gay man said recently.

On the whole, though, gay men's sexual harassment of women is less focussed on references to 'doing sex' than straight men's, but this does not make it any less contemptuous, as the above comment shows. Gay men are men who revere 'maleness' to the nth degree and, as we've said, male versions of reality confer superiority on men merely by virtue of their difference from 'inferior' women.

These angry and wayward generalizations assume that gay male sexuality is based on an absolute abhorrence of women – whether in political organizations or sexual situations. Clearly, Wise and Stanley's participation in the lesbian and gay rights movement in the 1970s was a bitter one since women were marginalized and misrepresented in some (not all) of those campaigns. Yet this specific experience is used to diagnose the essence of gay maleness – misogyny. Lurking beneath their analysis, there is the sense that gay men harass women (use, abuse, patronize, and rip them off – hardly an understatement) because we are made to feel 'inferior' to other men. Our masculinity, it seems, demands that we feel 'superior' to a subordinate group (women). Since we 'revere maleness to the nth degree', women are only to be despised. (Do we revere those straight men who beat us up, I wonder?) It is as if our *lack* of sexual interest in women makes us intrinsically *more* sexist than other men. Wise and Stanley thoughtlessly enable their restrictive analysis of sexual relations here to run more smoothly by ignoring the sexual harassment gay men themselves experience at home, at work, indeed in all aspects of everyday life. Harassment of gay men – particularly in the workplace – has increased in response to media reports of AIDS. Since Wise and Stanley's book shares the same historical moment as, for example, the government's alarming health warnings about the syndrome 'such as 'AIDS is not a gay disease'. Well, what *is*?), they are conniving with right-wing fears of gay men. As the papers peddle the myth that promiscuity among gay men is likely to kill off the entire population, these lesbian feminist authors tell the world that we hate women too. Wise and Stanley have, then, used the accusation of gay misogyny in the name of a homophobic feminism.

The invidious process of scapegoating – whether in the very different hands of the moral right-winger or the lesbian separatist – always involves establishing some unchanging *essence* which marks out the scapegoat as a convenient target for fear and loathing. For the moral Right, gay men are carriers of a plague. For Wise and Stanley, gay men are disgusted by femininity. The crazy idea that gay men are *essentially* misogynistic (who is the 'one gay man', so loosely cited? One from a random or highly selective sample? Wise and Stanley are, supposedly, *sociologists*) simply facilitates a reductive lesbian politics, one that would be rejected by lesbians who ally themselves with gay men and who realize that gayness and lesbianism are *not* sexual essences but statements about sexual preferences. Gay men can (and, of course do) relate sexually to women – as fathers, husbands, friends and, on occasions, misogynists. What, then, is motivating this ludicrous paragraph from Wise and Stanley's manual on how too deal with sexual harassment in everyday life? To discover the answer, it is necessary to return to the gay scene.

Misogyny is a disturbing but not an intrinsic feature of gay culture. The figure of the drag queen is sometimes pointed to by feminists as the epitome of gay men's innate hatred of women. However, it needs to be borne in mind that drag takes many forms – sometimes it vilifies femininity, sometimes it exposes and decries how men construct images of women (as in the performances of Bloolips). Like much of gay culture, drag is closely involved with political dangers and sexual risks. Writing in the late 1970s, Derek Cohen (1980, p. 185) argued that we needed to listen to a

'variety of gay cultural voices', represented not just on the
commercial scene but in theatre (Consenting Adults, Gay
Sweatshop, Brixton Faeries), film, fiction and so on: 'We
must acknowledge the different pleasures that each form
offers, and hence embrace their manifold political
potential.' Nearly a decade later, it feels as if the political
edge to gay culture has been blunted. Gay men are now
visible *and* invisible in popular culture – in that the 1970s
gay politics opened up a space in which a gay image might
appear in the mass media only to disappear (or, at least,
become partly obscured from view) in practically the same
moment. Cohen was writing at a time when a multiplicity
of gay images and styles (hardly an essence, like the one
Wise and Stanley choose to believe in) seemed a possibility.
But now, quite a few years later, the gay man in film, fiction
and theatre is often only barely seen for what he is. His
sexuality is hinted at, not affirmed. He is hardly an essential
type, let alone an upfront misogynist. Is this to be
welcomed?

Pop music, for example, has been interesting in this
respect since it is one of the few forms of cultural expression
where a diversity of racial and sexual images are relayed.
Although gay men have become more evident in pop, they
are largely silent about their sexuality. Managers and
record companies don't want potential stars talking about
their desires, and yet gay pop stars always attract publicity,
which can be used to a marketing advantage. Boy George,
notoriously, announced that sex is less exciting than a cup
of tea. The Pet Shop Boys dress up as leather men on the
cover of the teen magazine *Smash Hits* (12–25 August
1987) and yet, in flirting with this gay imagery, they are
addressing themselves not to gayness so much as to
stardom. However, it cannot be denied that their use of gay
imagery is not dissociable from their success. There is
nothing militant in the Pet Shop Boys' songs, although a gay
audience will detect gay allusions and subtexts in the lyrics
(such as 'Rent' – charting during October and November

1987). The popular press causes considerable excitement in disclosing who may or may not be gay – several stars from Elton John to those clean-cut models of youth, The House-martins, have been subject to the tabloids' relentless polic-ing. Gutter press gossip provides a sensationalizing repress-ive tolerance towards gay men in pop. (The papers actually *need* scapegoats – film stars dying of AIDS and so on – desperately.) No longer does the discovery of gayness necessarily mean the ruin of a pop star's career (it may well provoke interest in him). As long as the music is in demand and the money keeps rolling in, then gayness of a semi-visible kind is allowed for. One band, The Communards, has evolved from the Gay Youth Movement. However, their openly oppositional voice is drowned by the clamour of fans who don't always differentiate between the band's music and its politics. The Communards themselves might claim that there is in fact no difference between these two things. (One recent album is entitled *Red* with designer Soviet chic to match.) Consumers, of course, can choose what they want to hear.

Being gay, then, is no longer so much of a threat in this area of popular culture because it means that gayness is presented in a form that won't immediately pervert the masses. Likewise, given the marketing constraints under which they have to perform and the increased depolitici-zation of gayness, pop stars find it almost impossible to *be gay*. The more we look out to popular culture in hope of positive and identifiable gay images being presented to us, the more we have to return to the gay scene in order to have some control over *our* sense of what it means to enjoy a gay lifestyle.

If The Communards provide something of a popular image of gay politics and culture, it is interesting to note how the radical press responded to one particular aspect of gay men's lives – the contact advertisement. Several para-graphs ago, I pointed to feminist fears of homosexuality. In taking on board lesbian and gay rights, certain sections of the Left have been rather scared by the full range of implications that go along with our rights – one of which, clearly enough, is *our right to sexual expression*. In the past few years, the gay press, along with mainstream publications (including local papers), has welcomed, much to the advantage of its readers, a growth in the number of advertisements for escorts and masseurs. It is possible to hire via *Gay Times* and other regional gay journals all kinds of men – construction workers, Filipinos, schoolmasters – for a massage (which may well be what it says but may imply sex). Straight magazines carry ads for similar services, along with 'strippagrams' and other kinds of courier services. It almost goes without saying that unemployment is related to this kind of 'free enterprise'. (Are there Training Services Commission grants for such work?) One radical magazine which has carried a substantial number of advertisements for what it euphemistically calls the 'other scene' is *Marxism Today* – itself a commercially successful enterprise (sales around 15,000 a month) sponsored by the Communist Party of Great Britain.

Like most left-wing publications, *Marxism Today* endorses lesbian and gay rights. (The considerable time-lag after the heyday of GLF is conspicuous.) Whether support for our rights is in keeping with the sale of fetishistic goods or enabling masseurs to obtain work is, in the eyes of some Communists, an altogether different matter. The question of gay liberation, like women's liberation, has always posed awkward problems for a class-based politics. In the case of gay men, there is, inevitably, a lack of seriousness given to the question of homophobia. In fact, homophobia finds its way into the most 'enlightened' arenas of political debate. The absorption of any politics to do with sex and gender has led some revolutionaries (like Workers Power (June 1987)) to require that sexual relations be defined purely in terms of class struggle, thereby eliminating the autonomy demanded by many non-proletarian groups. Other parties (like the CPGB) have recognized the need for a politics

focusing on specific *issues* (anti-racism, women's rights, to
name but two) where autonomy within the Left is regarded
as vital. However, in accepting advertisements that origi-
nate in the commercialized gay scene, *Marxism Today* has
found itself with a difficult contradiction on its hands.
Some of its readers object to this kind of gay culture – a
culture that has been interpreted by some *Marxism Today*
readers as misogynistic, aggressively capitalist, and
extremely perverse.

A letter to *Marxism Today* from Jude Bloomfield
(March 1987, p. 11) expresses discomfort with the ads for
'personal services':

> the most disturbing adverts in the journal are those in the
> personal columns for escorts and masseurs. Again
> because they concern gay men, they appear immune from
> criticism. While I cannot find any basis for distinguishing
> one person's desire for silk with another's for leather –
> each to their own fetish – there is a basic principle
> governing sexual relations which is not a question of
> taste or choice, and that is that they are voluntary.
> Voluntary, not only in the sense of not engaged in or
> under the threat of violence, but freely chosen.
>
> In all forms of prostitution one contracting partner
> would not choose to have sex with the other were it not
> for economic inducement or gain. I am fed up with the
> dismissal, as moralism, of a feminist or egalitarian mora-
> lity of truly voluntary sex under conditions of mutually
> expressed desire. This is not to make any value judge-
> ment about the duration of relationships, or whether
> they are gay, bisexual, heterosexual, monogamous or
> multiple, but about sexual partners being on an equal
> footing.

Bloomfield's letter invites several responses. Michael
O'Dwyer, in a reply (*Marxism Today*, April 1987, p. 11),
points to Bloomfield's reactionary tone, stating that the

'carefully used words "taste", "choice", and "silk and leather" thrown off-handedly into her letter, convey ... a concealed heterosexist dismissal of homosexual identity'. Bloomfield is certainly disdainful towards sexual diversity, and she is not entirely clear about what 'voluntary' relations might be. What is more worrying is that Bloomfield's letter makes it perfectly clear how a specific left-wing vision of sexual relations refuses to see how sex and money might be brought into a much more radical alignment.

Sounding in some respects like a nineteenth-century rescue-worker campaigning against the pestilence of prostitution, Bloomfield wishes to dissociate sex from money. (We are brought up to believe that both things are dirty.) In this far from ideal world, sex has its workers, and more and more of them will appear as a result of lack of employment in other areas. The conditions under which they work must be improved. What is needed is legislation which guarantees a fair wage (better contracts) for those providing sexual services. The hiring of masseurs, and the circulation of pornography, has become a means for some gay men to change their erotic practices in the name of 'safer sex'. Moreover, since there is still a pressing problem for some gay men in being 'out' at work and also at home (many of us are, of course, married), there is a demand for certain sexual needs to be satisfied. Sex workers are not unionized – and it is precisely their lack of protection that leads to exploitation. Pimps and escort agencies – the illegal and the spuriously legal – continue to cream off the profits (and 'free enterprise' obviously encourages this). Bloomfield also wants to see sexual diversity – leather, silk, the lot – kept quietly in private, and not turning up as a 'politically incorrect' item on the Marxist agenda. Support lesbian and gay rights, yes, but please keep the culture that goes along with that out of sight. O'Dwyer calls Bloomfield's attitude 'heterosexist'; perhaps its roots also lie in a kind of homophobia – a fear of sexual change, a fear of many different erotic pleasures. It can all look so fetishistic, so frightening.

But it isn't. What *is* terrifying is male heterosexuality, a sexuality that makes life continually difficult for women and children (most obviously in the recent child abuse controversies). Straight men can be bearers of a sexual force that has always made me scared. I recognize now, as I did at school, that my desire for other men is related to a fear of them, and is not concerned with hating those people who seemed much more reasonable – women. At the present time, in the late 1980s, gay culture is in some ways trying to investigate how our desire can be (but not necessarily is) bound up with sexual fears.[2] These are fears we may choose to play with, but without harming one another. Perhaps SM is the safest sex that any of us might enjoy? But it might also be the most restrictive (not just if you're in bondage), the most tightly coded form of sexual expression. SM has to work with a precise range of sexual terms. Clearly, its pleasures lie in the accuracy of its definitions in relation to the thrills and fears it arouses. SM, however, is not, I think, the end-point of gay culture.

Gay culture will keep shifting its limits to where, perhaps, we are no longer defining ourselves as 'gay' but where we are truly polymorphous. For example, it's worth considering how the word 'gay' will be kept intact as more and more 'new men' (you know, the guys who have learnt to cry in public and run the crèche at the feminist conference) start to emerge and relate to us. And, to make a rather different point, in the city where I live a space has been bought up to provide some kind of alternative to the commercial scene. Some of us are bored with the scene – the almost exclusively Hi-NRG music, the same dress codes, the same rituals of beer and cruising. And some of us still want, need and enjoy the scene. The impact that these two things have on gay identity – locally and nationally – will be interesting to watch.

I think it's true to say that gay men need better networks through which to talk and organize (and this is not to discount the remarkable work undertaken around 'safer sex' and HIV). There is still much more work to be done in a serious and supportive way to discuss what our chosen identity is representing, about the fears that surround that identity, and how our love for each other affects everyone we meet. Attempts to stigmatize us will continue. Yet, in that ongoing interchange of dominant definitions and our counter-definitions of who and what we are there will be some sort of transformation, one that might, as Jeffrey Weeks (1985, p. 260), hopes 'take us beyond the boundaries of sexuality as we know it'.

In the meantime, we need to become more precise about one thing – and this sounds a contradiction in terms – we need to become precise about sexual meaning. We are – to the heterosexual world – walking definitions of sex. We *mean* sex. Our lifestyle is defined as a sexual lifestyle, a lifestyle that says 'fuck'. It is hardly a coincidence that it is one of the greatest insults to tell someone to 'fuck off'. Fucking has a power that is hard to define. Sex is still bound up for many people with explosive fears and volatile hatreds. It is also the thing that western peoples speak interminably about. The fascination of sex is endless. Gay men provide a convenient target for the displacement and projection of a widespread social *confusion* about heterosexuality on to a small 'perverse' group.

Although despised by much of our largely heterosexual culture, we, as gay men, are telling our haters things about themselves they would prefer not to know – that the anus isn't filthy, that two (or more) men's bodies fucking is not corrupt but healthy, that to have many partners is not immoral. Sex has been for hundreds of years in Judaeo–Christian culture some kind of dirty secret. One of these days the world will find out what we have already discovered – that homophobia and misogyny, and not the lifestyles of gay men, are central to the problems of our society.

Notes

1   Feminists here include the French writers Luce Irigaray and Julia
     Kristeva whose work is deeply informed by the Lacanian reading of
     Freud. The key right-wing proponent is Roger Scruton. Two articles
     which take the Freudian 'repressed homosexuality' thesis to pieces
     are Mandy Merck, 'Introduction – Difference and its discontents',
     Screen, vol. 28, no. 1 (winter 1987), pp. 2–9; and Craig Owens,
     'Outlaws: Gay men in feminism' in Alice Jardine and Paul Smith
     (eds), *Men in Feminism* (London: Methuen, 1987), pp. 219–32.
2   See, for example, the avant-garde lesbian and gay journal *Square
     Peg*. On the topic of the relations between sexual excitement and fear
     it's worth consulting Carole S. Vance (ed.), *Pleasure and Danger:
     Exploring female sexuality* (London: RKP, 1984).

References

Cohen, D. (1980), 'The politics of gay culture', in Gay Left Collective
    (eds), *Homosexuality: Power and Politics* (London: Allison and
    Busby).
Humphries, M. (1985), 'Gay machismo', in A. Metcalf and M. Humph-
    ries (eds), *The Sexuality of Men* (London: Pluto Press).
Millett, K. (1969), *Sexual Politics* (London: Virago Press, 1977).
Sedgwick, E. K. (1985), *Between Men: English literature and male
    homosocial desire* (New York: Columbia University Press).
Weeks, J. (1985), *Sexuality and its Discontents: Meanings, myths and
    modern sexualities* (London: RKP).
Wise, S. and Stanley, I. (1987), *Georgie Porgie: Sexual harassment in
    everyday life* (London: Pandora).
Workers Power (1987), *Lesbian and Gay Liberation: A communist
    strategy* (London: Workers Power, June).

CHAPTER FOUR

Business as usual: Substitution and sex in *Prick Up Your Ears* and other recent gay-themed movies

Mark Finch

In 1982 Hollywood companies produced and distributed a number of films whose narratives self-consciously drew on aspects of gay and lesbian identity. *Lianna, Personal Best, Cruising, Partners*, and *Making Love* incited much comment from within and outside the gay community, not as separate texts but as part of a self-contained thematic group – at worst, a cynical fashion; at best an apposite trend.[1] Yet more recently films like *Parting Glances, Kiss of the Spiderwoman, My Beautiful Launderette, Prick Up Your Ears* and *Maurice* – all distributed in the UK and North America between late 1985 and mid 1987 – have not been discussed in the same way and have successfully asserted themselves as different products, discrete and unrelated. Largely their difference has been asserted by marketing, which in all but one instance avoids mention of their investment in gay themes and images. When the gay press has given space to talk about these films it is in the same way as the publicists; gay people are as much consumers as any other group and could reasonably want to believe that each new product is different from the last. After the novelty of 1982's titles, there is no sense of continuity or criticism between cultural texts. The gay press has inherited its criteria from traditional journalism, with the fillip of critical interest devoted to whether each discrete text trades in 'positive' or 'negative' images of gay life;[2] consequently there is a sense that in the last half of the 1980s we are overwhelmed by an ever-expanding constellation of rich, diverse gay images.

This sensation of diversity and bewilderment is misleading and obstructive. Superficially, these films seem different; my argument is that nevertheless, textually, a number do organize around a set of central common interests – romantic love, monogamy/infidelity, confession and its consequences – and arm themselves with strikingly similar strategies – of substitution, metaphor, and ambitions to universality; and that although they sustain narratives of homosexual passion and romance, their ultimate allegiance is to heterosexuality. Explicit straight sex may have become boring – that is, unmarketable – for Hollywood, but these films work covertly to examine the conditions of heterosexuality; gayness is represented only in order to exhaust it, to see what it can be made to say about heterosexuality and gender. I want to look at the terms of this substitution – the recurrent features of its articulation – particularly in relation to *Prick Up Your Ears*[3] which is easily the most complex of this group; its unease and shifts of tone lay bare the contradictions of its bedfellows.[4]

Universality

Prick Up Your Ears focuses on two homosexual characters; nevertheless, 'It's a universal story' advises producer Andrew Brown (*The Media Show*, Channel 4, 22 April 1987), summarizing one of the dominant themes in the film's marketing. What this means is that 'they're just like us', where the speaker and the intended audience are marked as heterosexual. Who is being addressed is as important as who is being represented; in fact, knowing how the audience is being defined helps us make sense of the images. In this respect *Prick* is no different from *Parting Glances* – a gay-made day-in-the-life New York comedy – although the determining principle of that film is '*we*'re just like you'; that is, it starts out from the position of being gay. (*Parting Glances*' publicists were even so bold as to use the phrase 'a gay yuppie movie' on their posters.)

It is hardly surprising that both films should have so much invested in what at first seems a fairly common-sense premise; after all, 'We're just like you' has been the consistent reformist message of much of the gay movement since the late 1970s. Regardless of the importance of this message to a specific historical period and set of cultural–legal restraints, in relation to film it is bound up in a whole set of problems around representation. As Richard Dyer (1984) notes,

> Arguments about homosexuality are very hard to make on the terrain of existing definitions which do inexorably imply categories and types. Thus a statement like 'homosexuals are just like anyone else' already reproduces the notion that there are persons designated homosexuals.

In order to prove the thesis, cinema – particularly what we can call 'classic narrative cinema', of which *Parting Glances* and *Prick* are both a part – has to invent a way of representing the category homosexual in order to efface it.

The most common (and, historically, most recent) device for getting around this problem is, banally, in casting. For example, Scott Meek of Zenith productions (the company which produced *Prick*), commenting on another of their films, the TV movie whodunnit *Murder In Space* (1985), said: 'It was down to casting. I went to the casting sessions in Canada with one thing in mind – that the two men who played the gay astronauts should in no way "look" gay, like

gay stereotypes' (in Trenchard and Finch, 1986). Performers employed to play gay or lesbian roles are screened
for tell-tale anatomical signs. More than anything else, this
shows an unsophisticated regard for how stereotyping
works – it doesn't account for the constructions that
surround the performer, of lighting, costume, mise-en-
scene, music, editing and narrative placement.

In *Prick* the success and limitations of this avoidance of
visual stereotyping are apparent when, leaving Leicester
after his mother's funeral, Orton walks to a bus stop, where
a labourer in his mid 30s is also waiting; in the next scene
Orton and the labourer walk across the wasteland to a
deserted house for some quick sex. That shot of the two
men walking towards the house is there because we need
time to register the shock – not so much of Orton's
ceaseless promiscuity, which has been well hammered
home by this point, but of the labourer's homosexuality.
How often do we see plump, middle-aged, donkey-jacketed
working-class gay men on the screen? Yet even before this
moment our sense of recognition has been alerted. Why else
include a scene of Orton walking to a bus stop unless there
is some supposed significance? This is nothing to do with
stereotyping of physiognomy, but of narrative structure,
pace and editing.

Prick uses this strategy compulsively. It suits a film about
a promiscuous working-class author to shock us, and it
knows we will respond repeatedly to the revelation of
homosexuality in 'unlikely' places. Besides the Leices-
tershire labourer, Orton has encounters with a young man
on the Underground, an undertaker's assistant, a lonely
bachelor in a council flat, as well as initiating a utopian,
classless orgy in the Gents beneath Holloway Road. The
film's way of saying 'they're just like us' is to call up images
from outside the middle class – see, not all homosexuals
have penthouse flats in the city. Conversely, *Parting
Glances* – being devotedly about rich fags with well-
furnished SoHo lofts – uses a different tack; by portraying

the gay men and lesbians in various oppositions – slim/fat, healthy/with AIDS, single/coupled, has good taste/bad taste – the film asks us to believe that middle-class gays are just like middle-class straights because they share the same range of material (qua moral) values: 'Gays are just like straights because we're different in the same ways heterosexuals are different.'

Romance

The consequence of this emphasis on universality and equivalence is to set up transcendent categories of romance and romantic issues like fidelity. That is to say that, like other concepts, definitions of 'love' and 'romance' are precisely historically formed and culturally specific; day-to-day life, however, betrays a marvellous amnesia about this specificity and most of the time we live as if love and romance have always been there and always will be. Of course, the unanswerable nature of love has long been an *idée fixe* for Hollywood, but it is a fairly novel concept for its newly invented gay characters to engage with. What's astonishing about *Maurice* and *Parting Glances*, for instance, is their commitment to enacting romantic love between the same sex within old Hollywood conventions – the narrative structure of successive separation, ending in rhapsodic reunion; the symbolic value of costume; an excessive, swooning music score; and the emphasis on fate, chance, coincidence and fantasy sequence. *Making Love* (1981) probably marks the cross-over, being a 1980s twist on the woman's picture or weepie, in which the other woman is a man. As Simon Watney (1982) argues, *Making Love* is 'not about homosexuality ... [but] explores the meaning of marriage in today's middle-class America'. Frears and Bennett do something similar with *Prick Up Your Ears*; Orton's life is transformed into a statement – it's not sexuality but relationships which matter – and in

one swift stroke is erased the accumulated history of the
fight for gay rights. Says Cliff Hamer, the publicist for the
US distributor: 'An American audience aren't ready to deal
with the frankness of a homosexual relationship ... We
decided that [in the marketing] we would make it a
relationship movie, but leave it a little ambiguous as to
what the relationship was' (*The Media Show*, Channel 4,
22 April 1987).

Specifically, *Prick Up Your Ears* is about marital
relationships. As represented, Halliwell's inflexible commitment to playing the neurotic wife-figure gives the film its
central metaphor. The difficulties of heterosexual marriage
are both explored and relieved through this analogy (Bennett's script is introduced by Elizabeth Hardwick's comments in *Seduction and Betrayal* on the impossible role of
the wife in the marriage contract). Within the first few
minutes, one of Halliwell's whingeing monologues ('What
sort of day have you had, Kenneth?' 'Not unproductive ... I
caught up on a big backlog of dusting ...') is followed by
Peggy's visit to the Lahr household, where John Lahr's wife
is only the more submissive example of a poor professional
marriage. Secondary illustrations abound with coy self-
consciousness: Orton's sister is pictured in quarrelsome
relation with her husband; and Orton's mother and his
landlady are both caricatured in frivolous approximations
of marital tyranny.

Casting the gay relation as a carbon-copy of a heterosexual, institutionalized one gives us a spurious, moral way
of interpreting Orton's sexual adventures – they become
glaring examples of his multiple infidelities. It is as if the
film perversely wants Halliwell to be a pre-feminist
'heroine'; as an oppressed 'wife', his response to Orton's
promiscuity is articulate and liberating. We're even put in a
position of wishing such determination upon the film's real
women, particularly Anthea Lahr and Orton's sister. (In a
final scene dropped from the film, Lahr and Ramsay visit
Orton's Islington flat in 1980, and discover that the new

residents – a young heterosexual couple – are as nervous and insecure as the narrative's other couples.) Successful agent Peggy Ramsay stands apart from the other women, not so much a model of feminist achievement but as a mark of Vanessa Redgrave's star image, which is contemporarily bound up in anxiety about the suitability of gender roles.

At first sight, *Prick Up Your Ears* seems the least romantic of the new gay-themed films. It is obviously about the sourness of relationships, but its prognosis is locked in to the ideals of love and romance. Baldly, the film doesn't challenge the stereotyped Orton–Halliwell moral narrative – that Halliwell killed Orton out of sexual as much as creative jealousy – but adds that here is a lesson for all marriages. In this sense monogamy and promiscuity and boredom and jealousy are given the same shape in the film's gay and straight relationships. In real life, of course, these concepts (and the feelings they mercilessly engender) have a different timbre not only between the two communities, but across them. This is not to say that gay men and lesbians don't enjoy romance, or believe in it, or that films about gay people shouldn't be romantic; but that there is an historical and social particularity about being gay that makes this feeling different. In *Prick* as well as *Kiss of the Spiderwoman, My Beautiful Launderette, Parting Glances* and, spectacularly, *Maurice* homosexuality is denied a specificity in order to celebrate the longevity of romance in the domestic or personal sphere.

Sex

These contradictions cluster and wash around one moment in particular. In all the films quoted here there is a sex scene; even the absence of a sex scene serves as an index of the scene's primacy. The narrative of *Maurice* is from the beginning set upon a climactic sex scene, which pointedly occurs offscreen. *Parting Glances* is a little less frenetic; its teasing post-jog opening is the nearest we ever get, with shots of clothes flying through the air and landing on the way-signs of new gay materialism – a dinosaur art mobile, yucca tree, Asiatic hand-patterned rug, and other earthy, designer bric-a-brac.

On the subject of the sex scene, the following review – with its fascinated/terrified subtext – has a point: 'One's reactions to *Prick Up Your Ears* may be determined by how one reacts to the endless images of men sharing embraces and lingering kisses. If the couplings and recouplings were of a heterosexual nature, the film would seem repetitive and boring' (Mike McGrady, 1987). Of course – but the sex scene is important for three reasons. First, if they're just like us, or we're just like them, here is where the last in-eradicable bit of difference resides. The fascination with representing the sex act is a fascination with that difference. Ultimately, it is to the image of two men embracing (or kissing, or fucking) that all sides of the argument will be drawn, like murderers to the scene of the crime. Yet the much commented-upon sex scenes in *Prick* are not in fact scenes of sexual acts – in the coy manner of *Parting Glances*, they only delineate a before and after. Notably, the set-piece 'orgy' in the Gents under Holloway Road marks the film's most startling retreat into art movie conventions; that is, it takes the sex act away from the terms of one realism and into another more stylized one (the scene plays heavily on chiaroscuro and choreography).

Second, the sex act is used to explain and encapsulate the truth about homosexuality. Mandy Merck (1986) has described this tendency in relation to lesbian representation in art movies:

> [Gay] politics and art cinema are constituted within discourses which privilege the body, particularly its sexual functions, as a source of truth about social rela-tions in general ... In the art film ... everything tends to mean something else. The result is to assign that cinema-

tic convention, the love scene, a particular symbolic function: the ability to represent 'lesbian experience'.

Just as for Maurice a single night with the gamekeeper's assistant offers a meaning to his feelings and to his sense of alienation, in these other films the sex act is not only the culmination of textual anxieties, it serves as narrative motivation (an exception is *My Beautiful Launderette*, in which much effort is expended to de-emphasize the sex act, within the unquestioned terms of romance). Halliwell's seduction of Orton is automatic and conventional: a hand directed straight to the groin, he disrobes in a stately manner, and slips into bed (the crackly echo of the 1953 Coronation parodies this). These actions shape our understanding of his later jealousy and stagnancy. His final acts of murder are almost a reprise of the sex scene; sex explains his sexuality, which in turn, the film – contradictorily – proposes, accounts for his 'tiresome mean-mindedness'. Furthermore, in Halliwell's vulgar timing and Orton's mischievous nonchalance the film betrays a nest of worries about the sexually direct older man and the complicity of the boyish 'victim'.

Third, the gay sex scene is structured around heterosexual gender roles. If the gay relationships in these films are relentlessly focused upon the forms of heterosexual ones, the sex scene in particular replays old – that is, heterosexual – roles. In Orton's promiscuous adventures he is always shown as the active partner; Halliwell's envy is the jealousy of the woman who – 'essentially' – cannot take on the role of pursuer. (Besides his awkwardness in the seduction scene, an elaborate joke about his new wig and his sexual attractiveness confirms him in this submissive role.) Tops and bottoms is what it's about; the feminized man and the over-masculinized male partner. Many commentators have been alarmed at the cinema's interest in gay sex in 'the age of AIDS',[5] presumably in part out of desire to obliterate real homosexual desire; whereas in fact this is entirely explicable: images of gay sex allow free play for those forms of sexual behaviour which are outlawed by governmental and most medical misinformation. Men can be 'men' again in gay sex scenes – penetrative, promiscuous, compulsive. Undoubtedly, the identification is a complex one, and if there's any anxiety about this fantasy, the film-makers will remind us 'It's a very moral film – after all, they die' (Frears, 1987).

Metaphor

'Maybe Gays are especially good metaphors for misplaced people' muses director Stephen Frears (*Today*, 26 April 1987) on his reasons for being attached to them as fictional subjects (Frears also made *My Beautiful Launderette*). Frears's understanding of gay men in society is about as informed as the idea of humankind's universal commonality. Nevertheless, it locates a difficulty with the film, and how this relates to a standard film image. Traditionally, gayness has been used in a closed circuit of cause and effect with other marks of transgression: the gay man who kills is a killer because he's gay (*Cruising*, *The Eiger Sanction* (1975), *Victim* (1960)); the lesbian who is bitter and twisted is bitter and twisted because she's a lesbian (*Rebecca* (1940), *The Killing of Sister George* (1968), *Windows* (1982)). This is not the same as using gayness as a metaphor. In the traditional image, other marks of criminality, deviancy and buffoonery stand as metaphors for homosexuality.

What *Prick* and these other films propose instead is that the position of the gay man is a useful index of the position of the outcast. There are particular problems with this, besides the unspecific definition of 'the outcast'. To present the outcast's point of view means giving a gay character's point of view, and this presents a new dilemma. Writing about *Boys in the Band* (1970) and *Outrageous* (1977),

Alison Graham (1981) argues that Hollywood films have commonly used homosexuality 'as a metaphor for particular ways of perceiving the world'. The carrier for the metaphor in the films Graham discusses is the theatricality and artifice of drag and camp; *Prick Up Your Ears* and *Maurice*, as costume dramas, draw examples from history. In coexistence with claims to universality of gays and straights – the lack of difference, the commonality of love – both films inscribe the social and legal consequence – another *difference* – of being gay. The homophobia of characters such as the Islington librarian is both ridiculed and, regretfully, acknowledged to be the dominant force in 1950s Britain; and in *Maurice* an extensive addition to Forster's original novel describes the melodramatic downfall of Viscount Risley, a young politician who is prosecuted and ruined for pawing a soldier.

In *Maurice* this liberal position is sustained at the level of dialogue and narrative development; but there is a contrary visual emphasis, a sheer pleasure in the soft-lit trappings of the stuffy old England it condemns – dressing for dinner, punting on the Cam, shooting for grouse and beating the villagers at cricket. *Maurice* doesn't see that it cannot ask us to enjoy both its plea for tolerance and its seductive mise-en-scene, and the latter finally devours the former. *Prick Up Your Ears* maintains a struggle over point of view throughout. The story's self-consciousness about telling itself ('I remember ... and then ...') betrays a massive uncertainty. The film opens with a close-up of Halliwell looking straight to camera, after having killed Orton. From this point, Peggy Ramsay's seems to be the unifying perspective: she narrates both from her memory and from Orton's diary. Yet some scenes are played, without any preceding link, direct from the diary, while another – when the diary is read by Lahr's wife and mother-in-law – remains unvisualized. Who is narrator – biographer Lahr, eye-witness Ramsay, or the spectre of Orton?

For a metaphor, the point of view is remarkably unrestrained. There's a kind of chafing against this position, an uneasiness about providing a voice for a 1960s queer rebel. Furthermore, we know what Frears means when he describes Orton as a 'misplaced' person, but the connotations of uniqueness, of special talent, ride against the universality expressed by the marketing and, to an extent, the film itself. If Orton is exceptional, how can he be typical? The film deserts this dilemma in mid-point: its restructuring of Orton's life, bookended by suicide/homicide, and its dependency on 'Ortonesque' epithet and non sequitur provide a crafty but unstable closure.

Film demonstrably deals in the metaphorical: an image always stands for something else (*Prick* compounds this by being – reluctantly – a biopic, in which traditionally the protagonist's life stands for her/his work). Nevertheless, these films exceed their context of naturalism; their narratives are part of a more extensive substitution, around seemingly transcendent categories of romance and universality. Within this, the sex scene stands as the last bastion of difference – the spanner in the works for 'we're just like you' – and also functions to concretize more far-reaching explanations of homosexual psychology. But that explanation comes in the form of traditional gender roles.

As John Fletcher's essay in this collection argues, homosexuality always figures in the psychical and social construction of heterosexuality. 'Metaphor' suggests the substitution of one similar term for another; this may be the case at one level, but the attention to homosexuality in these films is also a delving deeper into the heterosexual gender system – a sort of inspection of the timbers for the dry rot. *Prick Up Your Ears* and many other representations of the late 1980s serve as an examination of the qualifications of heterosexuality. It is only through images of homosexuality that these films can afford to contemplate what really interests them.

Notes

1 For example, 'Hollywood's new homos?', *Body Politic* (March 1982), pp. 36–7; 'Hollywood's gay fling', *The Advocate* (29 April 1982), pp. 36–40; Al LaValley (ed.), 'Out of the closet and on to the screen', *American Film*, vol. 12, no. 10 (1982), pp. 57–64; and Mary Richards, 'The gay deception', *Film Comment*, vol. 18, no. 3 (1982), pp. 15–19; also Andy Medhurst, 'Notes on recent gay film criticism', in Richard Dyer (ed.), *Gays and Film* (New York: Zoetrope, 1984), pp. 58–64.

2 By the 'gay press' I mean British newspapers such as *Capital Gay, Gay Times, Man Alive, Gay Life, Gay Scotland*, but not *Square Peg* or some North American magazines (*The Advocate, New York Native*) which are able to discuss the media in slightly more complex ways. It is particularly worth recommending the work of Richard Dyer and Vito Russo.

3 *Prick Up Your Ears*, produced by Zenith (a company owned by Central TV), distributed in the UK by Palace Pictures and in the USA by Samuel Goldwyn; directed by Stephen Frears; written by Alan Bennett; starring Gary Oldman, Alfred Molina and Vanessa Redgrave.

4 Although this essay deals only with a specific aspect of gay male representation, Donna Deitch's lesbian romance, *Desert Hearts* (1986), works interestingly in many of the same ways.

5 This was the premise of *The Media Show* (Channel 4, 22 April 1987), and an interview in *Today* (26 April 1987), pp. 24–5.

Prick Up Your Ears and some of the other films mentioned here are available for 16mm educational and film society hire from Glenbuck Film Distributors (tel. 01–399 0022).

References

Dyer, R. (1984), 'Seen to be believed: Some problems in the representation of gay people as typical', *Studies in Visual Communications*, vol. 9, no. 2, pp. 2–19.

Frears, S. (1987), interview in *Today* (26 April), pp. 24–5.

Graham, A. (1981), '*Outrageous* and *The Boys in the Band* – The possibilities and limitations of coming out', *Film Criticism*, vol. 5, no. 1, pp. 36–42.

McGrady, M. (1987), review in *Newsday* (17 April) quoted in *New York Native* (2 May 1987), p. 22.

Merck, M. (1986), 'Lianna and the lesbians of art cinema', in C. Brunsdon (ed.), *Films for Women* (London: BFI), pp. 166–75.

Trenchard, L. and Finch, M. (1986), *Are We Being Served?* (London: Gays and Broadcasting).

Watney, S. (1982), 'Hollywood's homosexual world', *Screen*, vol. 23, nos. 3–4, pp. 107–21.

CHAPTER FIVE

Freud and his uses:
Psychoanalysis and gay theory

John Fletcher

The fate of psychoanalysis in the era of 'sexual politics' has been chequered and various. The first waves of feminist and gay politics found their voice in the United States in the late 1960s, in the shadow of a tamed and assimilated American psychoanalysis, sleekly and successfully absorbed into a conservative medical and psychiatric establishment. Americanized Freud had produced a school of ego psychology with its emphasis on adaptation to social reality. A theory progressively shorn of its rebarbative emphasis on the refractory and contradictory nature of psychic life, its priorities set by a native pragmatism dominant in philosophy and psychology, had materialized in the institutions of the 'psy-complex' as a technology of social control.

Understandably Freud and psychoanalysis featured prominently as targets of polemical attack and ideological critique among early feminist and gay writers. Summing up the bitter experiences of many women and gay men of a conformist therapeutic practice (Coleman, 1973), they pointed out the obvious role played by American Freud in the elaboration of a reactionary sexual ideology both in specialist psychiatric institutions and practices and in the wider culture. Kate Millett's radical feminist attack on Freud in *Sexual Politics* (1970) as a leading theorist of the 'sexual counter-revolution' is a classical instance of the early head-on collision of psychoanalysis and feminism. However, the relations between Freud and contemporary feminist theory were radically altered if not in the long run reversed by Juliet Mitchell's *Psychoanalysis and Feminism* (1974). This sought through a detailed exposition to rehabilitate Freud against feminist misunderstanding and criticism, and to put psychoanalysis on the agenda as the only systematic and useful theory of gender and sexuality for a radical sexual politics. In large areas of anglophone feminism this is now the case. That this transformation was inaugurated by a British feminist from a New Left Marxist background draws attention to the various national traditions of psychoanalysis and their different cultural histories, while signalling a point of appropriation between French Lacanian theory and 1970s feminist theory. Since then in various fields from sociology to cultural studies feminists have borrowed and developed psychoanalytical insights and arguments for a variety of projects, including a therapeutic practice by and for women informed by feminist commitments (Ernst and Maguire, 1987).

Nothing comparable has happened in the gay movement. Apart from a small number of *European* gay writers – the 'wild psychoanalysis' of Guy Hocquenghem and Mario Mieli, the sober if sketchy outlines of a theory of homosexuality by Martin Dannecker – there has been no systematic attempt to appropriate pyschoanalytic theory for a gay self-reflection on the constitution of homosexuality and its relation to gender, in any way comparable to the now extensive feminist use of psychoanalysis for reflection on femininity and female sexuality.

In his paper, 'Homosexuality and the problematic nature of psychoanalysis ...' given at the 1983 Gay Studies and Women's Studies Conference, Jeffrey Weeks remarked on 'the absence of a coherent psychoanalytic discourse in gay politics' (p. 5) and went on to argue that psychoanalytic theory could make a positive contribution to gay politics and theory, despite normative tendencies in Freud's own thought and the conservative role played by the psycho-analytic institution especially in America in the pathologiz-ing of homosexuality. In this essay I want to support Weeks's case for a gay appropriation of psychoanalysis and to elaborate further those elements which allow for a radical critique of the dominant heterosexual norms and their internal contradictions and difficulties. This enables us to situate the forms of homosexual subjectivity within the normative matrix in and against which they are consti-tuted. This essay will be particularly concerned with male homosexuality.

Freud's own positions on homosexuality differ markedly from the reactionary and homophobic consensus that Americanized Freud has been used to sanction (Bieber, 1965; Socarides, 1979). Though Freud continued to invoke the opposition between normality and perversion, these terms function as *descriptive* labels to discriminate between heterosexual genitality in the service of reproduc-tion and any other non-reproductive manifestation of sexu-ality. Homosexuality for Freud is 'perverse' in that it constitutes a non-reproductive *inversion* of sexual object. He polemicizes strongly against views of homosexuality as either innate or degenerate, recentring the category strictly around the issue of object choice (Freud, 1905). He breaks with prevalent notions of 'gender inversion' (for example the female brain or soul in a male body), whether in sexological science or the 'third sex' ideology of homo-sexual theorists such as Ulrichs and Hirschfield. Freud's usage of the normal/perverse opposition is without any *necessary* implication of mental illness or pathology. In an interview in 1903, he asserts: 'I am ... of the firm conviction that homosexuals must not be treated as sick people, *for a perverse orientation is far from being a sickness* ... Homo-sexual persons are not sick' (Marmor, 1980, p. 394). In the famous letter to an American mother in 1935, he wrote:

Homosexuality is assuredly no advantage, but it is

nothing to be ashamed of, no vice, no degradation, it cannot be classified as an illness; we consider it to be a variation of the sexual function produced by a certain arrest of sexual development. (Freud, 1970, p. 419)

The interest of this is not simply for a vindication of Freud's liberalism as against the homophobia of his epigones. The very *limitations* of such liberalism, evident in the slide from 'variation' to 'arrest', indicates a teleological model but also a gap or discrepancy between its motive force and its developmental goal. The notion of specific developmental tasks that might be met or not in individual cases, without any necessary implication of mental pathology, indicates that the *telos* or goal is culturally imposed not biologically guaranteed or determined. This is clear in Freud's fundamental commitment to the notion of a primary infantile sexuality that knows neither gender nor reproduction, and which he designates precisely as 'polymorphous perverse'. It is out of such a perverse primary condition that the norms of genital heterosexuality are constructed. This construction is culturally necessary, Freud thought, for historical progress and survival. Weeks refuses Freud's undifferentiated notion of a 'civilization' that requires repression and substitutes a neo-Foucauldian thesis, 'that it is social forms, categories and institutional practices that produce, organize and regulate sexual desire' (Weeks, 1983, p. 8). In Freud's thought the cultural 'necessity' is in the nature of an imperative, a task to be achieved. This occurs through the processes of repression and sublimation, of blocking and redirection of the drives. This cultural pattern of injunction and taboo involves, in Freud's account, a moment or scene of psychic violence whose ineradicable effects of splitting and division in psychic life are given in the concept of the Unconscious. An early essay such as ' "Civilised" sexual morality and modern nervous illness' (1908) with its picture of heterosexuality as a casualty ward of psychic cripples and walking wounded, of

male impotence and female frigidity – 'we may well raise
the question whether our "civilised" morality is worth the
sacrifice' (p. 55) – indicates that this emphasis on the
internal conflicts and the *cost* of normality – 'the preparation for marriage frustrates the aim of marriage' (p. 50) –
was a recurrent feature of his thought.

Psychoanalysis is important for gay theory because it
conceives sexuality not as a fixed biological instinct to
reproduce, but as a highly mobile psychical reality that is
organized *symbolically*, and so is always in excess of the
realm of biological needs and the cultural functions it is
made to serve. It stresses not just the drive but a symbolic
order that assigns positions and identities. It is the division
of the subject in the symbolic order that constitutes
identity and desire. The conflicts it describes are not just
between drive and identity, but are fundamental contradictions internal to the identities that are culturally
enjoined. The attempt to meet these demands produces
distress, disablement and resistance. Neurosis, Freud suggested, is the struggle of the ego against the demands of
the sexual function (1931, p. 347). Homosexual object-
choice and the fantasies that sustain it, I will argue, are not
a freestanding, innately determined possibility, nor a
developmental failure, but are one of the forms that resistance takes.

The Perverse Drive

If homosexuality is to be understood as a response to the
contradictory demands of what Adrienne Rich has called
'compulsory heterosexuality' (Rich, 1980), then the status
of cultural norms and the question of how they operate to
organize forms of identity and desire are central. Freud's
radical reformulation of the concept of the drive, which as
Weeks argues entails a *break* from conventional instinct
theory, means that the notion of reproductive hetero-

sexuality cannot be thought of as the expression of a given 'natural' instinct.

The notion of instinct here is crucial. Freud's own usage testifies to a systematic if implicit contrast between two concepts which he renders as 'instinkt' and 'trieb'. The Standard Edition in both French and English elide this distinction in Freud's German, collapsing it into a single term 'instinct'. 'Instinkt' indicates a set of pre-formed behavioural reflexes, hereditary in origin, tied to a set of biologically-determined needs and adapted to a set of pre-given objects, of which hunger and the eating/digestive processes are prototypical. By contrast the 'trieb' or drive is a borderline concept 'on the frontier between the mental and the somatic, [as] a psychic representative of the stimuli originating from within the organism ...' (Freud, 1915, p. 118). Sexuality as a *drive* is always psychosexuality, formed as a set of psychical representations. Freud deploys four categories derived from the biological theory of instincts. Like instincts, the sexual drive has a pressure, an aim, an object and a source. The pressure is a quantitative economic factor indicating the insistence of the somatic element in the drives: 'a measure of the demand made on the mind for work in consequence of its connection with the body' (ibid.). However, the differentiation of sexuality as a drive from the biological model of a reproductive instinct is clear in his analysis of source, aim and object.

The pre-given nature of the biological instinct, its teleological fixity binding a specific bodily source to a specific aim and object, gives way through reflection on homosexuality and the perversions to a radical contingency of sexual object, and an aim that includes under the generality of a pleasurable release of tension a series of acts related not to one but to various bodily sources, e.g. sucking, caressing, expulsion, muscular contraction, looking, penetration. The unity of a genital reproductive instinct is shattered and replaced by a set of multiple, fragmented sexual drives, dispersed around the body and aiming at 'organ pleasure'.

The core sites, mouth, anus, urethra, genitals, are physio-
logically destined as sphincteral orifices to being erogenous
zones, excitable breaks or turnings within the body surface,
points of bodily flows and exchanges between inside and
outside that attract parental care and pleasurable stimulus.
However, Freud makes it clear that 'erogeneity' is a
potential by-product of any bodily zone or activity that can
sustain a certain level of excitation, and that even intellectual activities can be eroticized and given sexual value.

The designated 'perversions' are explained by reference
to an original infantile sexual capacity that is autoerotic,
fantasmatic and knows neither gender nor reproduction.
This radical transformation and extension of the category
of sexuality as a set of pleasure-seeking drives has important effects for the understanding of the crucial relation
between perversion and the norm.

Perversion is understood traditionally as an alteration or
deviation from the fixed structure of the instinct with its
pre-given needs, reflexes and objects. The norm here is
biologically determined. It is clear that with Freud recasting
sexuality as a set of multiple local drives, 'normality' is no
longer guaranteed by the spontaneous unfolding of a
unitary reproductive instinct, genitally located and directed
at the opposite sex.

Through a detailed reconstruction of Freud's notion of
propping (*anlehnung* which Strachey translates unhelpfully
as *anaclisis*), the neo-Lacanian theorist Jean Laplanche
demonstrates that sexuality as such emerges as a *perversion*,
an autoerotic turning around and turning away from the
fixed structure of the instinct (Laplanche, 1970).

Taking Freud's analysis of the mouth and the oral drive
as the first sexual organ and the first sexual activity,
Laplanche demonstrates the distinctive structure of the
Freudian concept of the drive as it emerges in the infant
from the biological order of the pre-given needs and vital
functions. In the initial proto-sexual stage the infant's first
vital activity of sucking at the breast not only satisfies the

need for nourishment but produces the warm flow of milk and a pleasurable stimulus of the lips. This stimulus coincides with and is modelled on the satisfaction of vital functions (the satisfaction of hunger).

The second stage of infantile sensual sucking in the absence of hunger or of the milk as object of biological need marks the independence of the pleasure-seeking activity from the function that sustained it. In the turning from an external object of need to an autoerotic repetition of the memory traces of past pleasures, the object has become internalized, no longer the milk but the fantasized breast, through a relation of contiguity as a metonymic sign. In rhetoric a metonymy is a substitution whereby a part becomes the sign either of the whole, e.g. thirty sails for thirty ships, or of an adjacent part, e.g. smoke for fire. Anticipating adult object-choice, Freud concludes: 'The finding of an object is in fact a refinding of it' (Freud, 1905, p. 145). Laplanche comments that the object rediscovered is not the originally lost object of need but its substitute by displacement, the essentially fantasmatic and sign-like object of the drive. The emergence of sexuality in the drive is to be understood as an autoerotic repetition of sign-like traces in disjunction from the functional instinctual reflex with its fixed object. The absence of the real object of need, the substitution of an imaginary or fantasized memory trace or sign, its repetition through stimulus of the bodily site of previous pleasures, all indicate that a primordial sign-like or signifying structure is given in the very structure of the sexual drive. An unconscious metonymic chain of desired imaginary objects, open to successive displacements and diversions constitutes the field of sexuality as such.

In relation to notions of perversion and normality, Laplanche concludes that in Freud's analysis of the sexual drive, 'the exception – i.e. the perversion – ends up by taking the rule along with it ... undermining and destroying the very notion of the biological norm' (Laplanche, op. cit., p. 23). The whole of sexuality as a mobile field of

displaceable and substitutable signs and mental representations is a *perversion* of the order of biological needs and
fixed objects. The sexual is constituted 'in a movement that
deflects the instinct, metaphorises its aim, displaces and
internalises its object and concentrates its source on what is
ultimately a minimal zone, the erotogenic zone' (ibid. p. 23).
If the sexual drives are perverse in their very emergence, in
excess of given needs and functions, how are those relative
fixities, the norms of gender and genitality, constructed?

The Contradictory Norm

Despite Freud's emphasis on the 'vicissitudes' of the drives
(Freud, 1915), the teleology of the repudiated biological
model tends to reappear as a feature of an *endogenously*
determined psychosexual constitution taken as a whole.
Unfolding through set stages of development, oral, anal
and genital, it ushers in an active, phallic masculinity and a
passive, vaginal femininity clinched forever in their reproductive *pas de deux*. The resultant features of functionalism, teleology and 'a biology of mind' (Sulloway,
1979) have come to characterize the received wisdom of
conservative Freudianism. They are in ideological complicity with the heterosexual norms whose self-evident
common sense Freud had begun by challenging. The Freudian *oeuvre*, Jeffrey Mehlman has suggested, is a polemical
field 'in which mutually exclusive conceptual schemes may
be seen to be struggling ... to dominate ... a single
terminological apparatus' (Laplanche, 1970, p. ix). Consequently there are other elements in psychoanalytic theory
we can turn to in countering the dominance of this functionalist and normative teleology.

Lacan's structuralist reprise of Freud has reformulated
the Oedipal crisis as a movement from a two-term to a
three-term structure. The pre-Oedipal relations between
mother and infant Lacan characterizes as the realm of the

Imaginary, of the incestuous fantasies of mutual completion and identification. On the axis of identifications the infant lays down the groundwork of the ego through the imaginary incorporation of the absent breast, the maternal figure as a whole, and finally its own narcissistically-invested ideal image (Lacan's mirror stage). On the axis of desire the child desires the mother and her desire, to be the object of her desire, to be the maternal, phallic complement. As psychoanalysis understands the process of identification as a derivative of the oral drive, a metaphorical incorporation into the ego of the figure or object identified with, there can be no clear cut distinction between identification and desire, being and having, in the early stages. The two axes of identification and desire are only sharply opposed for the child by the transformations of the Oedipus Complex. The intervention of the symbolic Father as the Third Term, the representative of the Law and its interdiction on maternal incest, ruptures the mother-child dyad and precipitates the patriarchal symbolic order into the child's psychic life. This is lived out through what Freud called 'the primal fantasies' (Freud, 1916), a triptych of imaginary scenarios in which the paternal castration of the son, the paternal seduction of the daughter, are grouped around the central scenario of parental intercourse, the Primal Scene. This is a sado-masochistic fantasy of a primal rape or wounding of the mother by the father. The Primal Scene re-positions the formerly all-powerful pre-Oedipal mother as lacking the phallus and as the castrated object of paternal phallic aggression.

Laplanche and Pontalis have argued that the structuring function of the primal fantasies can be read as 'a prefiguration of the "symbolic order" defined by Lévi-Strauss and Lacan in the ethnological and psychoanalytical fields respectively' (1960, p. 17). I have commented on this elsewhere (Fletcher, 1986). Here I wish to stress their contradictory nature.

The symbolic order in question is patriarchal. The register of the 'primal' for Freud is bound to the symbolic Father and his Law which regulates the accession to heterosexual genitality. Its primal status claiming an imaginary pre-history ('In the beginning was the Father...') masks its actual operation as a form of what Freudian dream theory calls secondary revision. The supposedly 'primal' fantasies are in fact a secondary formation and revision. They rework the earlier pre-Oedipal organization of the drives bound to the maternal imago, the internalized figure of the mother, the infant's first object ('In the beginning was the Mother...'). Their intervention introduces the demands of the culture into the formation of the subject, making it a field of conflict and contradiction.

In 'The dissolution of the Oedipus complex' Freud casually asserts that just as milk teeth fall out, so the Oedipus complex is 'determined and laid down by heredity and ... bound to pass away according to programme' (Freud, 1924, p. 315). Yet it is here for the first time a radically different emphasis appears: 'What brings about the destruction of the child's phallic genital organisation is the threat of castration' (ibid. p. 317). A year later he asserts: 'The complex is not simply repressed, it is literally smashed to pieces by the shock of threatened castration' (Freud, 1925, p. 341). The fantasy of castration, so embarrassingly in excess of either biology or biography, an outrage on common sense and provocation to feminist indignation, becomes in the 1920s and 1930s the organizing category of heterosexual difference and the guarantor of reproductive genitality (even as it renders it fraught with anxiety).

Rather than a real organ, penis or clitoris, the phallus functions, Lacan insists (1958), as a signifier, concluding 'the organ that assumes this signifying function takes on the value of a fetish' (p. 84). In linguistic theory a signifier has meaning not independently but by virtue of its relation to other terms, by its differences, i.e. by relation to what it is not. Derrida in his critique of metaphysics has argued that the institution of traditional hierarchies, e.g. the masculine over the feminine, the rational over the sensible, operates by arresting and fixing the play of possible differences and combinations into a single binary opposition that is both static and hierarchical, but in which the apparent dominance of the privileged term is covertly dependent on its subordinate. This is the force of Lacan's designation of the phallus as signifier: its meaning exists only in opposition to castration. Not an organ that exists and might incidentally be lost, the phallus as a signifying or symbolic function is paradoxically an *effect* of castration. What erects the organ as phallic signifier is its fetish-like function of warding off castration. This paradox makes clear that it is not anatomy that is at issue but what and how the body is made to signify within a certain symbolic order.

In her appropriation of Freud for an account of the psychodynamics of patriarchy, Juliet Mitchell argues: 'castration bears the transmission of culture' (Mitchell, 1974, p. 79). The castration complex is the representative in the psyche of the Law of the Father and the Incest Taboo, and it is the symbolic submission to its imagined threat that maps out an Oedipal masculinity just as it is the acceptance of its symbolic reality that maps out an Oedipal femininity. It is crucial for our purposes that homosexuality and the 'perversions' are classically defined by psychoanalysis as the refusal or disavowal of castration. We have here the operation of norms with a vengeance. They are not, however, the smooth unfolding of endogenously guaranteed goals, but the shock and violence of a drama of disruption, turning on a set of symbolic oppositions (phallic versus castrated) and fantasies (the Primal Scene).

The law of the Oedipal polarity in effect states: 'You cannot be what you desire; you cannot desire what you wish to be.' Access to the mother is now regulated by the function or place of the Father and requires a paternal identification. Access to the father as libidinal object is through a feminine identification with the mother and the consequent loss of phallic prerogatives. The premise of bisexuality in the infant and the either/or structure of the Oedipal field means that there is no simple consignment of the biological individual to a given gender position. Gender positions are given in relation to each other (active/passive, dominant/subordinate), not to the anatomy of the subject who must negotiate certain identifications as the sanctioned mode of access to particular objects, just as the renunciation of particular objects is the price of sustaining particular identifications. The Oedipal order is a phallocentric symbolic apparatus that installs the heterosexual act of penetration – giving and receiving the phallus – as the authorized sexual act for both sexes.

Unlike the various animal species, human reproductive activity is not guaranteed by an innate biological programme. Human beings do not go on and off heat for set periods each year. Reproduction is not ensured by particular chemical triggers. This relocation of reproduction as a social function, from a biological to a psycho-symbolic level is premised on the mobility and 'perversity' of the drives and their vicissitudes with respect to aim, sources and objects. To secure the reproductive function in a patriarchal culture requires the conscription of biological individuals to a set of *symbolic* positions that turn on the circulation of the phallic signifier. The dropout rate is understandably considerable and seems to be increasing.

The range of Oedipal outcomes in individual cases will be the result of particular personal and family histories. Whether compliant or refractory they will be complex and contradictory, marked by the renunciation and splitting that constitutes the Unconscious. The contradictions I am concerned with are not the conflicts of individual histories but those that are structural and internal to the normative trajectories that are culturally imposed.

Gender and its maladies

Epigraph 'All women become like their mothers. That is their tragedy. No man does. That is his.'

Oscar Wilde. *The Importance of Being Earnest*

Freud had argued that the attainment of an Oedipal femininity was a far more fraught and difficult task than the path mapped out culturally for the male. This difficulty resides in the two extra tasks demanded of the woman: the change of object from mother to father, often accompanied by hostility to the mother; and a change of the dominant sexual aim and zone from the 'phallic' clitoris to the vagina, locus of heterosexual penetration, with the accompanying transformation of active, aggressive aims into passive, receptive ones. Joan Riviere paraphrases the psychical attitude of 'fully developed heterosexual womanhood', reached through renunciation, inhibition and reaction formation as: 'I must not take, I must not even ask, it must be *given* to me' (Riviere, 1929, p. 43).

This point of fracture, the turn to the Father that constitutes Oedipal femininity (which Lacan mischievously puns on as 'père-version'), undermines any simple opposition between norm and pathology, just as it renders impossible any conception of femininity as a 'natural' development. The ego will struggle against the demands of the reproductive function, and in particular Freud argues that the girl's intense pre-Oedipal maternal attachment is 'intimately related to the aetiology of hysteria' as 'both the phase and the neurosis are characteristically feminine' (Freud, 1931, p. 373). Hysteria involves the revival of the girl's active sexual aims and maternal object in protest against their renunciation. The hysteric is paralysed between compliance and rejection.

Juliet Mitchell in a recent essay has connected hysteria to a fundamental repudiation of femininity and passivity in both sexes: 'Hysteria is the woman's simultaneous acceptance and refusal of the organization of sexuality under patriarchal capitalism. It is simultaneously what a woman can do both to be feminine and to refuse femininity, within patriarchal discourse' (Mitchell, 1982, p. 289). This division of the subject, between desire and protest, renders graphically the psychic violence of that vicissitude fundamental to the demands of femininity as norm. Mitchell's colleague, Gregorio Kohon, describes hysteria as an inescapable moment when the subject is confronted with a choice between two objects, mother or father. Not a stage in a developmental sense but a permanent structural possibility: 'a place where something happens, in which a performance takes place, a drama is developed ... a distance between two stopping points' (Kohon, 1986, p. 378). This drama or performance poses the question which Serge Leclaire sees as agitating the hysteric: 'Am I a man or a woman?' (Leclaire, 1956). This oscillation, the impossibility of either position, the self-division of both, suggest that it is not just a choice of objects about which one might make up one's mind. It is an impasse of *meanings*, the Oedipal polarity between phallic or castrated, between being or having.

Hysteria as a pathology cannot be seen as incidental to an individual, a falling outside or away from a healthy normality. It is precisely a living through of that norm, its exactions, repudiations, seductions and demands. The space or stage of that performance is that of the primal fantasies. Mitchell designates hysteria as the daughter's disease. Having accepted a role in the romance of paternal seduction, the hysteric suddenly finds herself an understudy in the very melodrama of maternal castration she was wanting to avoid. Neither deviation nor failure, hysteria is internal to normality, the other side of its achievement. The shadow cast by femininity, it is simply part of the family.

No more than hysteria is lesbianism simply outside the norm. Female homosexuality needs to be seen not as a failure to proceed from mother to father, nor as a regression, but as an intelligible response to the same dilemma. In the classical summary by Otto Fenichel, 'the aim of homosexual object-choice is the avoidance of emotions round the castration complex' (Fenichel, 1946, p. 340). This should be seen not as a blind refusal of an object, the penis, or a person, the father, nor as a disavowal of genital difference, but as an attempt to contest or displace the meanings they carry, i.e. castration, its fantasies of mastery, loss, possession, subjugation and an avoidance of the destructive feelings they unleash, hostility, envy, shame, etc. If hysteria often seems to combine a flagrant seizure of the attributes of femininity – the masquerade, seduction – together with a bitter protest at its cost, lesbianism can be seen as a restorative strategy which seeks to *repair* the losses, denigrations, thwartings that a patriarchal culture inflicts on the girl in her primary relation to the mother.

Freud had suggested that in contrast to the difficulty of the girl's development toward femininity, the male trajectory is more straightforward. Unlike the girl, the boy begins with the 'advantage' of a heterosexual object, his mother, which he can keep, by displacement onto other women, into adulthood. He is not required to make the renunciations that both structure and imperil the path towards femininity.

In opposition to Freud the work of recent post-Freudian analysts such as Greenson (1968) and Ryan (1985) has described a similar point of fracture in the prescribed male trajectory, a 'père-version' not in the field of sexual orientation or object choice but in the field of identifications. The grounds for this claim are primary and pre-Oedipal. Not only is the mother the primary object of the drives but she is also the support of what Greenson calls, summarizing a widespread psychoanalytical consensus 'a primitive, symbiotic-identification ... on the basis of the fusion of early visual and tactile perceptions, motor-activity, introjection and imitation' (Greenson, 1968, p. 372). It is through this identification that the infant learns from the mother to perform key functions and behaviours, such as speaking, walking, self-feeding, sphincter control, etc. It is in this primary maternal relation that the groundwork of the ego and its primary differentiations, inside/outside, active/ passive, self/other are laid down. Where this core identification *reinforces* the gender identity of the girl, male gender identity can only be achieved through a process of dis-identifying with the mother and forming a counter-identification with the father (ibid., p. 373). This involves a *repudiation* of the primary maternal identification with its experiences of early infantile fusion, intimacy and support. As Ryan argues, it is never successfully eradicated but 'remains interwoven in the core of what we call masculi-nity' (Ryan, 1985, p. 26). Stoller is even more emphatic when he insists that 'the whole process of becoming mascu-line is at risk in the little boy from the date of his birth' (cited in Ryan, 1985, p. 26), and that the need to fight off this primary maternal fusion-identification energizes fami-liar stereotypical masculine behaviour. Masculinity is a doubly *defensive* structure, fortified against the return of the pre-Oedipal maternal relation as well as the inverted Oedipal homosexual relation to the father.

We might expect the point of fracture for the boy, the change from mother to father in the field of identifications, to form a pathogenic nucleus internal to the norm as we saw with the femininity–hysteria relation. Freud asserts: 'there is no doubt that hysteria has a strong affinity with femininity, just as obsessional neurosis has with masculi-nity' (Freud, 1926, p. 301). For the boy the normative solution to the trauma of castration that attends either Oedipal rivalry with the father or an inverted Oedipal identification with the mother is the paternal identification and the installation of the super-ego. In the theory of obsessional neurosis, however, it is precisely the relation to the super-ego that is the cause of the problem. Freud recognizes this when he admits: 'obsessional neurosis is only overdoing the normal method of getting rid of the Oedipus complex' (Freud, ibid., p. 269). The classical aetiology of obsessional neurosis locates it in a struggle by the ego to defend itself against Oedipal wishes which throw the libido back to the earlier stage of anal–sadistic organization. This regression from the genital leads to increased repression against the anal–sadistic impulses which replace the genital Oedipal wishes while still in some sense representing them. This regression to sadism effects the super-ego as a formation of the Unconscious, which grows more cruel and vengeful in consequence.

Otto Fenichel sees this regression as involving a return to the unresolved issue of masculine or feminine in a structure like hysteria but played out in anal terms:

> Vacillation between the original masculine attitude, now reinforced and exaggerated by the active sadistic component of anal eroticism, and the feminine attitude represented by the passive component of anal eroticism form the most typical conflict in the unconscious of the male compulsion [obsessional] neurotic. (Fenichel, 1946, p. 277)

Obsessional neurosis as an anal analogue to hysteria is marked by 'the relative predominance of punitive and expiatory symptoms over gratification symptoms' (ibid. p. 308), in contrast to hysteria. This preponderance of punishment over gratification is structural but suggests an ideological difference. Where hysteria is oppositional and protesting, obsessional neurosis is situated on the side of the Law.

The change of identification is the occasion for a punitive paternal super-ego locked in conflict with a stubborn and ambivalent maternal identification played out in the register of anality. The obsessive rituals of cleaning, ordering and regulation that characterize obsessional neurosis represent a continually renewed attempt to purge the male subject of that stubborn maternal anality, with all its connections to the active/passive oscillation and archaic states of merging. The psychopathic repetitive killing of women – for which there is no female equivalent – from Jack the Ripper to his recent Yorkshire namesake, writes large this impossible and interminable injunction to eliminate the maternal. The sterile paradox of obsessional neurosis, and the effect of its continual failure is, as Freud points out, the infiltration of the defensive mechanisms of the ego by the repressed wishes. These come to find their substitutive satisfaction in the very gestures and practices that seek to exclude them. Murdering the mother, that delirious separation of an imperilled masculine identity from an engulfing female object, becomes the last refuge and triumph of the ineradicable desiring identification that it struggles to defend itself against.

Male homosexuality

One of the most important things about Freud's reflection on homosexuality in the *Three Essays on Sexuality* (1905) is the way in which he uses the phenomenon of homosexual object-choice to break up the spurious unity and fixity of the popular category of sexuality. The resultant theory of sexuality as a complex and constructed psycho-symbolic form, made up of a range of refractory component drives, comes dialectically to call into question the unity and coherence of 'homosexuality' as a homogeneous category.

As part of his polemic against theories of homosexuality as either an innate or degenerate condition, Freud mobilizes the notion of bisexuality. He specifies this as a psychic bisexuality that is at best analogous to, but neither identical with nor caused by, anatomical hermaphroditism, the presence of organs of both sexes. He then considers the question of a psychical hermaphroditism, especially the inter-sex or third sex theories of Ulrichs (a contemporary homosexual spokesman and theorist) and Krafft-Ebing: 'a feminine brain in a masculine body'. This he rejects for two reasons: its biologism, notions of a feminine brain or brain centre have no physiological foundation: its assumption that the male homosexual is in some sense a woman. Freud argues that the notion of psychical hermaphroditism would have some substance 'if the inversion of the sexual object were at least accompanied by a parallel change-over of the subject's other mental qualities, instincts and character traits into those marking the opposite sex' (Freud, 1905, p. 53). He observes that while 'character inversion' does occur among men 'the most complete mental masculinity can be combined with inversion' (ibid. p. 53).

In Freud's hands, the category of homosexuality is moved away from notions of manifest gender inversion, a reverse heterosexuality, and recentred on the question of object-choice and its inversion. Bisexuality in men is not as the notion of 'hermaphroditism' holds: 'he feels he is a woman in search of a man' (ibid., p. 55), but simply the universal capacity to take as objects members of both sexes. Male homosexuality is posed as a vicissitude of masculinity. The later additions of 1910 and 1915 confirmed Freud's recasting of the category of homosexuality as one defined by object-choice. Polemicising against theories that attempted to separate homosexuals as a distinct group or gender with its own special characteristics, Freud insists on a universal and original bisexuality from which both heterosexuality and homosexuality emerge through a restriction of interests and objects that is only finalized at puberty. No more than homosexuality is heterosexuality a 'self-evident fact ... of a chemical nature' (ibid., p. 57).

Freud's most radical move, and one that returns later to skew his own categorization is to introduce the question of the Unconscious. He insists that

> all human beings are capable of making a homosexual object-choice and in fact have made one in their unconscious. Indeed, libidinal attachments to persons of the same sex play no less a part as factors in normal mental life ... than do similar attachments to the opposite sex (ibid., p. 56).

When the field of the Unconscious is introduced categories at a manifest level are implicated in their opposites. *Unconscious* homosexual object-choices are found at the heart of heterosexual normality.

Homosexuality as a manifest phenomenon is not exempt from this logic. Freud produces an early form of the classic schema of homosexual inversion which installs a repressed heterosexuality at its heart. Inversion proceeds from 'a very intense but short-lived fixation to a woman (usually the mother)' (ibid., p. 56). This maternal fixation is then converted into an identification: 'they proceed on a narcissistic basis, and look for a young man who resembles themselves and whom *they* may love as their mother loved them' (ibid., p. 56).

This bare and schematic account of homosexual desire does two things. It *reintroduces* at an unconscious level the question of identification banished from the category of homosexual object-choice. Desire isn't just for an object and so definable in terms of object-choice. We desire *as* someone, from a position. It involves a *relation* between two positions. The relation in question is here an imaginary heterosexual one, the mother's love for her son. It is narcissistic only in a special sense; the homosexual loves himself in another person, but not *as* himself, rather from the maternal position. This unconscious maternal identification played out through a desiring fantasy is structurally distinct from but combinable with conscious identifications and manifest gender behaviour of a conventionally masculine kind. Desiring from the unconscious position of the mother need not necessarily preclude a masculine gender identity in an overtly homosexual man.

Manifest phenomena have unconscious meanings which derive from unconscious fantasies and their scenarios, in which desire needs to be specified not just by its object, but as a relation *between* subject positions. There is no guarantee that manifest phenomena will turn out to be direct reflections rather than, say, contradictions of their unconscious structuring fantasies.

Otto Fenichel's monumental *summa* of classical psycho-analytical theory, *The Psychoanalytical Theory of Neurosis* (1946) draws together many of Freud's scattered remarks and presents a systematic exposition of the classical aetiologies which retains much that is valuably radical and disruptive of traditional and popular under-standings of male homosexuality. He retains the centrality of Freud's insight into the unconscious maternal identifica-tion, and situates homosexual object-choice, like hetero-sexual object-choice, as formed within the matrix of the Oedipal crisis and as a response to castration. What is striking about Fenichel's exposition is his refusal to essen-tialize homosexuality as a single, invariant structure and his insistence that its various component elements are to be found in heterosexuals as well. Conscious object-choice, whether heterosexual or homosexual, is the final manifest-ation of individual trajectories and negotiations, and com-posed of fantasies and symbolic elements common to a general masculine condition and the dilemmas posed by the Oedipal crisis. The unconscious structuring of fantasy and desire cut across the distinctions of conscious object choice.

Fenichel recasts Ferenczi's distinction between subject and object homoerotics around a distinction between different unconscious fantasies to be found in both hetero-sexual and homosexual men. What he calls 'subject homo-erotics' turn their genital wishes away from the mother because of castration and instead identify with her, substi-tuting an identification for an original object-attachment, and loving a phallic ego-ideal in the young men and adolescents they choose as objects. He sees a similar 'narcissistic' object-choice in certain heterosexual men who from an unconscious identification as feminine choose feminine partners and love the feminine parts of their own ego in them. This leads to the paradox of an apparently 'normal' heterosexual relation being based on an unconscious homosexual fantasy of love between mother and daughter, where the 'deviant' homosexual equivalent is based on an imaginary relation between mother and son. Each scenario internalizes a protective-defensive relation to the mother.

What is lacking in both these fantasies and the Freud-Fenichel analysis is either an erotic or theoretical recognition respectively of the place of the father. The father cannot just be absent; such an absence is not innocent. He is implied by the threat of castration that converts Oedipal wishes into the maternal identification in the first place. What we might divine in the form taken by desire, an imaginary mother-child relation (whether son or daughter), is an active *refusal* to identify with and take up the place of the father. If we pose the question, absent from both Freud and Fenichel, of the primary male identification with the mother, as described by Greeson, Ryan *et al.* then that refusal of the paternal phallic position begins to make sense. It is a stubborn refusal to leave the side of the mother, to change sides, even if the price paid is symbolic castration. The retention of the loving mother-son relation as the scenario of desire is an attempt to preserve the lost phallic ego-ideal in one's object, while bearing the burden of maternal castration oneself.

What Fenichel designates as 'object-homoerotic' is based not on a refusal of the paternal phallic position but on an imaginary appropriation of it for other purposes. Starting at the same point of maternal identification, Fenichel sketches out the classical scenario of the inverted male Oedipus complex, involving a passive, receptive sexual aim directed at the paternal phallus.

Fenichel sees this as virtually identical with the scenario through which the paternal phallic position is incorporated libidinally in the normal route to heterosexuality, and as part of a wider condition of 'femininity in men' regardless of object-choice. Commenting on the latent hostility that may accompany this passive submission he relates it to the 'apprentice love' based on 'an old and original [oral] identification with the father'. Both the normal 'every boy' and the homosexual 'feminine partner' are 'learning the secrets of masculinity from the "master" or ... depriving him of them' (ibid., p. 334). Such a scenario may range between the two extremes of killing the father in order to take his place or through submission being granted imaginary participation in the father's phallic activity.

Francis Pasche, in a fascinating reflection on homosexuality as a structure in all men, defines it as 'the sum total of behavioural attitudes which express a feminine relation to the father', part of the unavoidable, negative or inverted Oedipus complex (Pasche, 1963, p. 210). He writes of an unconscious fantasy, underlying certain homosexual object-choices, of a psychic hermaphroditism, 'father and mother at the same time, irreconcilable rebels before God and the Law whose place they endeavour to take' (ibid., p. 211). This composite luciferian fantasy which Pasche detects in wider cultural patterns, e.g. Goethe's Mephistopheles, Balzac's Vautrin, embodies the wish 'to correct, to remake, thwart, parody and finally destroy the divine creation, that is to say, the creature of the Father.' He locates here a passive Oedipal desire for the father and especially a wish 'to give birth to a child in anal fashion and the concomitant desire to manipulate, mould and "undo" the faecal material.' What is presented here as an apparently perverse anal fantasy can be read as a rebellious response to the Law that lays down such oppressive terms and conditions for being and desiring. It is a transgressive attempt to have the making and moulding for oneself, to refashion oneself or an image to one's desire *over against* the forms sanctioned by the paternal Law. Mary Shelley's *Frankenstein* [1818] (1968) elaborates such a fantasy in its narration of a seizure of the Divine prerogative to create life, by the hubrisitic Man of Science. Frankenstein, collecting his decomposing waste matter from the graveyard to construct a New Man in his 'Workshop of filthy creation' (p. 315), enacts the fantasy of a transgressive faecal parenthood.

In the two major classifications of Fenichel, the homo-sexual object-choice entails either a refusal to incorporate a paternal phallic position in the 'subject-homoerotic' (a more conservative-defensive position), or a rebellious/incorporative desire for the phallic position on different and other terms in the 'object-homoerotic' (a more aggressive/offensive position). Both trajectories involve possible *risks*, the playing out of aggressive and vengeful impulses in the closed space of their chosen *mise en scène*. They also indicate a ground or potential in the psychical structure of homosexual men for a *possible* opposition at the level of social and political practice to the dominant forms of gender and the patriarchal fantasies of castration and possession/submission that fuel them.

The crucial development is the emergence of the Gay Movement in which a potential or latent psychic structure (individual refusal, rebellious appropriation) is mobilized for the construction of a *new* collective identity – 'gayness'. Schematically one might say that the Gay Movement and gay male subcultures have tended to move from an early refusal of masculinity and phallic identity (the validation of effeminacy) as in the 'subject-homoerotic' scenario to an attempt to incorporate and transpose the terms of mascu-linity as traditionally established, through parody, nar-cissism, feminization, analogous to the object-homoerotic scenario. It is at this point that Pasche's description of the fantasy of a transgressive remaking of sexual identity and relations, of a seizure of the prerogatives of the paternal Law to regulate this domain is relevant. What is refused is not masculinity or the phallic in itself, but the polarity at the heart of the Oedipal injunction: 'You cannot *be* what you desire, you cannot *desire* what you wish to be.' The 'narcissism' that characterizes certain gay male erotic scenarios, turning on the images and terms of traditional masculinity and phallic positioning, often can be seen to have a reparative function, restoring an *alliance* between being and having, identification and desire. Perhaps only such a 'perverse' eroticism can release the male body from its subjection to the phallic function and enable a re-symbolization and re-investment of maleness which might heal the ravages of symbolic castration and its effects, the 'père-version' imposed by the Law of the Father and its polarities. With the easing of that psychic violence and the relations of domination and possession it supports, such a destabilizing of 'castration' need not entail a denial or disavowal of female difference, the reproach so often addressed to the male 'pervert'. Access to a psychical femininity (a different matter) is enabled through that stubborn maternal retention at the seat (so to speak!) of homosexual anality. This is not to announce a utopian vision but simply to begin to speculate on future *transitional* developments, strategies and directions.

Conclusion

This essay has sought to situate a sketch of common male homosexual trajectories within the outline of a general psychoanalytic account of human sexuality as such, and of a dominant Oedipal heterosexuality in particular. It has drawn on the work of Freud and especially certain radical elements and developments of Freud by theorists in the French tradition, notably Jacques Lacan and Jean Laplanche. It distinguishes sharply the opposition between psychological health and pathology from the opposition between normality and inversion/perversion. The latter distinction is subjected to a deconstructive critique by demonstrating in Freudian thought that the sexual drive is perverse in its very constitution (Laplanche). More controversially the work of Lacan is invoked to give an account of the relative fixing of heterosexual and homosexual outcomes, not as the results of a biologically guaranteed or stunted natural development, but as responses to the unconscious primal fantasies enjoined by the phallo-centric

Oedipal order and their 'père-version' (Lacan) or turn to the Father.

The account of the human sexual drive in its fantasmatic derivation and deviation from the biological order of fixed instincts might plausibly make claims to a universal application. The specific account of a particular Oedipal symbolic ordering of desire and identification, with its heterosexual and homosexual object-choices, is clearly more narrowly culture-bound and tied to historically distinct forms of the bourgeois nuclear family. Psychoanalytic theory is notoriously reluctant or unable to address the question of the culturally and historically specific conditions of existence and determinations of the psychosexual patterns it describes.

My necessarily partial sketch of male homosexual trajectories stays fairly close to Freud and the early Freudians, summarized by Otto Fenichel, before the petrifaction of a virulently homophobic orthodoxy set in in the 1930s and 1940s. In the twelve months since a version of this essay was given as a paper at the 1987 Amsterdam Conference of Lesbian and Gay Studies, three important new books on male homosexuality within a psychoanalytic framework and committed to a non-pathological account of homosexuality have appeared. *The Psychoanalytic Theory of Male Homosexuality* by Kenneth Lewes gives a near comprehensive account of the history of psychoanalytic theorization of male homosexuality together with a trenchant criticism of its increasingly conformist commitment to an ideology of reproductive heterosexuality as both a cultural norm and a prescription of psychic health. Fritz Morgenthaler's *Homosexuality, Heterosexuality, Perversion* and Richard Friedman's *Male Homosexuality: A Contemporary Psychoanalytic Perspective*, both advance different models of a non-pathological trajectory for male homosexuality. While the latter two work within the highly problematic frameworks of contemporary ego-psychology and self-psychology (entailing all the critical objections to these schools made by Lacan and the French tradition), all three books are of considerable interest to gay readers. They indicate a welcome break from the previous normative and homophobic consensus in which the psychoanalytic theory of homosexuality has stagnated for decades.

Bibliography

Bieber, I. (1965), 'Clinical Aspects of Male Homosexuality', in J. Marmor (ed.), *Sexual Inversion* (New York: Basic Books).

Coleman, J. (1973), 'My homosexuality and my psychotherapy', in *Homosexuality: A Changing Picture*, ed. H. Ruitenbeck (London: Souvenir Press).

Ernst, S. and Maguire, M. (eds) (1987) *Living with the Sphinx* , Papers from the Women's Therapy Centre (London: The Women's Press).

Fenichel, O. (1946), *The Psychoanalytic Theory of Neurosis* (London: Routledge & Kegan Paul).

Fletcher, J. (1986), 'Poetry, gender and primal fantasy', in V. Burgin *et al.* (eds), *Formations of Fantasy* (London: Methuen).

Freud, S. (1903), *Die Zeit* (Vienna, 27 October, 1903), cited in J. Marmor (ed.), *Homosexual Behaviour* (New York: Basic Books, 1981), p. 394.

Freud, S. (1905), *Three Essays on the Theory of Sexuality*, in A. Richards (ed.), The Pelican Freud Library (PFL), Vol. 7 (Harmondsworth: Penguin, 1977).

Freud, S. (1908), '"Civilised" sexual morality and modern nervous illness', in A. Dickson (ed.), PFL, Vol. 12 (Harmondsworth: Penguin, 1985).

Freud, S. (1915), 'Instincts and their vicissitudes', in A. Richards (ed.), PFL, Vol. 11 (Harmondsworth: Penguin, 1984).

Freud, S. (1916), 'The paths to the formation of symptoms', Lecture 23 in J. Stachey and A. Richards (eds), *Introductory Lectures on Psychoanalysis*, PFL, Vol. 1 (Harmondsworth: Penguin, 1973).

Freud, S. (1924), 'The dissolution of the Oedipus complex', in A. Richards (ed.), PFL Vol. 7 (Harmondsworth: Penguin, 1977).

Freud, S. (1925), 'Some psychical consequences of the anatomical distinction between the sexes', PFL, Vol. 7, ibid.

Freud, S. (1926), *Inhibitions, Symptoms and Anxiety*, in A. Richards (ed.), PFL, Vol. 10 (Harmondsworth: Penguin, 1979).

Freud, S. (1931), 'Female sexuality', in PFL, Vol. 7, op.cit.

Freud, S. (1935), *Letters of S. Freud 1873–1937*, E. Freud (ed.) (London: The Hogarth Press, 1970).

Friedman, R. (1988), *Male Homosexuality* (New Haven: Yale University Press).

Greenson, R. (1968), 'Dis-identifying from the mother, etc.' *International Journal of Psychoanalysis*, Vol. 49, pp. 370–3.

Kohen, G. (1986), 'Reflections on Dora: the case of hysteria', in G. Kohn (ed.), *The British School of Psychoanalysis: The Independent Tradition* (London: Free Association Books).

Lacan, J. (1958), 'The meaning of the phallus', in J. Mitchell and J. Rose (eds), *Feminine Sexuality* (London: Macmillan, 1982).

Laplanche, J. (1970), *Life and Death in Psychoanalysis,* trans. J. Mehlman (1976) (Baltimore: Johns Hopkins Paperback, 1985).

Laplanche, J. and Pontalis, J. B. (1960), 'Fantasy and the origins of sexuality', in *Formations of Fantasy,* op.cit.

Leclaire, S. (1965), 'Jerome, or death in the life of the obsessional', in S.Scheiderman (ed.), *Returning to Freud* (New Haven: Yale University Press, 1980).

Lewes, K. (1988), *The Psychoanalytic Theory of Male Homosexuality* (New York: Simon & Schuster).

Mergenthaler, F. (1984), *Homosexuality, Heterosexuality, Perversion,* ed. P. Moor (New Jersey: The Analytic Press).

Mitchell, J. (1974), *Psychoanalysis and Feminism* (Harmondsworth: Penguin, 1975).

Mitchell, J. (1982), 'Femininity, narration and psychoanalysis', in *The Longest Revolution* (London: Virago, 1984).

Pasche, F. (1964), 'Symposium on homosexuality no. ii,' *International Journal of Psychoanalysis*, vol. 41, pp. 210–13.

Rich, A. (1980), 'Compulsory heterosexuality and lesbian existence', in *Signs: Journal of Women in Culture and Society*, Vol. 5, no. 4, Summer 1980, pp. 631–60.

Riviere, J. (1929), 'Womanliness as a masquerade', in *Formations of Fantasy,* op.cit.

Ryan, T. (1985), 'Roots of masculinity', in A. Metcalf and M. Humphries (eds), *The Sexuality of Men* (London: Pluto Press, 1985).

Shelley, M. [1818] (1968), *Frankenstein, or The Modern Prometheus,* in P. Fairclough (ed.), *Three Gothic Novels* (Harmondsworth: Penguin English Library).

Socarides, C. (1979), 'The psychoanalytic theory of homosexuality etc.', in I. Rosen (ed.), *Sexual Deviation* (Oxford: Oxford University Press, 1979).

Sulloway, F. (1979), *Freud: Biologist of the Mind* (London: Burnett Books, 1979).

Weeks, J. (1983), 'Homosexuality and the problematic nature of psycho-analysis, etc.', in *Among Men, Among Women,* Gay and Women Studies Conference (Amsterdam, 1983).

CHAPTER SIX

Theories of sexual identity and the masculinization of the gay man

Jamie Gough

Since the early 1970s the style and image of gay men in North America and Western Europe has undergone a dramatic shift. Whereas previously the most characteristic practice and most pervasive popular image of the male homosexual were effeminate, over the last twenty years the predominant styles of gay men have become increasingly masculine. The most obvious aspect of these new styles is clothing. The central styles have been the 'clone', partially supplanted in the mid–1980s by the sportsman. Alongside these have grown other, more specialist images: the leatherman/biker, the construction worker, the squaddy, the skinhead, the cowboy. Many, though not all, of these styles of clothing mimic those of occupations and pursuits which are strong male preserves. But the prescribed forms of masculinity extend beyond dress to gestures and 'body language' (no longer the limp wrist, no more 'mincing'), to ways of speaking (no more screaming and lisping), to language (we are no longer to be 'Miss So-and-so'). The change is also present in the body: hours in the gym are required to create, not necessarily an inflated muscle man, but a male-athletic body. The category of the sportsman, and to a large extent that of the leatherman, is centred on this notion of the masculine body. The opposition here is not merely femininity/masculinity but male/female: the body is to be what-is-specifically-male, thus apparently rooting the new gender style in physiology, the social in the biological.

Of course, this change has been very uneven. It is more pronounced among gay men whose social life is centred on the scene, and, within this, more pronounced in the scene in the large cities; it is clearer among younger than older gay men; and so on. The older cultural traditions survive, and not only among older gay men. But the shift is clear.

One of the aims of this essay is to explore the adequacy of different theories of sexual identity in explaining this change in the gay identity. But the new masculinity is also important from a political point of view. On the positive side, it has shaken an important element of previous anti-gay ideology, that gay men and gay sexuality are inherently effeminate; whatever the merits of this idea of effeminacy (which I examine further below), set within a wider sexist ideology it results in gay sexuality being seen as both unnatural and demeaning. Traditional ideology has seen gay men as effeminate in both a social and a physio- logical sense; the latter has formed a part of the medical model of the homosexual developed in the nineteenth century and constantly appearing since (Marshall, 1981, pp. 142–5). The form taken by the contemporary masculi- nization of the gay man tends to undermine the view of gay men as effeminate in both the social and physiological senses.

But there are problems in the way in which the new styles reassert – in a sense recycle – masculinity. The distinction masculine/feminine is purely social, based on the oppres- sion of women and on what is now an historically obsolete sexual division of labour. The category masculine is there- fore a wholly reactionary one. The fact that no *individual* can choose to live outside the social system of gender, and that all of us therefore participate in masculinity/

femininity, does not remove this reactionary content (Gough and Macnair, 1985, pp. 36–41, 57–9). The new styles therefore present a real political problem.

To be sure, gay masculinity is not, in any simple way, 'real' masculinity, any more than camp is 'real' femininity. It is more self-conscious than the real thing, more theatrical, and often ironic. As the Village People and Frankie Goes to Hollywood affirmed, it is hard to take cowboys very seriously in the middle of Manhattan. And this gives rise to a further contradiction, since this self-consciousness of the gay masculinity is itself feminine: it is women who have to worry about their appearance, whereas carelessness and a pseudo-naïve 'naturalness' are essential parts of masculinity. (One effect of the contradiction embodied in the necessarily feminine aspects of the new masculinity is a great *variety* of styles: the contradiction can be negotiated in many different ways.) Nor is the newly-masculine gay man necessarily more misogynist than the camp queen: the gender styles do not in themselves determine the man's form of participation in real gender relations, in the active oppression of women.

But the new styles *are* in many ways oppressive to women and to gay men themselves. For gay men the immediate problems concern sex. As I argue below, for gay men the masculine styles are based on a new self-consciousness as *sexual object*. They involve a sexual desire focused on the masculine, which is a particular quality abstracted from the person, and which within this desire substitutes itself for the person (which we may call asexual 'fetish' (Gough and Macnair, 1985, pp. 41–5)). To the extent that this is a socially dominant sexuality, one is both required to conform to this abstract model in order to be attractive, and at the same time to be sexually attracted to it in others. Yet no one is, or could be, nothing-but-masculinity, essence-of-masculinity, so these aims are logically unattainable and must to a considerable extent remain fantasies. Masculinity as a sexual fetish, is, therefore, oppressive not simply for dictating a certain norm, but for demanding something which cannot be achieved. (This is in fact a contradiction of all fetishistic sexualities, not only of the fetish of masculinity.) The new style of sexual attractiveness is all the more tyrannous in that, as we have seen, it prescribes not only social behaviour but also physiology.

The problems of the new styles are also of gender and class. They appear as a part of the reassertion of traditional gender styles in society as a whole that has been taking place (albeit unevenly) in the 1980s. And some gay masculine styles imply, and to some extent must encourage, admiration for, or condoning of militarism and fascism (Theweleit, 1988).

The theoretical problem, then, is to understand how and in what sense gay masculine styles represent and are part of 'real' gender relations. I shall argue that the new masculinization arises from changes in the gender system as a whole and specifically from the changing organization of the gay scene and the sexual relations within it. This analysis leads to distinct political conclusions. Existing writing on the masculinization of the gay scene (and more generally, on fetishistic sexuality) has tended to adopt one of two schematic political stances: either moralistic injunctions on individuals to reject this behaviour as oppressive; or a bland acceptance of it as a harmless 'game', a product of sexual consumer demand freed from reactionary shackles. I will argue that these stances rest on superficial explanations of the phenomenon of masculinization, and that an approach which locates masculinization in the materially-based organization of gender and of gay sexual relations can provide the basis for a more realistic, but also more critical response.

Sexual identities

A rather obvious, but neglected, initial point is that a change in the form of a sexual identity can only be understood within a theory of sexual identities themselves. As is now widely acknowledged (McIntosh, 1968; Plummer, 1981), the notion of heterosexual, lesbian and gay *individuals* is a modern one. An historical–materialist account of why and how this is the case was developed in Gough and Macnair (1985, Chapter 2). We theorized the emergence of individual sexual identity as the product of a contradiction within capitalist social development. We argued that in all patriarchal societies, sexual choice has been sharply limited by (amongst other things) the importance of the family structure and by the sexual division of labour in and outside the family. But within capitalist society, in particular, the exploited majority of the population are free labourers, in distinction to slaves and serfs. That is, they are free by virtue of capitalist relations of production to work for whom they please, and therefore to live where they please and to arrange their own domestic lives. Moreover, capitalist economic development itself has strong tendencies to weaken the family. The family declines as a unit of socially-recognized production in favour of individual wage labour; much domestic work organized within the family is replaced by the purchase of commodities; subsistence becomes increasingly possible outside the family economy; and capitalist demand for labour power often directly (and brutally) breaks up families. These developments can open up a greater freedom of sexual choice; thus, in the economically advanced countries, sexual choice has become an increasingly important consideration in the formation of households or families. But this choice is still made under the gravitational pull of the family and the sexual division of labour and their attendant gender roles; thus there is sexual choice, but this sexuality still 'has to be' heterosexual. Prospective partners, then, are no longer made desirable by their economic attributes alone, but by their quality of wanting heterosexual sex and of being sexually attractive to the opposite sex; hence the emergence of the heterosexual individual. Equally, those who do not want heterosexual sex increasingly have to, *and* are able to, lead a different kind of life as a result of their sexual desires: hence the male homosexual and the lesbian. The heterosexual *and* homosexual identities are thus founded on the capitalist relations of domestic production and wage labour (which we may call 'economic' in the broadest sense). A necessary starting point in examining changes within the gay male identity such as 'masculinization' is therefore change in these economic relations.

The account so far takes as given heterosexual and homosexual *desire*, and leaves open the question of how it is formed. I will not put forward a positive theory of this here; it is, however, necessary briefly to criticize a theory which bears directly on our subject, the gender styling of a sexual identity. Fernbach has argued (1981, pp. 82–91) that for men in patriarchal societies, gay sexual desire is a product or aspect of an effeminate gender identity, which is in turn the result of a failure of the boy to be separated from the maternal culture by the father or straight society. The boy, by virtue of being effeminate and living in a heterosexist society, inevitably sees himself narcissistically as an object of male desire and seeks to subordinate himself sexually to men (p. 86), or is unable to 'compete for' and to dominate women and thus becomes homosexual by default (p. 87). If this argument is right, then the question of masculinity of gay men would be short circuited: 'gay men ... really are effeminate' (p. 83). Sexual identity (gay) and gender identity (effeminate) are one. Apparent masculinity of gay men can be no more than a very superficial cover-up, and thus of little theoretical or political significance.

Fernbach's thesis is empirically shaky. In all patriarchal societies there are many men who have both homosexual desires and practice who are also normally masculine; in those with institutionalized man–youth sexuality (many hunter-gatherer societies, ancient Greece), these men are the majority. Conversely, in some patriarchal societies (contemporary Britain, for example), some effeminate men are heterosexual. These oversights result from Fernbach's rather mechanical and functionalist reasoning. Fernbach sees *subjective gender identity* (the boy seeing himself as effeminate) as leading to particular *social practices* (seeking and getting men and not women), and social practices as determining *sexual desire* (desire for men). But neither of these connections works in this mechanical way. In this case, the fact that a man feels himself to be effeminate does not stop him practically in 'competing for' or dominating women; nor does the fact that he carries out these social tasks inadequately stop him desiring women. For Fernbach, in a heterosexist society heterosexuality is completely over-whelming: an effeminate man is like a woman, therefore he must desire a man; and there is no real homosexual desire, only pseudo-heterosexual desire. But in reality sexual desire, while it is always *formed* partly by social relations, does not only take forms which *reinforce and perpetuate* those social relations. We therefore cannot *merge* sexual identity with gender identity as Fernbach would wish.[1]

So far I have focused on the choice of sexual object between woman and man, leaving unspecified *what it is* in the woman or man that is desired. Again, I will put forward here only a negative thesis, which is nevertheless necessary for the argument below: that in a gendered society it is not only the physiological features of the woman or man that are desired, but also their social nature; not only their sex, but their gender. Some considerations make this assump-tion plausible. First, if one allows that sexual desire is socially constructed at all, then it is extremely unlikely that the social category of gender does not enter into it. Second, for the infant, other than in breastfeeding the distinction male/female enters through the different caring roles of men and women, that is, as gender rather than sex. Third, infants and, in some cases, young people and even adults, have had sexual desires specific to men or women without knowledge of their physiology. Thus we may assume that the sexual desire for men is *desire for the masculine* as well, perhaps, as the desire for the male body. Of course, what is meant by 'masculine' varies enormously both between particular gendered societies and within these societies.

The traditional gay roles

We can now look more closely at the gender references of the gay male identity. The discussion will be abstract, concentrating on logical connections and structures rather than attempting a concrete history.

Schematically, we may say that from the emergence of a definite homosexual identity in Britain in the late seventeenth century (Bray, 1982) up until the 1970s, gay male sexual *activity* centrally involved two types of individual. The first was the homosexual, whose sexual practice was exclusively homosexual and who, because of the conditions of capitalist society described above, was able to be involved in a homosexual milieu and compelled to regard himself as a fundamentally different kind of person from the norm. The other was the man who had sex with other men, but did not otherwise frequent a homosexual milieu, typically was married, and regarded himself as essentially heterosexual. There was a strong tendency for the homosexual to be seen, and to see himself, as effeminate. This gendering of the homosexual arose not from the normalcy of heterosexual *behaviour* as such but precisely out of the existence of the heterosexual *individual*: if normal individuals are heterosexual, then someone who desires men is like-a-woman. This effeminacy of the self-conscious homosexual is evident very early, with the 'mollies' of the early eighteenth-century scene in London (Bray, 1982). As Marshall (1981, pp. 137–48) has shown, the dominant homosexual identity remained strongly effeminate well into the twentieth century, systematized in the biologistic theories of the 'invert' and the 'Third Sex'. The man who merely had occasional sex with other men, on the other hand, was not gendered in this way precisely because he did not *organize his life* around his homosexual activity and thus did not have a deviant sexual identity.

These two types of actor were not just two separate possibilities, but were to some extent involved in sexual relations with each other and were to that extent the contradictory parts of a single reality. For, in order to find apparently masculine, and thus desirable, sexual partners, homosexuals tended to look beyond the milieu of other, necessarily effeminate, homosexuals. Their partners thus tended to be either the men who had gay sex occasionally from choice, or other men who were economically coerced ('trade'). The initiative for these relationships might also come from the other direction. For the non-homosexual seeking homosexual sex, a homosexual and therefore effeminate partner allowed him to see his own sexuality as quasi-heterosexual, to see himself as 'the man' in the encounter.

On the other hand, there was also a milieu of sexual relations *between* men who did not define themselves as homosexuals; this sex was therefore not 'queer', was in a sense asocial, 'merely sex', and thus raised no problems of gender. It was (and is) on a continuum connected to the subconscious and naïve homosexuality which is a component of all male society. Indeed, precisely because of this advantage of gender style, some self-defined homosexuals (Joe Orton is a well-known example) tried to adopt and use a masculine style by immersing themselves in this milieu.

Thus the effeminacy of the homosexual was reproduced through, as well as partially determining of, the forms of *sexual relationship* he entered into. This shows that, contrary to Marshall's argument (1981, p. 135), the homosexual identity was indeed a *sexual* identity and not essentially a gender one, even though the gender style was very marked.

As already hinted, there was also a *partial and tentative* construction of a more masculine homosexual identity, though very different from the modern one. This identity escaped by various means the process by which the homosexual was constructed as effeminate. The most important means was the use of *age difference*: an older man could have exclusively homosexual relations, socialize with other homosexuals and still be butch if he had sex only with young men, and was presumed to be the 'active' partner; the young men were thereby constructed as effeminate. A difference of class often reinforced this gender differentiation. When this sexuality theorized itself, it was typically as a 're-creation' of the masculinist and misogynist culture of ancient Greece; examples are the Community of the Special in 1920s Germany, and the significantly-named contemporary French magazine *Samauri*. However, it is easy and convenient for men in this situation not to see themselves as truly homosexual, especially given the existence elsewhere of a strong effeminate homosexual identity. This sexuality is therefore only a partially-formed sexual identity, the participants tending to see themselves as 'neither heterosexual nor homosexual'. This is reflected in the harking back to ancient cultures, the attempt to theorize this sexuality in pre-capitalist terms, that is, in terms of sexual behaviour before the advent of the heterosexual and the homosexual. This refusal of individual sexual identity is also connected to the prevalence of this sexuality within classes with strong pre-capitalist cultural survivals, such as the English and Prussian capitalist classes: due to the 'organic' nature of the transition from feudalism in these countries, their ruling classes have maintained strong aristocratic (non-bourgeois) traits. Male homosexual activity has been carried on in the British upper class without the implication of homosexual identity that it has had, for example, among ruling-class men in the USA. This evasion of sexual identity meant that the dominant homosexual identity remained elsewhere and effeminate.

The causes of masculinization

The sharp change in the style of the gay scene is rooted in changes which took place during the boom of the 1950s and 1960s and which have not been reversed despite the subsequent economic stagnation. After an initial stabilization, the boom generated a further erosion of the sexual division of labour and thus of gender roles; wider use of contraception tended to separate heterosex from reproduction. As one would expect from the previous discussion of sexual identity, these developments produced a widening and deepening of the male and female heterosexual and homosexual identities. They enabled, from the late 1960s, a massive expansion of the size of the gay scene (including in the latter gay relations carried out in private).

These processes produced a contradictory movement in ideas: homosexuality became both more and less 'deviant'. First, the strengthening of the heterosexual identity tended to make homosexuality seem more deviant, and actually strengthened one aspect of gender roles (the sexual). Second, however, the weakening of gender roles in other respects meant that a particular sexual behaviour could be conceived of as less strongly associated with a particular sex. In particular, the notion of gay male sexuality as a sign of effeminacy tended to be weakened. The very growth of the gay scene and its increasing visibility also tended to weaken the view of it as deviant.

But the change within homosexuality was not merely in its ideological place. A crucial part of its transformation came from *changed practices* deriving from the growth of the gay scene. The greater number of participants in the scene encouraged homosexuals increasingly to seek sexual partners *among other identified homosexuals*. This activity may indeed have become more necessary: the strengthening of the male heterosexual identity tended to mean that *fewer* 'normal' men would have occasional and casual gay sex, since this now more clearly carried the stigma of being a queer. The increase in sexual relations among homosexuals meant that *homosexuals became not just the desirers but the desired*. And this, following my assumption that it is gender as well as sex that is desired, required a masculine identity. The increasing adoption of this masculine identity then further encouraged the pattern of homosexuals seeking partners among other homosexuals.

This shift also involved a deepening of a specifically homosexual identity at the level of sexual practice. Whereas the effeminate homosexual was assumed to seek only a 'passive' role (though desire, and to a lesser extent practice, may have been different), now all possible roles in homosex are available to be played by homosexuals. Thus the *central* distinction shifts from the effeminate–passive man contrasted with the masculine–active man to the homosexual *tout court* contrasted with the heterosexual.

This explanation of masculinization in terms of choice of sexual partner explains my earlier observation, that the change in gender styling has been most pronounced among those whose social and sexual life centres on the commercial scene. But the change also runs through the scene in the widest sense, that is, through all social relations between gay men. It operates wherever gay men form *and* continue with sexual relationships with each other, or where such relationships are imagined. And, of course, the new styles are propagated as fashion, through imitation and through the media. The change in social relations is thus clearest within the commercial scene, but by no means limited to it.

The masculinization of the homosexual, which began in the 1970s, has been joined in the 1980s by the increased masculinization of the heterosexual man. These two trends have tended to reinforce each other: a masculinization of men in general. The masculinization of the heterosexual man is a result of the increased freedom of heterosexual women, at least in the middle class, to choose their sexual partner (a deepening of the female heterosexual identity itself), with heterosexual men, like gay men, becoming objects of desire. This process is therefore similar to that involved in the masculinization of gay men, and could be said to be part of an increased (though socially very uneven) sexualization of social relations in general. But the masculinization of men in general also has underpinnings which are more retrogressive: an ideological reassertion of traditional gender roles (even against the grain of current changes in the sexual division of labour), reflecting both a reaction to the insecurities generated by the economic crisis and the impact of right-wing propaganda. The contemporary masculinization of (all) men therefore is not a unified 'idea', but rests on contradictory trends in social practice and the ideas that these incorporate.

Other approaches

My approach may be contrasted with other accounts of the masculinization of the gay scene, based explicitly or implicitly on other theories of sexual identity.

1   An approach which sees *sexual identities as formed essentially at the level of ideological production ('discourse')*. Both Humphries (1985, pp. 72, 77, 84) and Blachford (1981, p. 200) explain the masculinization of the gay scene as an attempt by gay men to make themselves more respectable. Empirically this is dubious in that the styles adopted do not actually look 'normal': even a clone outfit does not look 'normal' and, far from being a disguise, advertises you as gay. The logic of the argument is also hard to understand: why should gay men seek to make themselves more respectable at the very time that the space for homosexual relations was widening? Indeed, the argument begs the question: why was this strategy not adopted until the 1970s? This problem points to the weakness of all theories which operate only at the level of ideology (the most influential being that of Foucault, 1979). They give no

account of how the ideologies which they describe are constructed, sustained and contradicted by material practice; they therefore fail to explain both the historical evolution of these ideologies and the way in which these ideologies fail to completely dominate their subjects, their areas of *in*effectiveness.

2   An approach which sees *sexual identities as arising purely from increased sexual freedom*. The expanded 'market' is seen as allowing and calling forth more varied 'commodities' (identities) (D'Emilio (1982, p. 11)) this is also a popular 'common-sense' view of the phenomenon). This explanation neglects the continued constraints on sexuality, whether immediate social and economic constraints or their psychological mediations. As I argued above, these constraints are an essential part of the construction of sexual identities, where they are expressed in a fetishized form (Gough and Macnair, 1985, pp. 50–1). Thus gay masculine style reflects a *combination* of sexual freedom with the *un*freedom of the institution of masculinity (i.e., of the gender system). A theory which sees only sexual freedom pitted against some undifferentiated 'anti-sexual' reaction cannot explain why sexual identities take the particular form that they do. It therefore has to fall back on a notion of 'natural' or self-generating sexual taste (just as neo-classical economics, which the theory closely parallels, relies so heavily on unexplained consumer taste).

Each of these theoretical positions can lead to either of two political lines, which are, at least superficially, opposites:

a   The first political perspective is *that the masculine gay identity is reactionary pure and simple and should be consciously rejected*. The ideological–Foucauldian theorization (1 above) can lead to this conclusion (Kleinberg, 1987; for a systematic exposition of this politics, see Heath, 1982). The message borne by the style of the newly masculine gay man, that is, the purely ideological aspect of the phenomenon, is indeed purely and simply reactionary. And if masculinization is an ideological 'strategy' (the term used by Foucault), then it can be combatted purely by an ideological counter-strategy – conscious rejection. Hence the strongly moralistic perspective. This view thus misses two crucial points: the politically contradictory aspects of masculinization (its reflection of both freedom and unfreedom); and the need for change in *materially-based* social relations in order to confront it.

A similar political conclusion can be underpinned by the 'market' theorization, as among some feminist critics of the male gay scene. This theorization sees male sexuality as fetishistic, and therefore reactionary, *by nature*; the view of sexual taste as outside history, characteristic of 'market' theories, is evident here. The reactionary essence of male sexuality is then seen as being realized via increased sexual freedom, via the 'market'. The political solution is therefore self-control, less promiscuity. This view thus reverses the real relation of the social forms of sexuality (fundamentally the effect) and the material relations of gender (fundamentally the cause), and thus comes close to right-wing moralism.

b   The main current alternative political perspective is *that the masculine role should be celebrated as simply one variant among many possible ones.* The Foucault school generally tends to this kind of liberal/anarchist conclusion: if ideologies can so easily structure the whole of social practice, then there is little scope for rejecting or combatting them. Furthermore, if these ideologies are really independent of material life, or from any notion of fundamental human needs, as the Foucault school holds, then there is anyway no firm basis from which to criticize them. Consequently, there is a tendency to see different sexualities merely as 'games', which are without wider social significance. Thus Humphries (1985, p. 83) suggests that masculinity could and should be confined within sexual practice, made independent of 'real' gender roles outside.

This perspective, then, takes these roles essentially as facts of life, and seeks to ring new changes on them (p. 85). Within the market theory of sexual identity, the 'free market' in sexualities can be welcomed as a realization of freedom of choice (D'Emilio, 1982, p. 248). If the role of oppressive structures in constructing these identities is ignored (p. 11), then there is no reason to criticize them.

It is significant that each of the theories criticized here lends itself to opposite, equally simplistic political conclusions. Both theories make unjustifiable abstractions in their view of sexuality: of its ideology from its material social practices, or of the basis of sexuality in nature from its social construction. The central social contradictions, and thus the social instability, of sexuality are therefore missed. Inevitably, then, the political prescriptions offered do not include social action, but are either fatalistic, or rely on asocial, individualistic action.

If, as I have argued, the masculine sexual identity is grounded in concrete social practices, it cannot be regarded merely as a 'game'. However, by the same token, it *is* possible to combat this masculinity, through the struggle against those practices that underpin it: namely, the gender system and the class system within which it is embedded.

Calls for individuals to reject the masculine gay identity will not be effective. But we have seen that this identity itself is far from monolithic, as it appears in both the theories criticized above, since it has foundations which are both contradictory and shifting. We have seen how sexual identity is based on a contradiction which consists of a degree of sexual choice set alongside continuing oppressive relations. This can be experienced emotionally as a tension between the excitement of playing a sexual role and the constriction which it at the same time imposes – a tension which many gay men feel with the various masculine sexual roles. These roles also have their particular contradiction, that of a desire for the masculine on the part of people who (still) violate the masculine role. The masculine role models themselves are anyway unsteady due to the obsolescence of the gender system: the male manual worker, the sports*man*, the cowboy are not what they were. And as with all fetishistic sexuality, there is often a strongly-felt conflict with the need for nurturance and companionship. All these contradictions open up possibilities and needs, limited but real, for individual gay men to question and limit the masculine identity.

Note

1   Fernbach at some points of his argument (e.g., p. 83) appears to be distinguishing the desire of the gay man from the desire of the man who has gay sex, and to be theorizing only the former. But his arguments in fact apply equally to the latter. Marshall at one point (p. 135) comes close to Fernbach's conclusion, though on a very different theoretical basis.

References

Bray, A. (1982), *Homosexuality in Renaissance England* (London: Gay Men's Press).

Blachford, G. (1981), 'Male dominance and the gay world', in K. Plummer (ed.), *The Making of the Modern Homosexual* (London: Hutchinson), pp. 184–210.

D'Emilio, J. (1982), *Sexual Politics, Sexual Communities* (Chicago: Chicago University Press).

Gough, J. and Macnair, M. (1985), *Gay Liberation in the Eighties* (London: Pluto Press).

Fernbach, D. (1981), *The Spiral Path* (London: Gay Men's Press).

Foucault, M. (1979), *The History of Sexuality*, Vol. 1 (London: Allen Lane).

Heath, S. (1982), *The Sexual Fix* (London: Macmillan).

Humphries, M. (1985), 'Gay machismo', in A. Metcalf and M. Humphries (eds), *The Sexuality of Men* (London: Pluto Press).

Kleinberg, S. (1987), 'The new masculinity of gay men, and beyond', in M. Kaufman (ed.), *Beyond Patriarchy* (Oxford: Oxford University Press).

McIntosh, M. (1968), 'The homosexual role', *Social Problems*, vol. 17, no. 2, pp. 262–70.

Marshall, J. (1981), 'Pansies, perverts and macho men: changing conceptions of male homosexuality', in Plummer *op. cit.*, pp. 133–54.

Plummer, K. (ed.) (1981), *The Making of the Modern Homosexual* (London: Hutchinson).

Theweleit, K. (1988), *Male Fantasies*, Vol. 2. *Warfare, Male Bodies, Homosexuality* (Cambridge: Polity Press).

CHAPTER SEVEN

You don't need bars to build a jail: The politics of sexuality in care

Ben Perks

'Cor, I'd give her one' grunted the male adolescent as he lay on the cushions in the TV lounge, at an uncomfortable angle – so he could stick his chest out and his shoulders high enough to keep the presence of his physical superiority while he relaxed. 'I know what you mean – ', a second neanderthal voice added from the other side of the room, 'What about you, Stephen?' Gulping at my own incriminating silence, I managed to half-heartedly agree, though despising the obligation to do so.

I have nothing academic to offer on the subject of young people in care: I am, however, an expert. This may sound a contradiction in terms, but the first thing one has to accept about young people in care is that only those who have lived in care understand the reality of life in care. It is wrong for 'child-care experts' to be called such, just as it is wrong for white people to claim to be experts on racism.

Before one looks at the problems caused by being gay and in care, one must first look at the special problems for

young people in care. Because care – particularly residential
care – is so isolated and divorced from the community at
large, people learn about the care system mainly through
the media. According to the papers people read and the
television and radio they watch and listen to, they may have
several different stereotypes of young people in care. There
are two main stereotyped images of young people in care
and those who have lived in care: the first is the 'children in
need', 'charity' image, which in my own experience is the
picture portrayed in the tabloid press and lower quality
television and radio programmes, and is perpetrated by
upper working-class people (by this I mean those from
'skilled workers' ghettos'). I have also found that middle-
class people, and poorer people, have an image of young
people in care as 'deviant, criminal' and 'in care through
fault of their own'. *All* people tend to view young people in
care as less intelligent than those outside care, and many see
young people in care as pathetic and helpless. Sometimes
their views are the same with regard to those who have left
care.

Both of these groups – the upper working-class and
middle-class people – would probably consider young
people in care, and those who have lived in care, to be
illiterate and not very bright. All of these views are totally
divorced from reality, and are taken on board by callous
media and an uncaring education system.

The outcome of these negative stereotypes is discrimination against young people in care, and those who have lived
in care, throughout housing, employment, education and
all other public services. Neither the Left in general, nor
anti-discrimination groups (such as the National Council
for Civil Liberties), tackle this discrimination in the same
way they do with other minority groups. This is because the
Left has the same negative attitudes to young people in care.
Indeed left-wing local authorities have much in common
with conservative ones in their unjustified ill-treatment of
young people in care. Southwark Council, for example,

sent police and their own officials to The Hollies children's home in 1984 to remove physically the children who had barricaded themselves in because they were frightened of being moved from their home. Both Lambeth and Southwark have regularly bowed down to the viewpoint of union officials when children have complained about being abused.

Most people are brought up by one or two adults. Those young people who are in care are brought up by bureaucracy, by a council system, by paid full-time employees. Those in foster care are brought up by people who have high expectations of the young people they take on. Both groups have files kept on them, have statutory case conferences and six-monthly reviews held about them, and have a team of six or seven adults dealing with their lives. The majority of local authorities don't involve the young people with either the files, meetings or management of their lives.

Young people in care are always the ammunition for political battles; they are seen as being of 'some use' to childless adults; by their mere existence they create jobs. As far as the authorities go, most of them tend to let their sympathies lie with the people who work around or foster young people, as opposed to their clients.

There are added problems for other minority groups in care – particularly Black people who may be brought up with white people, and therefore be alienated from their own identity and culture, as well as suffering direct racism from the people they live with (this, of course, is something they wouldn't suffer if living with their own families). Young women and girls often have to ask *male* members of staff for sanitary towels, which are stored in bulk and carefully logged when taken. Disabled young people suffer even less consultation about their own lives, and their sexual and emotional needs are often ignored.

The care system is based on a legal obligation to care for children and young people under several criteria, from neglect and abuse to loss of parents. A minority of young people will be placed in care for truancy and crime. The obligation is set out more through a set of restrictions than a clear idea of what care should be. There are two types of care: residential care and foster care. Residential care is a modernized version of the Dickensian children's home; foster care is where a family care for a child, and this often leads to adoptive care, where the child legally becomes part of the family. Secure accommodation is a form of residential care where restrictions on liberty are imposed; for example, being locked up in a room all night and only being allowed out to go to school in the same part of the building. In my opinion secure units are used unnecessarily and too much. It is very much easier for a local authority to initiate a secure order for someone already living in care than it is for someone not in care. This situation is largely responsible for the criminalization of young people in care.

The majority of young people who go into care, it could be said, are the victims of the breakdown of the family. As young people, and people in general, are extremely 'patriotic' about their family, then that 'failing' of their own family is an embarrassment. The care system therefore presents itself as a smug, self-righteous, 'better' alternative – particularly with regard to fostering and adoption.

I described earlier the image some people have of young people in care being 'deviant'. Despite that image, only 12–17 per cent of those who go into care do so for reasons of crime or law-breaking, and only one in seven is under 5 (the vast majority being over 13). Many male young people will go straight into either a single-sex home or a mixed teenage home, and will therefore be confronted by a macho male atmosphere, with clearly defined sex roles and little personal privacy (due to what could be described as 'overcrowding', where there can be up to four to five to a room). Going into care might be compared to starting a new school; but I would argue that in care one has to spend 24 hours a day with the peer group, and one has little chance to sit alone and reflect on things or to develop any individual personality. In fact, to many young people residential care is an extension of school. In these conditions it is extremely difficult to hide gay sexuality. When it is discovered, it is very likely that the news would be passed around your school and local community very quickly, as it is almost certain that at least one boy in the home would attend the same school and most of them would be involved with local young people. Both the staff and the young people auto-matically assume that one is heterosexual; the system is not geared to promoting the positive aspects of living away from a family, such as personal freedom and individual personality.

Going into a new foster home can be just as traumatic, particularly in the first couple of days when one would be extremely anxious to please. To go into a foster home is, in effect, to go to live with a family that has 'succeeded' far better than one's own; this in itself works to ensure the foster family's supremacy and often has an image of 'setting an example of how to be'. Many adults seek to become foster parents because of their expectations resulting from the stereotypes outlined earlier: some may be looking for a child in the same way they look for a pet, someone to cuddle and pat on the head; another type may be the ex-sergeant major and his wife who are keen to put a corrupted young man on the right tracks, to whip him into shape.

In some of our meetings we have talked about fostering. Most of us in the group have been fostered in the past, although now we all live in homes. Although fostering sometimes works it is not always the answer. Some of us feel that we were treated differently from the foster parents' own children and we were given fewer privileges. Social workers do not always visit you enough and tend to take sides with the foster parents against you. Some-times you feel as if no one will listen to your point of view. Maybe you need a separate social worker for yourself and another one for the foster parents. We also think that young people in care should go and talk to groups of foster parents, to tell them what it is really like to be in care.

Whilst I was in there, in one year, I held myself in so much that I hardly ever felt able to release the built-up tension. This was because there I was, the charity girl! Always to be reminded of my good fortune and ingratitude. Maybe foster parents do this for social status – Christian Act! How kind they are – but are they? Don't they realise the damage they can do? Selfish. They play and use us for their goodness. I could never be myself there. They only knew the nice me, a one-sided personality caged in respect and expected gratitude, but now in a Children's Home where they accept my anger, moods, and bad days, I can be myself and feel free! (from the NAYPIC booklet, *Sharing Care*, 1985).

Most entries into care involve a court order of some kind, and the legal system itself, even when dealing with something as sensitive as parental rights, will apply heterosexism and homophobia (in relation to this, see also Les Moran's essay in this volume). The sexuality of any party in court proceedings can often be taken into account when reaching a decision. Specifically, young gays have either been placed in care or referred to psychiatrists. Obviously the judiciary regularly scapegoats gay men for child sex abuse. This is a threat to all gay men either living or working in care. The passage below may help you to understand this threat:

The sunset fell over the roof-tops in the south-west of Birmingham like only Sunday sunsets do. The peaceful clean street was interrupted by the appearance of a middle-aged woman in a fur coat and dyed black hair who was clambering awkwardly out of a battered Cortina car. Two scruffy children ran before her from the car into the side-gate of the building. The woman was met by a middle-aged man at the door. She demanded an explanation for something that her children had told her during their weekend leave. 'Why are they sharing a room with a queer child-molester?' she screeched, as the bedroom-window light highlighted the Marlene Dietrich eyebrows on a battered face. 'They are sharing a room with another child. How can another child be a child-molester?' the man retorted. 'He's queer, isn't he?' Her voice rose a few decibels, and before the man had chance to answer she continued: 'Well, I am worried about the children and want them moved into another room.' At this, a head, which had been leaning out of a window at the far end of the building, was quietly brought back in. Inside the building the word went round fast, and the queer was very quickly cornered by three older boys. The woman got back into her car and was driven off. But the quiet street was soon again interrupted, by the screams of a teenage boy in agony.

This is a real-life experience of a young gay man brought up in care in Birmingham.

Young gays in care are in the front-line of both sex abuse itself and the stigma attached to it. The status value of young people in care is itself low, and being gay only adds to the problem. Sex abuse is about power; those in care have the least power, are the least cared about, and are therefore the most vulnerable. One home in Northern Ireland was virtually converted into a meat-market by all sorts of people from outside, and for years nothing was done. There is far more sexual abuse in care than we hear about, and there are many reasons for this – including the authorities' lack of respect and trust for those in care, and the client's fear of a big impersonal system. I remember being raped outside of the home by two men I didn't know: within hours of telling a member of staff *in confidence*, all his colleagues were asking me about it.

When teenagers first go into residential or foster care, masturbation – let alone sexuality as a whole – becomes an embarrassing problem. I am sure I speak for many when I say that, between 13 and 16, masturbation was always in the bathroom with the door locked and the tap running in case anyone was listening at the door. Even with such discretion I was caught out at least a few times.

It goes without saying that physical and verbal abuse are supposedly 'justified' by the sexuality of gay men. Although this is the same at school or in the workplace, young people in care are particularly vulnerable – because of the high tensions of those in care and because of the number of different people involved in a home. The strain of suffering this for 24 hours a day, in and out of school, is often beyond endurance and the end result has sometimes been tragic. Indeed, many young people have decided that they are safer living on the streets, and have used begging and child-prostitution as their only means of survival – some never being heard of again.

Heterosexism and homophobia are just as apparent in care work as in any other field of work. The powers of care workers aren't quite as extensive as those of parents, but they do have ultimate power over young people. Adding to this the fact that they are unlikely to have the same love and devotion for that young person, he may be left feeling extremely vulnerable. I have met, and know, hundreds of care workers up and down the country, yet I have never met an out-gay man working in care. Although the highly respected Association of Young People in Care (NAYPIC) voted for more positive discrimination, to reflect the gay population in the community at large, no steps have been taken to promote this. NAYPIC also voted for encouragement to be given to lesbian and gay foster parents, but, with the exception of the more radical boroughs, little has been done.

For these reasons, and many more, young gay men in care often feel the need to get away from the system. Some attempt suicide, many run away. There is no safe provision for those who run away, since it is illegal for an adult to put a roof over a child runaway's head (which is 'harbouring'): the law seems to think it is better to leave the young people out on the streets. The vast majority of runaways are also too young to get employment or claim dole money, and they have to keep hidden from the police. Therefore, the young gay man on the run may have illegally to obtain money and find somewhere to sleep, as well as taking to a world of dark back-streets, and generally being at the whim of others. Recently, seven rent boys were interviewed in Birmingham by a tabloid newspaper: it turned out that five of them had run away from care and the other two had officially left care; some were sleeping rough and the others were staying with older men. The social services departments, in conjunction with the police, often seek an easy answer in locking young people in secure accommodation.

After reading this it will not need a great deal of intellectual reasoning to work out that young gay men in care get a raw deal. The issue never seems to have been tackled in mainstream politics before. The biggest insult to young gays and lesbians in care has been the Left, and the gay and feminist, movements' insistence on campaigning for gay men and lesbians' right to foster and adopt. Young people in care *do* want gay and lesbian foster parents, but they object to the idea of groups of people protesting because they can't buy us, as they'd buy a pet, because of *their own* sexuality. Any fostering or adoption should be for the benefit of the young person, not the potential parent. We also object to this issue being either prioritized over, or set against a background of a lack of, other general changes to the care system which should benefit the gay consumer, but which, instead, merely benefit gay and lesbian friends of and voters for the local authority – by offering young people in care as pets.

Local authorities now need to recognize that not all young people in care are heterosexual. Local council lesbian and gay working parties should recognize that their biggest responsibility is to those in care. They must take steps to co-opt young people in care with full voting-rights on to all of the lesbian and gay working parties, and more importantly on to the social service committees that affect any decisions about young people in care.

The media feed off the controversies over child-prostitution, sex abuse and the sexuality of young people in care. Justified by their own naïveté, they call for a return to moral values and for a more caring society. The section of the public which believes that young people in care need charity would be put out if told that those young people had a sexuality, and offended if told that some of them were gay. Those who treat young people in care with suspicion would nod their heads if told they had a sexuality and that some were gay. They would put it down to the general deviancy.

Changing the system is like being on an island in the middle of a huge ocean: having to convince the establishment that it is *their* problem, and having to tell the Left and the gay movement that the problem is not a trivial one.

In this essay I have briefly outlined a few of the problems young gays in care face. I must stress again that only the young people in care themselves are the experts. To those who fit into this group, their persecution is not trivial and any view to the contrary is totally divorced from reality.

CHAPTER EIGHT

The contradictory politics of SM

Mike Macnair

In 1985 the lesbian and gay movement in this country was divided by a sharp debate about who could use the London Lesbian and Gay Centre, with some groups arguing for the exclusion of (among others) SM groups. The debate is now over, but the issues grumble on: they are fundamental to the movement's image of itself, of the oppression it is fighting and of the rights, or liberation, it is fighting for. I want to discuss the issues behind the debate: the politics of SM and its relationship to lesbian/gay liberation. I aim to cast a critical eye over the arguments about SM, and perhaps suggest an alternative approach.

The arguments about SM circle around two issues. The most basic is the nature of lesbian/gay liberation and of the movement for it. Does this movement include all groups of lesbians and of gay men, however diverse their aims and concerns? Or is it defined by some specific aims and practices? The second is the personal and cultural–political significance of SM sex. Does it, as supporters claim, play an enabling role, offering catharsis, and a fuller understanding of self? Or is it an obsessive dead end which distracts us from tackling our real problems? Does it expose and parody the order of power in society – or does it mimic and reinforce it?

The movement: liberal democracy
or counter-culture?

The simplest argument for the participation of SM groups in the movement is a traditional one in the male gay movement: that the liberation of the oppressed involves *accepting people as they are*. One form of this argument is the classic liberal position: society should not interfere with individuals' behaviour unless what they do harms, or interferes with the liberty of, others. A lesbian/gay liberation movement is needed because society, through the state, interferes with our individual liberty (by laws against us, etc.) and does not protect us from interference (discrimination, etc.) by other individuals. This sort of argument applies with equal force to SM people — if the argument itself is accepted.

Pro-SM writers, and supporters of the right of pro-SM groups to participate in the lesbian and gay movement/s, have placed great emphasis on the issue of democratic rights (Califia, 1982; Rubin, 1982), arguing that their opponents are in effect lending support to the right-wing, pro-censorship lobby and to police harassment. It is this sort of emphasis on democratic rights which leads most pro-SM writers to stress the consensual character of SM sexual practice.

The state is certainly absent from the arguments of most contributors to the radical feminist collection *Against Sadomasochism* (Linden *et al.*, 1982): these writers place a great emphasis on the rather minor violence, domination and symbolism of domination of SM, but ignore the monstrous agency of violence and domination that is the state under which they live, and *its* all-pervasive promotion of the symbolism of power and subordination. But the opponents of SM are not without counter-arguments. In the first place, the liberal argument depends on the argument from consent and individual freedom, and some opponents argue that consent in the context of SM is either a contradiction in terms, or predetermined by the social order, in the sense that (for instance) women are brought up to imagine that they ought to give men sexual service, so that their apparent 'consent' to this state of affairs has moral implications.

But second, it is possible to defend SM groups against the state without accepting that these groups are part of the movement – as Sarah Lucia Hoagland points out in her contribution to *Against Sadomasochism*. Simply within the general liberal-democratic framework, in defending SM groups we are defending freedom of the press, and freedom of association – the freedom of citizens to organize groups, parties and societies on issues of common concern without interference from the state. But in deciding who is, and who is not, a part of the movement, we are exercising these freedoms ourselves. Freedom of association is freedom to choose who you will and will not associate with. It involves freedom of *dis*association. If lesbian/gay coalitions decide to exclude SM groups, this is not an attack on SM people's freedom of association: it is defining the limits of the association of lesbians/gay men. The issue of democracy in itself provides no solution to the problem.

To the argument that the purpose of the movement is precisely to fight for democratic rights for lesbians and gay men against state oppression and public prejudice, feminist opponents can legitimately respond that the oppression of women works, precisely, through the free and 'consensual' expression of the heterosexual culture of male dominance and female submission. Any movement for the liberation of lesbians therefore has to fight against this culture; for gay *men* to defend 'freedom' in this context is like Margaret Thatcher's defence of her 'freedom' to use private medicine.

One way to preserve the liberal conception of the movement against this objection is to argue that sexuality is something which is not simply chosen by individuals; whether sexualities are seen as biologically, or as socially formed, we do not experience the shape of sexual desire as something which can be moulded to fit in with our political or religious ideas. So discrimination against lesbians and gay men is wrong for the same reasons that discrimination against women, or Black people, is wrong: it is wrong to penalize people for something they 'can't help'. This argument doesn't really hold water, however; nobody would argue (to suggest an extreme example) that people who could only achieve orgasm by killing other people should be allowed to do so. Our claim to liberation is founded, in the end, on the claim that 'Gay is Good'; we can't evade the necessity to make some evaluative judgement of SM as such.

The opponents of SM, however, reject altogether the view of sexuality as something we don't choose. They see sexuality as a social or ideological construct, which can be changed in adult individuals by the construction of a social practice opposed to traditional norms. For the supporters of this view, sexual desire and practice are areas of conscious struggle, in which we work together to change ourselves and the world at the same time. This is the struggle for liberation; and it involves rejecting our 'worse selves' – where SM groups exalt them. It is this view of sexuality and of the nature of the movements for liberation which gives political force to a negative view of SM.

The problem with this approach to the movement is that it has already been tried and doesn't seem to work very well. Attempts to construct new and freer 'alternative personal relationships' have led, for many of the participants, merely to a new morass of contradictions and despair. Moreover, the 'struggle against oppressive forms of personal behaviour' lets loose in the movement an immensely powerful force for division and splits. Once the principle that would exclude SM groups on these grounds is accepted, there is no stopping point short of the dissolution of all organizations into tiny cliques of those who imagine that they are without sin, and ultimately atomized and demoralized individuals.

The underlying problem is that the conception of the liberation movement as a counter-culture remains within the framework of liberal ideas of personal responsibility, founded on the autonomy of the individual. Individuals are asked to 'leave all and follow me' (me in this case being the movement), or to behave as though they lived in a free and equal society, while in fact they grew up and still live in a hierarchical one. But human beings are not autonomous individuals. We are born dependent on others, and take a long time to grow. When we get old and our bodies begin to become decrepit we become dependent again. And in reality we are dependent on others all through our lives, in ways that only become obvious when something goes wrong and disrupts the ordinary course of life. We are dependent on the existence and functioning of human society.

There is, in truth, no escape from the society in which we live, and the idea of a realm of individual sexual desire and practice purifed from power relationships in the midst of a society systematically structured around inequality is an illusion. This does not, however, mean that change and liberation are impossible. But change takes place because society as a whole, and social institutions, develop – in a contradictory way. To make the processes of change work in our favour, we need to understand sexuality as a social institution, and its development – and the possibilities opened up – as elements of contradiction and change in society as a whole.

Jamie Gough and I have argued (*Gay Liberation in the Eighties*, 1985) that distinct fetishized individual sexualities are a product of the contradiction, inherent in capitalism, between the social institutions of the family and the market; and that the socialist reorganization of society would entail the disappearance of both these institutions and of the contradiction between them, and therefore of the social form *heterosexuality* and its various alternatives, the various specific deviant sexualities – leaving behind sexual capacity, the physical capacity to take and give sexual pleasure in diverse ways. We argue that the liberation of people who are oppressed for their particular sexualities is a necessary part of this process, which leads ultimately to the end of the distinct groups as such.

On this analysis, what a *movement for liberation* needs to be about is not simply celebrating diverse sexualities as they are and fighting for our 'right to do as we please with our bodies'; nor, however, can it be about constructing a new and politically correct sexuality. Rather, we argue, the movement needs to concentrate on attacking the legal-political, economic and ideological instruments of our oppression, which are also constraints on the straight majority. The liberation movement cannot set itself loftily opposed to the cultures of the oppressed as they exist, which anyhow contain some 'seeds of the new'. Nor can it refuse criticism of their defects, *which in themselves are oppressive to others* – like the elements of sexism in the male gay scene. But this framework still requires us to make some evaluative judgement of SM. Does it contain within it *any* 'seeds of the new'? Or is it purely a manifestation of the old order?

The meaning of SM sex

Supporters of SM argue a positive value for SM sex in four ways. The first is that the need for explicit consent to particular acts in SM actually heightens awareness of the needs, rights and autonomy of the sex partner as compared with 'vanilla' (i.e., non-SM) sex. A second argument is that SM is 'cathartic', offering a way of working through and releasing conflicts in relationships. I find these arguments unconvincing. The evidence in favour is the personal experience of individual radicals involved in SM, and it is easy to find other individuals who offer other and negative experiences: a compulsion which evades real conflicts (Elizabeth Harris in *Against Sadomasochism*), or grows over to shape the whole relationship into one of dominance and submission (Marissa Jonel in *Against Sadomasochism*).

A third argument is that SM, both by asserting that sex is recreation and by the sheer variety of activities that can be involved, demystifies, defetishizes, or even 'deconstructs' the God Sex (Jeffrey Weeks, 1985, pp. 239–41). Where is the 'natural core' of which it is a 'perversion' to enjoy being bound, or whipped, or humiliated, etc., etc.? The *existence* of SM, according to this argument, makes nonsense of religious or naturalistic claims of the 'purpose of sex'. In this framework, as Weeks argues (pp. 240–5), 'sexuality' as a category begins to disappear. I am sceptical about this sort of argument; as I will show, it seems to me that SM sex is less far from vanilla sex than this would make it seem.

Fourth, SM play is said to undermine power relationships in society, because it caricatures and mocks the order of power in society. In *S and M*, Califia argues that: 'In an S/M context, the uniforms and roles and dialogue become a parody of authority, a challenge to it, a recognition of its secret sexual nature. Governments are based on sexual control' (Weinberg and Kamel, 1983, p. 135). The opponents of SM turn this argument on its head: for them, far from parodying or undermining the sexuality of power in society, SM merely mimics it, in a way that can easily grow over into a real oppression of one partner by the other; and that this mimicking legitimizes the real power system and insults those who are really oppressed. Thus, in *Against Sadomasochism*, Karen Sims and Rose Mason, and Alice Walker, argue that the master/mistress–slave image in SM is racist, and Susan Leigh Star attacks the use of symbols of oppression and domination.

Pro-SM arguments based on the premiss of the 'parodying' or 'exposure' of power relations in society are, I think, no more than special pleading by radicals involved in SM. It may well be that people who start out with radical ideas can use the rituals of SM for these purposes. But there is no serious evidence that this is either intended or experienced by the majority of people who practise SM. These ideas are markedly similar to those which floated around the old Gay Liberation Front about the radical significance of camp and of drag; but these ideas offered only a temporary uplift to the individuals involved, and hardly changed the world.

It seems to me that many of those on both sides tend to assume that the order of power in society is mainly about sex. I think this assumption is blinded by the recent past of the 'developed' countries, where starvation has largely gone away. There is an old tag, 'first eat, then philosophize', and it applies with equal force to sex as pleasure. For most people in the world, most of the time, life is dominated by the need to get food and shelter, and the necessity to work to achieve these goals. Sex is important, and is surrounded by symbolic meanings; but the order of society is governed by control over resources and work, and control over sex is a by-product of these powers. Both sides of the argument over SM give too much emphasis, I think, to the importance of sexual desire, practices and pleasure in the social order; and this informs both what Jeffrey Weeks (1985, p. 239) calls the 'latent imperialism' of pro-SM claims, and the determination of their opponents to exclude pro-SM groups from the movement.

Finally, and, I think, centrally, it seems to me that the arguments on both sides understate the physical component of SM or fail to theorize it; and that the anti-SM arguments are wrong to assume that the SM of the SM subcultures is simply modelled on the social order of male dominance and female submission in the larger society. These two points need elaboration.

Physical pleasure and pain

My starting point is an observation which may appear to be banal and obvious, but which is worth making in view both of the emphasis in some pro-SM writing on catharsis, and of the suggestion that SM in some way involves the 'deconstruction' of genital sexuality. My observation is that SM scenes are in general engaged in with a view to producing genital (genital-centred) orgasms. The stimulus may not involve direct stimulation of the genitals; the response is none the less a complex of sensations centred on the genitals. This is something that SM shares with vanilla sex.

The specific physical activities involved are chiefly what is done to the 'bottom' (submissive partner). What the 'top' (dominant partner) gets out of it may be sexual service in the sense of a closer attention to particular desires (as is suggested by Gosselin (1985, p. 131)), it may be the sense of power, or it may be the response of the bottom as a stimulus in itself (both are suggested by Califia, 1982). Both statistical studies, like that of Andreas Spengler (in *S and M*), and anecdotal evidence, suggest that there are more bottoms than tops, and that a significant number of those who act as tops see themselves as able to take either role, and/or started as bottoms. Both SM as a subculture, and its physical apparatus, are to a considerable extent organized around the desires of the bottom; that the physical element is real and not merely an accessory to domination by the other partner is suggested by the widespread 'autoerotic SM' reported by Spengler (p. 69).

The variety of the particular acts which stimulate particular bottoms perhaps obscures the fact that the stimuli in SM sex have not ceased to be particularized, just as the stimuli in vanilla sex are. We are *not* in the realm of the general exploration of the potentialities of the body. Sex and turn-ons are merely particularized in different ways. Moreover, these physical turn-ons are not that varied and limitless, though individuals re-combine different elements in different ways. The lesbian erotica printed in *Coming to Power* (Samois (ed.), 1982) confirm in an impressionistic way the results of Andreas Spengler's study of gay men and of Gosselin and Wilson's survey (in Howell (ed.), 1984): SM physical activities are not that diverse. Elements re-combined in different ways include physical restriction and restriction of the senses (bonds, gags, blindfolds); the infliction of pain by various means, but to the same physical locales (thighs, buttocks, back, neck, nipples, as well as directly to genitals); and the use of fetish materials (leather, silk, rubber, being relatively typical). The areas stimulated to the point of pain are, therefore, broadly similar to those likely to be deliberately stimulated in vanilla sex. It may be added that restriction, in the sense of limitation of free individual movement, and the limitation of the senses, in the sense of their concentration upon the sex partner, are inevitable characteristics of vanilla sex, though less extreme than in SM.

In fact, SM is (in its specific physical aspect) less different from vanilla sex than might at first glance appear. The difference is as much as anything else in the overlap in SM between pleasurable and painful physical stimulation. However, the boundary between pleasurable and painful sensations is not identifiable apart from context. The classic example is, of course, the difference between consensual sex and sexual assault; but it is also clear that the boundary between pleasurable and painful stimulus in 'normal' sexual behaviour varies in different societies and cultures (Ford and Beach, 1952, pp. 55–65).

There seems to me to be no serious objection to these physical aspects of SM. The risks of SM practice are not greater than those of many aspects of everyday life, and the practice is not in itself injurious to health; unlike smoking, to which two writers in *Against Sadomasochism*, Vivienne Walker-Crawford and Paula Tiklicorect, compare it. What sort of movement for liberation is concerned to liberate us from the potential of our bodies for different forms of pleasurable activity? The problem, however, is that these physical activities do not exist in a vacuum but in the context of rituals of domination and submission.

The multiple meanings of domination and submission

It is not clear that the 'SM scene' of which in a certain sense gay male and lesbian SM groups are a part is – as many anti-SM writers assume – formed *directly* on the basis of modelling from the behaviour of heterosexual dominant men and submissive women. The dominant and even brutal man and the woman who really wants to be dominated are, as Wagner correctly points out, constantly celebrated in popular fiction, and are only regarded as deviant in very extreme cases (Linden *et al.*, 1982). Conscious SM sexual practice is, in contrast, unambiguously regarded as deviant by straight society; it is also distinguished from the ordinary run of male violence against and coercion of women by the fact that an express consent is required by the subculture, while in the predominant culture consent is assumed to be forthcoming without much investigation.

I remarked earlier that, in reality, SM practice seems to be largely organized around the needs and desires of the 'bottom', and I suggest that this is a pointer to the origins of the subculture. Male heterosexual masochism has existed as a distinct sexuality, whose needs have been satisfied (among the upper and upper middle classes) by prostitution for a long time – specialized prostitute services of this sort are reported in London in the early eighteenth century, at about the same time as the early male gay scene (Bullough, 1976, p. 479; and compare Bray, 1984, chapter 4 for the early male gay scene). It seems plausible to suggest that the larger gay male SM scene draws on this tradition for elements of its culture (dominance of the desires of the 'bottom'), and physical technique and apparatus (notably the whip, which can hardly be said in view of the time-lag to be drawn directly from the widespread use of the whip in society), as well as drawing for its primary underlying impulse on the mutations of the search for 'rough trade' discussed by Jamie Gough (elsewhere in this volume). It is from this gay male scene, in turn, that both lesbian SM groups like Samois and the emergent heterosexual 'SM scene' draw a culture – or ideology – of an SM practice structured around consent. But in heterosexual SM groups and publications, this ideology sits uneasily together with the perfectly ordinary, non-deviant, straight ideology according to which women provide sexual service for men, even if the service provided is domination, for the sake either of money or of 'love' and that amalgam of the two, marriage.

At the heart of the eroticization of ritual domination and submission in the practice of SM is something which is the half-conscious assertion of a profound truth. We *are* all dependent on each other, in each other's hands. We *are* all responsible for each other. In SM the bottom must accept that dependence on the top; the top must accept that responsibility for the bottom. The dominant culture denies these truths in two ways. It offers a division of roles in which men must be assertive, independent and responsible, and women must be passive, dependent and irresponsible, and in which sex is about men doing things to women. In their different ways, not only gayness/lesbianism, but also male heterosexual masochism reflect the inability of individuals to fit into the moulds offered by the dominant culture and challenge its ideology by their existence.

Second, the dominant culture offers a vision of a world of free, equal and independent individuals. This vision, the vision of the free market and liberal-democracy, is in some ways in conflict with the sex-role division (which is ultimately based on the family and male power). It denies alike our dependence on each other and our responsibility for each other. Homosexuality as such, and in particular gay male culture as it developed up to the advent of AIDS,

offers no challenge to this ideology of individual autonomy; if anything it often expresses a particularly frenetic
search for an illusory personal freedom from dependence
and responsibility. All varieties of SM practice, in contrast,
challenge the claim that we can escape from the condition
of dependence on, and responsibility for, others.

To this extent SM in its ritual aspect, as in the physical
practices which extend the boundaries of pleasurable sensation, does indeed assert a human reality, a human
potential, which are repressed and denied in the sexual
culture of capitalist society, and the liberation of SM people
is indeed part of the same movement of liberation as the
lesbian and gay movement/s. This point also implies that
Susan Griffin's characterization (in *Against Sadomasochism*)
of SM as an aspect of the 'revenge of culture on nature' is
misplaced; besides the fact that this opposition is in general
unhelpful, here is an aspect of SM which is the assertion of
something in our nature as against the 'cultures' of masculinity and of individual autonomy.

But there are also negative sides to the picture. In the first
place, the practice of SM may be a means, in certain cases,
of reconciling the participants to the roles prescribed by the
social order; in particular, among men, of 'releasing' the
tension between individual personality and the norms of
masculinity, the difficulty experienced by the individual in
playing the role of the dominant man, which led this
individual to be something other than a 'normal heterosexual' in the first place. The classic example of this is the
forceful and aggressive man, often in a position of considerable power, who practises sexual masochism – usually by
employing prostitutes. It is plain that there is a conflict
involved, but sexual masochism may well be acting as a
'safety-valve' which allows the individual involved to feel
no real conflict over his general oppressive behaviour.

A more subtle example of reconciliation is the gay male
SM 'career' described by Kamel in *S and M*, in which the

individual starts by looking for something more masculine than people on the vanilla gay scene, passes into the SM subscene as a bottom and in turn becomes a top, taking on in this way a classic masculine role. Presented thus gay male SM seems to have a striking similarity to those rites of passage by which a boy becomes a man in many primitive societies; rituals sometimes involving institutionalized man–boy relations, and sometimes involving the demonstration of strength through the acceptance of pain. There is a dangerous closeness here to the rituals of male solidarity *against women* which persist in many traditionally all-male areas of society: apprentice initiation rituals, and the degradation of new recruits to the army and to police forces.

This poses the second problem. If SM challenges classic individualism and liberal ideology, legitimacy of SM may legitimize more traditional conservative ideologies of acceptance of the social order. The far Right, after all, also insists on interdependence and responsibility – but claims that these can only be realized through a permanent hierarchy of power and dependence in society (compare, for example, the arguments of Roger Scruton, 1980). The reality of this danger is evidenced by things like the casual use of Nazi insignia by SM people, attacked by Susan Leigh Star in *Against Sadomasochism*.

Third, SM practice approaches very closely to the appearance of sex as a commodity, diverse species of experience which are 'traded' in a sort of market, which runs through capitalist society. The 'rise of SM' is in one respect the appearance of a new and different commodity on the sex market; and in SM ritual we may escape more completely than in vanilla sex from the humanity of sex partners. This is a weak argument as an objection to SM, because the fetishism of particular characteristics completely dominates sexual behaviour in modern capitalist society in any case, so that SM is not unusual in this; but it is none the less a negative feature that SM shares with all sexualities, straight and gay alike.

Finally, SM relationships may indeed involve the exploitation of power imbalances; and this fact is by no means altered by role–reversal, or by the fact that the participants are members of the same 'sexual caste' (as Weeks, 1985, suggests). A woman who is induced to dominate a man for money or love, against her own desires, is sexually exploited by him as much as where the SM roles conform to the order of social power; and the same is true where the power of class or economic power is employed between gay men or between lesbians. Again, SM is not unusual in this; again, it is an obstacle to seeing SM simply as liberating.

In short, the 'SM phenomenon' is not so radically different in its political implications from the phenomena of 'deviant' sexuality in general. It contains both 'elements of the new society' which a movement for liberation should be seeking to set free, and elements of the old order against which we fight. The heat in the debate is not there because SM poses us with radically new questions, but because it reminds us of old questions and old debates which we have not, as yet, managed to resolve.

References

Ardill, S. and O'Sullivan, S. (1986), 'Upsetting an applecart: difference, desire and lesbian sadomasochism', *Feminist Review*, no. 23 (summer).

Bray, A. (1982), *Homosexuality in Renaissance England* (London: Gay Men's Press).

Bullough, V. L. (1976), *Sexual Variance in Society and History* (Chicago: Chicago University Press).

Califia, P. (1982), 'A personal view of the history of the lesbian S/M community and movement in San Francisco', in Samois (ed.), *Coming to Power* (Boston: Alyson).

Cant, B. and Roelofs, S. (1985), 'Sexuality', *Lesbian & Gay Socialist* (autumn).

Cant, B. and Roelofs, S. (1986), letter in *Lesbian & Gay Socialist* (spring).

Ford, C. S. and Beach, F. A. (1952), *Patterns of Sexual Behavior* (London: Eyre & Spottiswoode).

Glenny, T. (1986), 'Ideology, desire and sexuality', *Lesbian & Gay Socialist* (spring).

Gosselin, C. (1985), 'The rituals of pain and pleasure', *New Society* (24 January), p. 130.

Gough, J. and Macnair, M. (1985), *Gay Liberation in the Eighties* (London: Pluto Press).

Gough, J. and Macnair, M. (1985), 'Sexuality, SM, politics and proscription', *Lesbian & Gay Socialist* (winter).

Gough, J. and Macnair, M. (1986), letter in *Lesbian & Gay Socialist* (summer).

Howells, K. (ed.) (1984), *The Psychology of Sexual Diversity* (Oxford: Blackwell).

Linden, R. R., Pagano, D. R., Russell, E. H. and Star, S. Leigh (eds) (1982), *Against Sadomasochism: A radical feminist analysis* (East Palo Alto: Frog in the Well Press).

Rubin, G. (1982), 'The leather menace: comments on politics and S/M', in Samois (ed.).

Samois (ed.) (1982), *Coming to Power* (Boston: Alyson).

Scruton, R. (1980), *The Meaning of Conservatism* (Harmondsworth: Penguin).

Weeks, J. (1985), *Sexuality and Its Discontents* (London: RKP).

Weinberg, T. and Kamel, G. W. Levi (1983), *S and M, Studies in Sadomasochism* (Buffalo: Prometheus).

CHAPTER NINE

Black, *Brown* and White

Sunil Gupta

The issues

In any gay London night-club, on any given night, it is possible to observe that there are but a handful of Black-gays. Of these, the non-Afro-Caribbean contingent might be represented by just one or two people. The dichotomy of 'Black' and 'white', as it is framed at the moment, essentially negates the experiences of people from other cultural backgrounds. Here I will argue for the need to recognize that, not only Black, as in Afro-Caribbean, gays need to be recognized in their own right, but also that Indiangays, as in 'Brown', exist as a separate group, with their own specific needs.

Not only the commercial scene, but also gay liberation ideology, which developed over the last fifteen years, has ignored the specific needs of Black/Brown gays. Therefore, in 1987, you could walk into Gay's the Word Bookshop in London and not even find a general Black section. However, the oldest Blackgay group in the country has been meeting at a site next door for several years. This group has traditionally included all non-white races in its definition of Black, resulting in a mix between largely 'Afro-Caribbean' and some 'Asian'. Meanwhile, published documentation, what little exists, stems almost entirely from the Blackgay American experience.

A number of key issues need to be addressed in the context of Black/Brown gays in this country. The carrying over of racist stereotypes into the gay subculture, the meaning of difference as the basis of desire, the reconstruction of a gay identity in relation to the family, the impact of AIDS seen as both an African and a gay disease, and the public construction of gay identities through works of art and the media. Throughout there are similarities within a shared gay experience for all races and differences based on colour, culture and class.

The commercial scene

The commercial scene is a barometer for what is permissible both within and by the gay community. In Britain, as opposed to other Western countries, it has been governed hitherto by the particular licensing laws existing here. Also in the heady expansionist days before AIDS, Britain was almost unique in not having gay saunas. This social conservatism has had its negative impact on the place of Black/Brown gays.

Compared to gay American centres, London seems like a very white society, just like the movies. Now in New York, although there is a certain amount of racial mingling, there is a much more clearly defined separation that spills over into the commercial gay scene. That does not seem to exist over here. There is no specifically Black/Brown gay space.

The vocabulary around race is oppressive. Non-white people are being called Coloured; not Black, Indian, Chinese or whatever. Casual conversations are often maintained by white gays in terms of their understanding of the 'Coloured' problem, since that is as far as their knowledge of these 'other' people goes. I have had the startling experience of being chatted up by being placed at the receiving end of a diatribe against 'Asians'. They, it was claimed, had taken over Southall, were not only importing

Portrait of two men in front of the Coronet Cinema

their culture but edging out the whites by buying up all the property. Evidently I was not one of 'them' as I looked more gay than Indian!

That is the major problem facing Indians on the scene. Every time you go into a gay bar you feel obliged to leave your cultural baggage at the door. You can either be gay or Indian but not both, and unlike the Blacks, there is a feeling of the impossibility of creating your own identity, just a pull towards either the Black or white camp. The sensible option appears to be to go with the whites. There are more of them and they call the shots. Since Indians come in all shades between white and Black, they can pass for any number of non-threatening exotica. But merely 'passing' without a history and without a voice just renders them invisible. And that is the most frequent comment about Indians on the scene: they are *invisible*.

Blacks, however, are very visible. On the one hand, the more overt variety of racism is directed against them, and, on the other hand, there is an acknowledgement that their culture has played quite a large part in informing gay urban night life, which forms the core of the night-club scene. Blacks have responded by setting up an essentially Black night-out that moves around venues in London. Then there are the private parties that fill in for the lack of a separate Blackgay club.

One great gay mythology is that in this arena of desire we are all equal, and that there is a great crossing of barriers: class, race, etc. Well, that is clearly not the case. There is some provision for the fulfilment of fantasy, and there are institutionalized settings for white men to meet the other races. In these settings, racial stereotypes about the other races seem self-fulfilling for both parties. The Long Yang Club in London exists to bring together 'Orientals and interested Westerners' in a social setting where racial assumptions can hardly be challenged.

Gay liberation

Political gays in this country are most aligned with the
parties of the Left (although there do exist the official gay
caucuses within the Tory and Social and Liberal Democratic Parties). A consequence, then, of identifying a
group along the lines of sexuality, as we all know, is to
produce gays of all political shades. The debate around
this thorny issue is well documented, on a weekly basis,
in the pages of *Capital Gay*. Traditionally, politics have
been a white arena; of whatever shade, they were emanating from a white mainstream, and the first generation of
immigrants appear not to have engaged in them, at least
in a formal sense. The groups that did exist, like the
Anglo-Asian Society or the Anglo-West Indian Society,
were firmly in the Tory camp, furthering policies of
appeasement.

But now there is a younger generation of Black and
Brown constituents who want a share in power, and the
Labour-controlled metropolitan authorities were quick to
realize a new power-base. The Greater London Council
(GLC) showed that it was possible to operate a coalition of
gays, ethnic minorities, women, pensioners and all the
other disadvantaged groups in society. Black now became a
positive label and opened doors to jobs. 'Ethnic' is discredited, and the two largest non-white minorities have
become Black. Asians resisted, mildly; the Blacks liked it
and the whites liked it – so who were the Asians to resist the
label? It seemed so unsportsmanlike. After all, 'Asian' is
more geography than politics, and Black has both history
and power. It goes back to South Africa, Attica and Watts.
But it does not go back to India . . .

In the 1970s, the emerging gay liberation theory was
taken up by the broad gay Left. Looking back on those
days it is hard to think of any Black or Brown faces,
although there they were, among the troops. Coming out
and establishing your credentials was the rallying cry.

There was *Gay News*, London Gay Switchboard and the burgeoning organizations' world to participate in.

Very few Blacks or Browns participated. Arguably because they would have felt unwanted, outnumbered and possibly irrelevant. After all, few were making inroads into mainstream politics at the time. No one realized that coming out might mean, for Blacks and Browns, a turning away from their own communities, which had been providing essential support.

Perhaps it has also to do with the weakness of the Left to sell itself. The exclusion of American Blacks from the gay movement in the USA was to be repeated in Britain. This was ironic, considering their movement was based on the American civil libertarian movements, which in turn were influenced by the Black Power struggles of the 1960s. It has taken a decade for gay politics here to embrace the politics of colour.

One of the significant products of all the movements was the documentation that was produced, both as statements of personal experiences and as political tracts. For those who had not been around or had been in the closet, there is a vast resource with which to engage. Americans led the way in gay studies and now there are books from *Tearoom Trade* to *The Male Couple*. Neither American nor British political gay literature has much to say on the gay Black/Brown subject. It is as if we were not there, but we know that it is not true.

Cultural representation

We look for validation of our experiences in the realm of cultural representation. We look for proof that, yes, we were there, through cultural documentation. In the rush to represent gays in literature, theatre, movies, the visual arts, etc., Blacks and particularly Browns are missing. It's the old invisibility trick again, with a few exceptions.

My Beautiful Launderette presented for the first time a

India. Two men lying in the grass in front of a monument

gay Indian character in mainstream cinema. The film was a huge success both here and abroad. Pauline Kael gave it a long rave review in *The New Yorker*, and one of its principal charms was this unproblematic gay Indian character. I find this unproblematic aspect very disturbing because it is completely against what little shreds of evidence we have about Indians coming out, where the problems can seem insurmountable. However, it does fit in with the cynical 1980s, where style is everything and there is 'no problem'. If things were that easy for Indiangays then I would not be writing this essay.

Going back further there are the two most quoted gay examples of the British colonial romance with the Raj: *A Passage to India* and 'The Raj Quartet' (better known as the television epic *The Jewel in the Crown*). While the David Lean film of *Passage* was a complete mess, with a coloured Alec Guinness, the original novel remains of interest. It is one of the few major works that even attempts to describe a personal relationship between a white man and an Indian with any kind of subtlety. The whole presentation of the unfulfilled desire across the races, with the unresolved question of whether the white woman was really raped, was right on the mark as it dealt with the central preoccupation of the politics of race – the penetration of white (women, in this case) by the Coloured. No easy way out here. It still remains almost a starting point for my dealings within British society today.

Scott's epic, *Jewel*, is practically a reworking of *Passage* with a more popular audience in mind, but also with a much more overt gay theme. Against the unresolved question of a white woman's rape by an Indian is the other question of desire, this time a white man's homosexual desire for the Other. Caught up in his own class contradictions and repressed sexuality he is finally murdered in native costume by local rent boys. It is the most powerful gay image dealing with the impossibility of fulfilling desire across racial boundaries that I have come across. Again, for obvious reasons, the film does not do justice to the books, but for a work dealing with the big issues surrounding homosexuality – of race, SM and desire – one need look no further. It is very easy to dismiss these works as mere colonial stereotypes, but I think that they have left us with the few serious works that attempt a discourse around the colonial white/Brown homosexual relationship.

Currently, the overwhelming domination by white heterosexual film culture is being challenged by independent companies like Sankofa, who in their film *The Passion of Remembrance* challenged both the racist and heterosexist stereotypes held by men on both sides of the colour divide. *Passion of Remembrance* is a unique film by a Black film company in so far as it alludes to questions outside those of race. The film has references to the 1984–5 miners' strike and, above all, to gay politics: there is footage of Pride marches, the two central characters are gay. The narrative interweaves two situations: a fantasy one in which Black women and men argue about Black politics and feminism; and a more straightforward one in which two people in London watch videos. The film was groundbreaking in the way it made links with other struggles, principally the gay one.

The teaching of art history in this country is generally Euro-centric, the producers and consumers of art are assumed to be white. All other works of art are 'primitive' and the natives/immigrants need training both to create and to understand. The training comprises a learning of European and then American master-works. In the visual arts these assumptions are now being challenged, as in the film industry. There are, and have been recently, several exhibitions by Blacks that include the question of sexuality. In the arena of 'theory', work on the gay Black subject has been under scrutiny. The best-known exponent of homoerotic art, the photographer Robert Mapplethorpe, has had his work, on Black men, analysed in the pages of *Screen* and elsewhere.

A lot of this activity got start-up funding from local authorities like the GLC. Many questions were raised about the community and about definitions of colour. This is when the crunch came and the world split into Black and white. Therefore very little film and photographic work exists to support the needs of the Indiangay community. What passes for Asian expression, like Tara Arts, the theatre company, is more interested in dealing with national cultural stereotypes than in challenging its audiences' assumptions about sexuality.

There is a great unwillingness to raise the question of sexuality among the Indian community both here and back in the home countries. It is often defended by knee-jerk arguments about relevance and priorities. The stagnant Victorian morality that has infected the Indian ruling classes and set an example to the others has ensured that the question of homosexuality has no place in public life.

What this means today is that while there is some progressive work being done around the cultural representation of Blackgays there is virtually none being done around Indiangays. It has been a theme in my own work, however, and one that has been sustained largely by contact with gays in India rather than an Indiangay culture in this country. A commissioned piece of work, currently touring the country as part of a photographic exhibition called 'The Body Politic', was produced by me to address the concerns surrounding gay identity in India.

In a climate where gays are struggling to reclaim their own cultural history, it is very important that Black and Brown gays are not left out of the process.

AIDS

No discussion of homosexuality can be complete these days without acknowledging the impact of AIDS, both as a very real physical threat and also as it has been used in the public arena to re-create a diseased image of gay men and, latterly, of Africa as an origin of viral infection.

The threat it poses to gays and the gains made in the 1970s are well documented. Here it is worth noting that when the African connection was first mooted, it was seized upon by some gay men as a way of escaping the hatred of the media. They went along on the flimsiest of evidence and denounced Africa as a source of the 'plague' and disassociated themselves from it.

An early public London meeting held by the Terrence Higgins Trust, involving some gay doctors, that I attended was still a nervous mixture of anxiety and anger. In the course of the meeting the medical expert, who was gay, made a reference to 'darkest Africa' and immediately I felt distanced from this scene. In the time since then I have been very wary of getting involved with the AIDS debate, in which gays are getting drawn into a health problem that is often presented as a white issue. It is worth remembering that there are people who are also gay but who are being excluded by the white displays of complete collusion with racism in society at large.

So complete has been the displacement of Blacks and Browns from the activity surrounding AIDS within the gay community, that it is only recently that they have begun to seriously question the risk to themselves. The Black and Brown communities have just begun to take it upon themselves to address the issue and the threat it represents to them. In 1986 in New York, a small fund-raising event for AIDS produced the usual motley collection of white gay men who paraded all the clichéd prejudices about the other threatened groups: Blacks, women, etc.

Asians, like everyone else, displayed their own prejudices by responding that it is either a Black or a gay disease so it does not affect their communities. In 1986, the Indian government began testing all African students for the antibody, starting a programme of expelling all those who were positive, whose photographs and names then appeared in the papers. The only affirmative note was sounded when a few enlightened university chancellors and some student bodies refused to allow the Africans to be singled out in this manner. Prior to that the only other AIDS cases were, of course, traced to visits to New York.

In this complex situation the average response has been so pathetic that it can only enrage if thought about. But it is possible to see what the priorities are when money begins to be spent in the name of public policy. In Britain, sadly, as we all know, not a lot is being spent on research or care, and the advertising that came through the television and via leaflets was clearly aimed at some average white British audience. There were never any people other than white in the imagery, and the only language I have encountered the information in is English.

So, while AIDS restarted the whole campaigning side of gay life, as we have not seen since the gay liberation days of the 1970s, it also focused the ignorance and prejudice white gays display towards the Blacks – the Indian subcontinent not having been seen to be the source of the 'plague' yet.

Desire and fantasy

A lot of critical work is being done in this area based upon psychoanalysis and the currently-fashionable semiology. In an article (in *Ten*. 8, no. 22), 'Desire and black men', I studied the photographic constructions surrounding Black men with particular reference to the images that had a currency in the popular magazines that substituted for the lack of a gay press in the 1950s. These were *Physique* and its rivals. Against these there are the art images of Mapplethorpe. What I found was that there were parallel ideas between the prescribed idealized bodies of the former and accepted notions, in the latter, that Black men exist as consumer goods in a gay context.

In this area, of course, the obvious stereotyping begins to

be made plain, and somehow also here the differences between the races become more marked. Black men are perceived to be the possessors of the highly desirable big dicks of white men's fantasy. There is the related idea, then, that these exist to penetrate white flesh. It's an exact duplication of the idea that all white women are under threat of rape by Black men; and one of the biggest problems in both the colonies and the American South has always been this underlying fear of white women being penetrated by Black men. This fear finds its antithesis in desire in a particularly gay fantasy of being penetrated by the 'other'.

In defence of all the photographic interest in Black dicks, all one could say is that the entire range of gay male fantasy is centred on dicks, and perhaps in this context (when the dicks happen to be white) it is not remarkable. However, since this is virtually the only form of representing Black men, it begins to be worrying. Kobena Mercer's article in *Photography Politics: Two*, 'Imaging the black male sex', deals with this area. It follows the feminist line and draws analogies by replacing the position of white women as objects of desire by Black men. The difference, in the case of Black men, is that the images are so severely truncated as to leave them devoid of any personality at all.

Curiously the other races do not get photographed or imaged a lot. Certainly there is nothing circulating in England which begins to deal with Indian men in this way. And there is nothing in India either, barring some ninth-century temple sculptures and some photographs circulating privately.

In a British context Indians are passive, which translates into the gay scene as the idea that Indians are sexually passive and have littler (*sic*) dicks than whites; and they are therefore less desirable than Blacks, given that the basis for gay desire is dick size. However, there is a marginal area, again reflected from society at large, which has a particular interest in things Indian, so there are occasional people with an interest in Indians.

The most overt indication of this desire in the colonial foreign body is expressed in London venues that specialize in Orientalgays – Chinese takeaways, as they are popularly known.

The family

The family has been identified from the earliest days of gay liberation as the site of oppression and self-hatred. The rallying cry has been to 'come out' and take a stand against it. What gay activists failed to realize was that for many Black and Brown gays such a step might be more than simply moving out of a traditional nuclear family situation. For the immigrants the family was the source of both material and communal well-being.

In a hostile white environment, for the first generation the community was their only hope of comfort and security. To turn your back on it was to cut yourself off from both this security in real terms and from a sense of identity that was/is separate from the whites.

As it is, the Black family has been systematically under threat from the days of slavery. In this period of reconstruction in Britain, it was not going to be easy to leave it and join some white movement.

For Indians the traditional extended family network has meant a significant way of keeping caste and community going. There was also the time-honoured tradition of arranged marriages, which meant that you did no more than give your consent at the appropriate moment and allowed a bond to take place, not just between two individuals but between two families. To deny your family these bonds seems both selfish and foolhardy in the precarious financial situation most immigrants find themselves in. On the whole, as my father said, they could not care less as long as you provided them with these marriage ties, and hopefully went on to produce children.

Now, the complete absence of immigrant representation

of gays has gone a long way to bolster the myth among these families that there are no gays within the community and that being gay is just a matter of catching a white disease. Arguments like this were – incredibly – given air-time on television recently in the form of the ethnic minority of the Parents' Rights Group in Haringey who were busy denouncing these white homosexuals who are teaching their children how to be gay.

Those who came out in the 1970s were virtually shut out of the community and went into a white-identified gay lifestyle. Nowadays there is much talk about returning to the family and bringing enlightenment to the community. Realizing that we had such a marginal role to play in gay politics and culture until recently, it seemed better to identify along the lines of colour.

But there is no guarantee that these families would be much different from their white counterparts. In fact there is every indication that they are more likely to be conservative. This is certainly the case for Indian families, who demonstrated a national swing of 30 per cent to the Tories in the 1983 general election. And that is not surprising since most come from closely-knit rural backgrounds in the subcontinent.

Therefore, while there is much useful work to be done in educating our own communities about the relevance of gay lifestyles, it is unlikely that they will find it much easier to be accepting than do white families in general. On the other hand, having created a network among some white gays it seems a waste simply to turn your back on the whole gay identity issue, especially when white gays have provided some of the strengths.

Is there a resolution?

Accepting that there is a racial problem in gay culture, its resolution can only be attempted if reality is faced more honestly. First of all, one must accept that not only is racism rampant on the scene, but has been also in the movement, although here it might be more subtle. However, the results are still the same.

There has to be a recognition that Indians are not the same as Blacks, although we share several factors in common, such as colonial history and an isolation from the mainstream in this country. Culturally, however, we are standing on completely different ground.

Although Black as a term has gained a certain coinage, especially in radical circles, it will not reach out to those gays from the subcontinent who cannot so readily identify with it. The time has come to resist the pressure, from both whites and Blacks, to merge us together into one category of Black.

Blacks have been moderately successful in creating both a space and a network around themselves: but no similar arrangement exists for Indians. The only alternative is to look back to the subcontinent, from where not much is emanating.

There is one broadsheet called *Trikon* that, typically, comes from California: it is aimed at a gay audience from the subcontinent which is dispersed around the world. Coming from Silicon Valley its political leanings are very suspect, except that like all gay American ventures it has a certain evangelical fervour and energy. It has been going for several issues and can be found in London and also in New Delhi. *Trikon* reports the success of tactics such as an Indian presence in Gay Pride marches in San Francisco which caught the attention of the Indian press in North America in much the same way as the Black press has featured members of the Gay Black Group in London.

The relationship with white gays continues to be problematic. Having remained invisible, there is a lot of catching up to do for immigrant gays in terms of cultural history. At the same time the fact of the relationship cannot be ignored and some ideas have to be taken on board. The time for pure separatism appears to have passed. In any event, in a purely Indian gay context the numbers are so few that it would hardly make sense.

What must be done is to begin to counter the racism that exists. Work has already begun, particularly for Blackgays, and there are a few American precedents. However, for Indiangays this appears to be a starting point.

References and contacts

Beam, J. (ed.) (1986), *In the Life/A Black Gay Anthology* (Boston: Alyson Publications).

Gupta, S. (n.d.), 'Exiles', *Body Politics, Ten.8*, no. 25.

Mercer, K. (1987), 'Imaging the black man's sex', in P. Holland, J. Spence and S. Watney (eds), *Photography Politics: Two* (London: Methuen).

Mercer, K. and Julien, I. (n.d.), 'True confessions'/Gupta, S. (n.d.), 'Desire and black men', *Black Experiences, Ten.8*, no. 22.

Sankofa Film Collective (1986), *The Passion of Remembrance* (London).

Smith, M. J. (ed.) (1983), *Black Men/White Men* (San Francisco: Gay Sunshine Press).

Stambolian, G. (1984), 'A black man', *Male Fantasies/Gay Realities* (New York: The Sea Horse Press).

Black Lesbian and Gay Centre Project, Annexe 'B', Tottenham Town Hall, High Road, London N15.

TRIKON/Indian Subcontinent Gay Support Group, Box 60536, Palo Alto, CA 94306, USA.

CHAPTER TEN

Sexual fix, sexual surveillance: Homosexual in law

Les Moran

It's 1.55 a.m. on a June morning; it could be this year but in fact it's 1984. We are on Oxford Street in London. A couple stand at a bus stop. They are cuddling each other and kissing each other on the lips. The hand of one rubs the back of the other. The hand travels further down the body. A scene of passion. Two other couples walking along Oxford Street notice this passionate event. They point and shout, neither words of encouragement nor support but words of abuse. 'You filthy sods. How dare you in front of our girls'. The police arrive. The kissing and cuddling stop. The couple are arrested and removed from the street, charged and found guilty of an offence (s.54(13) Metro-politan Police Act 1839) of using 'Threatening, abusive or insulting words or behaviour with intent to provoke a breach of the peace.' Their appeal to the High Court (Masterson, Cooper *v.* Holden 1986) fails. The court decides that the magistrates' finding of guilt was perfectly lawful: *the ordinary everyday embrace criminalized.* Is this another example of the law being an ass? Is this the Orwellian '1984' fantasy made 1984 reality? No. This is *the everyday tale* of the law responding to *two men, to relations between men,* to their public display: an otherwise ordinary everyday event, the passionate embrace, transformed into crime when undertaken between two men.

As Masterson and Cooper, the convicted parties in the scenario above, demonstrate, to be gay is to have the potential to experience justice and law in a way different from the non-gay experience. Where others might seek and realize rights and justice, the gay experience is victimization and discrimination. An everyday socially acceptable action becomes outlawed. A dismissal from work that would otherwise be unreasonable, unfair, becomes reasonable, fair. An eviction, otherwise unlawful, becomes lawful. The *fundamental rights* embodied in these instances – the right to privacy, to a family relationship, to a sexual relationship, and others such as the right to freedom of speech, to freedom of assembly, to health care – are systematically denied (Crane, 1982). For gay men, both before AIDS and now amplified by the AIDS phenomenon, all the rights and protections others take to be central to, and solid in, the law melt into the air of its discriminatory practice.

The origin of the law's discriminatory position is distant. English legal writers in the thirteenth century noted and supported the practice of the courts of the church to condemn acts of sodomy. In 1533 Henry VIII introduced the condemnation of the practice of sodomy into the secular realm of statute law when buggery, which included in its definition the practice of anal intercourse between men, became an act punishable by death in the King's courts of law (Bray, 1982; Weeks, 1981). The primary concern of this essay is not to describe the long history of persecution, nor to catalogue today's legal rules that name these forbidden practices, nor to catalogue those rules that build upon them to regulate behaviour between men outside the criminal law. Those rules are legion. Their documentation has already been undertaken by others (for example, Crane, 1982). This is not to suggest that such a task has been exhausted nor to deny its continuing import-ance. The experience of Masterson and Cooper demonstrates that the rules need to be known. Further, those who have been subjected to AIDS-related discrimination and who seek to go to law to secure fundamental rights, access to fundamental goods and services, demonstrate a new dimension to this established practice that reveals a new urgency in such a project. In going to law they face a body of legal rules and practices that must be known.

My concern is related but different. I want to take a second look at these rules, to explore some general themes that cross and recross this world of rules that uses the language of 'truth', 'fairness', 'reasonableness', 'justice', as the central theme in the production of 'law'. I want to explore the requirements that have to be satisfied to put homosexuality 'in the true' in law. I want to look at how to *make* sense of 'homosexual' in law. In doing this I want to explore the image of homosexuality that haunts *every* legal confrontation where homosexuality is on the agenda. I want to explore that image of homosexuality which is given legitimate form in the lawful practices of officials of the law – be they judges in the House of Lords, Court of Appeal or the magistrates in the local Magistrates' Court, be they Chief Constables, beat bobbies, central and local government officials – or by officials using law but 'outside' the law – the building society officials, insurance company officials, employers and so on. I want to explore the institutionalization of lawful discrimination.

The two phrases in the title of the essay, 'sexual fix' and 'sexual surveillance' provide the structure for this exploration. 'Sexual fix' provides an opportunity to explore the origins and contemporary form of the idea of homosexuality that is produced and reproduced within the legal mind. 'Sexual surveillance' refers to the process whereby the eye of the law subjects the social world, in particular the male body and male behaviour, to rigorous scrutiny in its search for sexuality, for the truth of the sexuality of the man in question and of relations between men. My objective here is to begin to expose the sexual politics that speaks and masquerades as 'truth', 'justice', 'law' which will have to be confronted in any gay-related engagement with the law.

Sexual fix

... [homosexuals] connote an inversion of moral characteristics ... [they] seek habitual gratification of a particular perverted lust, which not only takes them out of the class of ordinary men gone wrong, but stamps them with a hallmark of a specialised and extraordinary class as much as if they carried on their bodies some physical peculiarity. (Lord Sumner, Thompson *v*. The King, 1918)

This observation by Lord Sumner in the House of Lords marks neither a beginning nor an end to the law's attempts to produce the 'truth' of homosexuality in law. The quotation is of interest here because it illustrates a conscious attempt by a senior judge to fix in law the 'true' nature of homosexuality. In doing so it illustrates in the realm of the law two persistent interrelated themes in the history of this process that I want to pursue in this section. First, 'homosexual' is represented as an *extreme difference*. For example, this is demonstrated in the way Lord Sumner resorts to overstatement and extravagance in his depiction of homosexuality: homosexual men are not merely men who have gone wrong, they are taken 'out of the class of ordinary men gone wrong' – they are to represent a profound difference. A second illustration of this required extremism is found in the idea of 'inversion'. In this word is depicted 'the ordinary world' (men desiring women) completely turned upside down (men desiring men). Again, the image is not of the sameness of heterosexual and homosexual: it is an image that depicts the two as polarities, an image of excessive difference, violent difference. In depicting homosexuality as such a radical difference Lord Sumner must resort to sensationalism. This manifests itself in his suggestion that the homosexual man is an 'extraordinary class' of men, and in the extravagance of the idea that homosexual men carry about them special marks that separate them out from other men 'as if they carried on their bodies some physical peculiarity'. Homosexuality is thus produced as *extreme 'Otherness'*, a positioning which neither originates nor ends with this judgement.

Second, in his reference to 'inversion' Lord Sumner demonstrates *the poverty of the law*. In producing a legal knowledge of homosexuality the legal process draws upon non-legal knowledge of sexuality – in this instance 'inversion', a concept that originates in sexology. Here he demonstrates the law's practice of selecting, taking and inhabiting ideas produced elsewhere and then using them to produce effects in law. In this judgement we have one attempt to fix the homosexual identity in 1918. What of the homosexual fix in law today?

The sexual fix of 'homosexual' in contemporary law is a complex phenomenon. It is manufactured through storylines that are recounted, repeated, varied (for example, the seduction story: boy meets man and falls from heterosexuality to homosexuality), through a set of ideas, through a restricted vocabulary, through a set of rules as to who can speak of such things. (For example, one technique through which an alternative voice is denied is the use of the idea that when homosexuals speak of homosexuality they are necessarily involved in seduction, this not being a factor in talking of heterosexuality.) Through all of these means the 'truth' of homosexuality is produced in law. Here I want to concentrate upon one aspect of this complex phenomenon, the language of the sexual fix that works to generate 'homosexual' in law. The language might be said to fall into two primary categories, a Christian tradition and a medical tradition.

The language of the Christian tradition has the longest standing place in the law. A contemporary commentary on the wording of the statute of Henry VIII (Lord Coke, 1644), which outlaws the practice of buggery, demonstrates the use of a Christian vocabulary through which to speak of relations between men. It shows how the new law speaks through the old established Christian vocabulary relating to sodomy. This provides a ready-made language for the law. It works to legitimate the law's condemnation of buggery (a word that fuses together a Christian and a secular condemnation of an action) by reference to the biblical condemnation of sodomy, which represents an already established tradition of condemnation. It soaks a new law in a mysterious lofty past. It uses an established way of seeing and speaking about things in a new context. At the birth of buggery within the secular legal tradition the law took over a language, a set of ideas, through which to produce its own language of condemnation.

What was this language that the law entered into? Within the medieval Christian tradition sodomy, as an act between men, is represented through a series of metaphors that are ordered around the question of man's relationship with God. To be a sodomite is to be without God, to be possessed by the Devil, a condition that is represented in many forms: for example, to be evil, impure, unclean, diseased, irrational, unnatural, animal, and, of course, womanly. To be a sodomite is to have fallen from a state of purity and grace to a state of corruption. These metaphors work to achieve a condemnation of sodomy through their relationship with their antithesis; that is to say, the significance of 'Devil' comes from its relationship with 'God'. They work to produce a clear, violent separation. These binary relationships, God/Devil, Good/Evil, Pure/Impure and so on, produce a hierarchy of high/low, superior/ inferior, venerated/condemned. In the language of the Christian tradition, sodomy is monotonously positioned as low, inferior, condemned, *the Other*. In condemning buggery (sodomy) the law entered this language, this world of ideas; to speak of buggery in law was to speak *this*

language. In inhabiting this Christian tradition the law
inhabited the language and ideas of this tradition of condemnation. The legal knowledge of particular relations
between men was fixed through this Christian register of
knowledge. Through a collection of metaphors (only some
of which have been referred to here) that sought to name
human experience, a complex picture of the human male
condition in law was produced. But this is a picture of law
in a medieval world and a renaissance world. Is such a
world in evidence in law today? Before considering this
question it is necessary to consider the second major
tradition, the medical tradition.

The origins of the medical tradition are more recent and
the language is more familiar. It is a tradition where sexual
relations are understood by reference to man's position in a
'natural' biological world, in nature. Science purports to
describe this world. In this world, homosexuality is nature
gone wrong; a stage in development, an evolutionary freak,
a biological error. It is the *'Other' in nature*. Medicine
brands homosexuality as the Other when it sees it as an
illness, a handicap, a retarded and frustrated psycho-sexual
development. Heterosexual sexuality is the norm, the
healthy. Homosexuality is its violent antithesis, a separate
and distinct category, 'abnormality'. Heterosexuality is
portrayed as the inevitable end of a 'natural' biological or
psycho-social process. Heterosexuality is psycho-sexual
maturity, adulthood. Homosexuality is deviance, perversion, perpetual sexual adolescence. It has to have causes, it
has to be explained (no one asks for the causes of heterosexuality). The 'causes' are multiple, possibly congenital,
biological, natural (hormones, genes). More probably, it is
thought to be acquired by contact: sexuality as contagion.
Nature is given a fixed single objective, reproduction. The
non-reproductive is that which has become deviant: led
astray, pushed off its natural course, seduced and corrupted
from what nature intended.

In this world the scientific sexual fix 'homosexuality' is

produced through a language of hormonal abnormality, gene defect, immaturity, retarded development, mental abnormality, neurotic behaviour, severely damaged personality, personality defect. While science can and has been used to explain and justify the normality and the naturalness of homosexuality, it has also been effective in attempts to outlaw homosexuality. The scientific sexual fix sustains the violence of the oppositions and works to secure homosexuality within this hierarchy as the low, the inferior, the condemned. In medicine the language of the binary oppositions shifts: healthy/unhealthy, natural/unnatural, sane/insane, mature/immature, and so on. Homosexuality occupies the unhealthy, the unnatural, the insane. The extract from Lord Sumner's judgement above illustrates in the word 'inversion' the seepage of medical (specifically here the sexological) knowledge of male sexuality into the law. A more recent example, and one that reflects the current status quo of medicine in law, is the Wolfenden Committee Report (Wolfenden, 1957) where the emphasis is on homosexuality as an incomplete, immature, psycho-sexual development.

How do these registers of language work in law today? While the 1967 Sexual Offences Act has slightly reduced the opportunity for the law to speak of homosexuality, opportunities still abound. They can be observed in their most unrestrained form in situations where sexual relations involve an individual under the age of consent. In 1973 Lord Justice Lawton (R v. Willis, 1973) provided a particularly extreme illustration of these registers at work. He described homosexuality in the following terms. The homosexual is the 'disordered', the 'depraved', the 'wicked', the 'revolting', the 'damaged', the 'effeminate', the uncontrolled ('[the] driving force of lust'), the 'corrupt[ed]', the 'mentally ill', a 'symptom in the course of recognised mental or physical illness ... '.

Here he weaves together the two registers of language,

Christian and medical: 'Lust', 'disordered', 'wicked', 'effeminate' (womanly) from the Christian; 'symptom', 'ill', 'illness' from the medical. They have different origins and are based on different ideas about the nature of 'man' and the truth of 'his' world, but both are sustained within and are made to work towards the contemporary production of homosexuality in law. The medieval register of condemnation, that originated in a universe which is almost unrecognizable in a world dominated by science and medicine, works *in conjunction* with that radically different universe. The law produces homosexuality through a curious collage of languages, medieval and modern. This mixture of the old and the not so old helps to sustain the idea that law has both a timeless and a modern aspect. It helps to produce in us the feeling that the law represents a natural and necessary development, that it is an unearthly power, that the answers are always already in a timeless legal past. It tends to blind us to the fact that the Christian and the medical are put to work to service modern needs. In this conjunction the law fixes homosexuality through many moments: sin and sickness, evil and illness, bad and mad. In their legal manifestation these languages come together to construct a supposed sexuality of the radically different, of homosexuality. They both work to sustain the production and reproduction of the *extreme Otherness* that is the image of homosexuality which is manifested *and legitimated* in law.

It would be premature to close this description of homosexuality in law without a reference to the importance of danger in the sexual fix. In law homosexuality is not a mere sexual category, it is a category of danger. It is represented as a dangerous sexuality, *a dangerous Other*. At its most extreme this danger appears in the idea that words themselves are dangerous. Legal texts referred to sodomy and buggery as crimes 'not to be named amongst Christians'. To speak the words was to release an evil force. Danger appears in the idea that homosexuality is a danger to the *self*. In the nineteenth century, the bare idea of being thought to be homosexual (a sodomite) was said to be 'more terrible than death itself'. Such an accusation produced a fear of 'losing character' and a 'fear of losing life itself'. In the twentieth century the threat to self manifests itself as loss of adulthood and maturity, as the possibility of perpetual immaturity, perpetual disability, perpetual childhood, with their attendant dependency and loss of 'adult' rights (Policy Advisory Report, 1981; Wolfenden, 1957). Homosexuality is presented as a danger to *others*. The law considers it to be reasonable to hold the belief that a homosexual man is a danger to *all* children, even in the face of medical evidence that the particular man in question has no desire for sexual relations with children (Saunders *v.* Scottish National Camps Association, 1981). Homosexuality 'is' a danger to the *family*. The homosexual father is a 'risk' to his son, his contact with him may 'scar' the son for life; the homosexual father has 'nothing to offer his son at any time in the future'. The homosexual father must be removed from the family otherwise the family will be destroyed (Lord Wilberforce in House of Lords case: Re D, 1977). Finally, homosexuality is represented as a danger to the *Nation*. It is the decline and fall, treason, the impossibility of patriotism. Lord Devlin, a retired Law Lord, considered that homosexuality caused 'decay' and 'disintegration', arising from 'weakness' resulting from the 'loosening [of] the moral bonds' of the nation state. His support for the 1967 reforms was based upon the belief that homosexuality could be confined and thereby made tolerable (Lord Devlin, 1965). Homosexuality in law is therefore not only the Other, but it is also seen as a great force, a great power, a great danger that – unless contained and kept in its place, unless sustained as something 'other' and marginal – will bring down all: the self, the family, the nation state. The law works with an extravagant image. It sensationalizes, magnifies, stoops to immoderation in its production of the idea of homosexuality.

Therefore, in the language of the law homosexuality is produced and reproduced as the *dangerous Other*. The 1967 reform provided little space within the law whereby the monotonous reproduction of this sexual fix might be challenged. This is not surprising. The language of that reform was toleration. Homosexuality was to be endured. Deviance would be allowed to exist, but it would firmly remain deviant. It was to remain locked into an already constructed language and set of ideas which named, and continues to name, it wicked, wrong, corrupt, ill, immature. To talk otherwise in the law would be to talk in a language which the law does not recognize. The law does not know the word gay. Any confrontation in law where homosexuality is directly addressed is already shaped and loaded in the language of the law. Any direct confrontation will have to negotiate that labyrinthine sexual myth of homosexuality in law.

Sexual surveillance

Sexual surveillance is the second dimension of this analysis of homosexuality in contemporary law. It has two noteworthy dimensions. First, we should follow the logic that provides the motivation for surveillance. Where homosexuality is represented as a dangerous sexuality, its containment *must* be achieved. As Lord Devlin said in response to the 1967 reform, homosexuality can only be tolerated providing it does not threaten the status quo. Where it is a danger, its mere presence is itself a threat. This is the inspiration behind the disproportionate investment of police time outside and inside the gentlemen's public toilet: the gentleman constable voyeur peering under the toilet door or precariously balanced on the slippery toilet seat looking over the cubicle wall. It is the driving force behind police harassment in the street and the reluctance to investigate anti-gay offences; every little helps to keep the queers in their place. It motivates that arrest on Oxford Street, the raid on the disco. It works outside the criminal law in the office, on the factory floor, in the family. If the goal of containment is to be achieved, the eye of the law must be ever vigilant. Homosexuality has to be hunted down and put in its place. This brings me to the second dimension of surveillance. In surveillance the law is obsessed with the pleasure of looking; it is the great voyeur. Its obsession with looking for detail comes from the belief that in the minutiae it will discover the deviant: in the minutiae behaviour which on the surface appears to be normal is rendered abnormal.

Prior to 1967 the eye of the law knew no limits. It penetrated the most intimate and the most secret parts of the heart and the home. As a result of the 1967 Sexual Offences Act, when sexual relations between two consenting men over the age of 21, in 'private', were taken out of the criminal calendar, the primary focus of surveillance has been 'limited' to the 'public' sphere. Three notes of caution need to be sounded. First, the eye of the law knows no limits where consent and/or the age limit are not satisfied. Second, what happens in the private sphere may slip or be forced into the public sphere. For example, the fact that you might have a stable gay relationship in the privacy of your home may become known in the workplace and may result in a fair dismissal from a job. The idea of a neat schizophrenic existence in two hermetically-sealed spheres is riddled with contradiction and practical impossibility. Third, even within the narrow confines of the 1967 Act the meaning of 'private' may be elusive. The definition of the private may be clear only *after* the event. It is in fact still 'good' law that there is no strict definition of the private – you have to look at all the surrounding circumstances, the time of day/night, the nature of the place, the likelihood of a third party coming on the scene, and so on (R *v.* Reakes, 1974). The divide is contingent rather than absolute. The barrier to the prying eye of the law may dissolve when you least expect it to.

Within the realm of legitimate surveillance, whose boundaries are so elusive, the eye of the law has two functions: to probe and to interpret. The two are inextricably linked. The moment of observation is the moment of interpretation. The law observes and renders significant. The gesture speaks the truth of its sexuality. The structure of surveillance is extravagant in its attention to detail. The law watches the movement of the head, the direction of the eyes, the shape of the mouth, the movement of the mouth, the colour of the mouth and face: 'he smiled in the faces of gentlemen, pursed his lips ... the face and lips were artificially reddened'. The law watches the movement of the body: 'he ... wriggled his body' (Horton *v.* Mead, 1913). The law watches the position of one body in the context of another: 'One of them had ... his penis exposed and the penis was erect, and the other had his anus turned towards the first ...' (R *v.* Hornby, 1946). The law watches the touch:

> Cooper rubbed the back of Masterson with his right hand and later Cooper moved his hand from Masterson's back and placed it on his bottom and squeezed his buttocks. Cooper then placed his hand on Masterson's genital area and rubbed his hand around this area. (Masterson and Cooper *v.* Holden, 1986).

It watches the spoken word – 'Hello' (Dale *v.* Smith, 1967) – and the written word. It sees what is said and what is left unsaid:

> ... I am coming to Blackpool for a week. I will look out for you on Tuesday night about 7 o'clock where the boat sails for the I.O.M. at Fleetwood. Please don't forget. Don't be afraid to make yourself known to me ... (R *v.* Cope, 1921).

or:

Alert young designer, 30, seeks warm, friendly, pretty boy under 23 who needs regular sex, reliability and beautiful surroundings ... (Knuller v. DPP, 1972).

or:

Young dolly boy seeks sugar daddy. (ibid.).

While some of these cases may be old, while the 'guilty' have long since been punished and passed away, the experiences in these cases are still recognizable and potentially repeatable today. They are *all* potential precedents that relate to legal rules that are part of the arsenal of the searching eye of today's law: s.32 Sexual Offences Act, 1957: persistently soliciting or importuning (Horton v. Mead; Dale v. Smith); s.13 Sexual Offences Act, 1956: gross indecency between men (R v. Hornby), or an attempt to procure the commission of an act of gross indecency (R v. Cope); s.54(13) Metropolitan Police Act, 1839: (Masterson and Cooper v. Holden), and acts outraging public decency (Knuller v. DPP).

This small collection of illustrations does not exhaust the inventory of signs through which sexuality is discovered in law. The genius of the process may be that the inventory is inexhaustible. The collection serves two purposes. First, it shows the law's concern with reading the minutiae of the human body and human relations: *gestures*, the way you move your hand; *movements*, the way you walk; *words*, the way you talk; *thoughts*, your innermost secrets, are all subjected to scrutiny. Second, it demonstrates the diversity of the opportunities whereby the law may fix a sexual identity. They may all be used to fit you into the already waiting category of 'homosexual' in law. The relationship between the surveillance inventory and the sexual fix is that the former is the gateway through which the latter enters. Through the 'discovery' of the signs and the imposition of

meaning, a sexual identity in law is produced. Your *every*
move is being watched.

The place of law within gay politics

What conclusions can be drawn from this analysis to help
us see the place of law within contemporary gay politics?
First, where any engagement with law directly addresses
homosexuality, the monolithic image of homosexuality I
have been exposing as *the dangerous Other* of sexuality
will necessarily arise. This sexual fix is labyrinthine in its
diversity, held together by fear to the self, the family, the
nation, constantly reproduced and re-legitimated in the
daily practices of those actors in law who carry out the
interpretation and application of those standards of
'reasonableness', 'fairness', 'justice' that play such a central
role in the rules of law. The image breeds, feeds and justifies
persecution through the law. Second, we should not forget
the poverty of the law. The law does not speak of diversity.
In its image of homosexuality it speaks almost exclusively a
language of vilification and condemnation. To speak in law
of the happy homosexual, of gay sexuality as a sexuality
outside of condemnation, is almost an impossibility. It is
not recognizable by the law as it is not a part of the
vocabulary of law: being gay does not exist in law. The
necessary language is not available in law, and its availability outside the law – awaiting incorporation into law –
is almost equally in short supply. It will be necessary to
work towards increased resources outside law that portray
the normality and stability of homosexual sexuality and to
work towards their incorporation into law, as well as
working to manipulate the language already in the law. At a
time when the law is being used directly to outlaw the
availability of alternative ideas and an alternative language
of sexuality (Clause 28 of the Local Government Bill to
outlaw the 'promotion' of homosexuality by local authori-

ties), such a battle takes on a new and dangerous dimension. Further, at a time when the relationship between homosexuality and danger is being re-invigorated through the Western response to AIDS, the difficulties outlined above suggest that strategies of direct confrontation are likely to meet a re-awakened hysterical resistance.

The use of strategies in law other than direct confrontation has shown some success. For example, in the case brought against Gay's the Word bookshop – which attempted to restrict the import of gay literature – a victory was secured by the shop through the laws of the European Community dealing with the free movement of goods. In Northern Ireland, resort to the language of human rights secured some success in the European Court of Human Rights (Dudgeon v. UK, 1981) in bringing the law in Northern Ireland into line with the rest of the UK, though it failed to secure a reduction in the age of consent from 21 to 18. Evidence of the success of human rights strategies in the UK domestic courts is depressingly absent. In the USA in the face of AIDS-related discrimination, gay men discriminated against have had some success in using laws to protect the disabled. Significant in these examples is the use of a vocabulary outside of sexuality. Fighting a battle through a vocabulary that has already been successful in combatting victimization elsewhere may be an effective strategy, in that it detracts from the inimical, already established fix of homosexuality. Perhaps the most effective strategy will be refusing to play the game of homosexuality in law, using an armoury fashioned for another purpose to achieve the desired ends.

If the law is resistant to direct and even indirect confrontation, is it relevant to a gay politics in the 1980s? The answer must be yes: a *political* engagement with the law must take its place with other political activities. To privilege it over and above all else would be to expend energies that may be more successfully employed in other directions which might be less resistant to change. To ignore law altogether would be to miss the opportunity to renegotiate the political terrain in law. While every dispute does not provide an ideal setting, every dispute involves a degree of negotiation, a degree of confrontation, the potential for change, no matter how small. Such political opportunities should not be readily abandoned.

Further, we should not forget that the law is a vehicle through which the persecution of sexual practices is brought to bear on life in a direct and sometimes devastating way. The eye of the law is already in place to subject us to its extravagant surveillance and control. In the past the law has been used to secure punishment by death. Today the punishment continues, but its techniques have changed. The maximum term of imprisonment for buggery continues to be life (s.3(1) Sexual Offences Act, 1967). While a life sentence is the exception rather than the rule, criminal convictions for this and other homosexual offences which give rise to lesser penalties are more than likely to have widespread repercussions, jeopardizing one's job, home, family, friends, and so on. These effects show that sexuality is policed not only through the criminal law. It is policed through many dimensions of the law; through employment law, family law, the tax laws, the laws of inheritance, housing law, local government law, to name but a few. The law works towards this social vulnerability, and compounds it through the lack of protection in the law.

In the context of AIDS-related discrimination, the failure of the law in this respect is already being illustrated in the law's response to the needs of gay men in the workplace (Buck *v*. Letchworth Palace Ltd, 1987). If this pattern is sustained elsewhere the law is unlikely to secure other urgently needed goods and services, such as health care, or a home. Further, the response to AIDS suggests that victories already won in the sphere of law reform are not battles that have been won for all time. They represent at best a temporary regrouping of forces.

The late 1980s may demand that battles already won be

fought again with new weapons according to new rules. To abandon law as a political objective would be to contribute to the legitimacy of discrimination and victimization already practised in law. It would be to condone the myth of impartiality, the myth of objectivity, the myth of universality. It would be to abandon a terrain of politics to the forces of reaction and oppression. A gay politics cannot ignore the institutions of discrimination that systematize violence and brutality.

References

Bray, A. (1982), *Homosexuality in Renaissance England* (London: Gay Men's Press).

Coke, Lord (1644), *The Third Part of the Institutes of the Laws of England* (London).

Crane, P. (1982), *Gays and the Law* (London: Pluto Press).

Devlin, Lord (1959), *The Enforcement of Morals* (Oxford: Oxford University Press).

Policy Advisory Committee on Sexual Offences (1979), 'Working paper on the age of consent in relation to sexual offences' (London).

Weeks, J. (1981), *Sex, Politics and Society* (London: Longman).

Wolfenden Report, The (1957), *Report of the Committee on Homosexual Offences and Prostitution*, Cmnd 247 (London: HMSO).

CHAPTER ELEVEN

A conversation about pornography

Richard Dyer

A comprehensive overview of gay pornography would take a book in itself. The conversation which follows centres on some quite specific – and important – concerns, taking a particular cultural and political context more or less for granted. This brief headnote is designed to indicate that context, in a necessarily rather schematic way.

We had in mind, for instance, the well-worn cultural distinction between 'pornography' and 'erotica'. Basically, the first is defined as exploitative and reifying – treating people as objects – and the second as not so. In what circumstances can gay pornography be said to become 'simply' erotica? Or to put it the other way round, is our erotica – the sexual images we manufacture and consume within our subculture – *necessarily* pornographic, debasing, dangerous, damaging?

The cultural distinction between pornography and erotica is of course highly articulated politically within and between feminism and the gay movement. It is this context rather than that of 'public morals' that we wanted to address: though a problem for us may sometimes be one of distinguishing between the two contexts. This is not to join the small chorus of gay individualists who resent 'intrusions' from feminism upon their pleasures, but rather to describe the shape of a problem.

Simon Watney's recent analysis in *Policing Desire* (1987) describes the ease with which certain anti-pornography positions taken up in the name of feminism slide into alliances with the new moral Right. He speaks of a 'tendency to fudge over straightforward and crucial political issues of censorship and legal moralism, and further confuse the simple yet central distinction between coercive and consensual forms of sex, sliding endlessly between "representation" and "the real"' (p. 71). For Watney, 'pornography' does not have a fixed content with always predictable effects, but instead the 'pornographic' is felt to be such by different individuals in differing situations; there is a range of sexual fantasies, a variety of possible identifications with an image, which are not recognized if we see pornography as a single coherent entity. Indeed, he suggests, to use the term 'pornography' is automatically to force us on to sides, whereas we ought to question the validity of the whole debate.

Accepting Watney's position or not, the relationship between gay men and women, as *potentially* represented in 'pornographic' images, still needs exploring. One central question underlying our discussion remains whether gay erotica/pornography necessarily *exploits* women, or reproduces the *conditions* for their exploitation.

For instance, some women hold out the possibility of a non-exploitative lesbian erotica (some of its makers would insist, 'porn') made for and by – between – women. Its removal from the realm of male power distinguishes it fundamentally from heterosexual porn. This is quite clearly not a question of *superficial* content – witness the plethora of pseudo-lesbian images in male hetero porn.

But the argument cannot run in the same way with gay porn because gay porn involves images of men. Much recent feminist work – campaigning as well as criticism – has focused on the issue of violence against women as a

pervasive fact of our culture, and has identified pornography as a major source of the ideological and emotional
construction of such violence – as the slogan has it:
'Pornography is the theory, rape is the practice'. The
structures of pornography, and especially the way in which
images of men and masculinity are constructed within it,
create a culture of rape. When these feminists have looked
at gay porn, they have seen exactly the same structures and
images, and have felt that gay porn simply partakes in the
culture of rape rather than being any sort of escape from it.

Some people (including some gay men) argue that the
superficial content of gay male porn, in the sense of there
being only men represented, has no bearing on its status as
pornography (bad) or erotica (good). They ask rather who
the material addresses, and how. It can be seen as either
celebrating men, and hence 'manhood' in the sense of men's
power over women, or as reproducing the exploitative
relationships implicit in heterosexuality. (Heterosexuality
as a system, that is: the cultural and legal principle of
exclusive heterosexuality as well as particular heterosexual
relationships.) Male homosexuality and heterosexuality,
and the cultural objects they produce, are seen as being
inescapably bound together. They are seen as merely two
facets of the same thing – patriarchy.

Arguing along these lines, the macho/military/slaving/
posing *images* in some current gay porn are only a symptom
of their deeper content. Even if these specific images were
subtracted (though, of course, there are arguments as to
what these images actually constitute, what they mean),
gay male pornography would inescapably – indirectly,
perhaps, but still inescapably – exploit women. Even 'non-
violent' images would take part in a whole range of
practices that objectively did violence to women.

And there is, of course, the possibly secondary question,
as to whether we as men can produce an erotica that
doesn't exploit *each other*? We don't need to use any
essentialist notion of 'men' – as somehow biologically

programmed to be forever brutal – to ask this question. We can consider men as things are: men within – however marginally or oppositionally – patriarchal capitalism.

Most gay men enjoy porn to some degree or other, but many political gay men also feel the force of the feminist arguments just outlined. It seems important to try to understand the appeal of porn from the inside, as it were, without an *a priori* position of moral superiority, but at the same time without abandoning critical awareness. We knew that Richard Dyer was both an 'out' porn fan and someone with strong feminist sympathies, as well as being someone who has written about gender and sexuality in the media, and this is why we suggested that we have a conversation with him about the issues – and pleasures – that porn raises for gay men. And besides it gave us an opportunity to return some porn that we'd borrowed.

Shepherd: It may be best to begin with one of the most vexed areas: the relation of gay male pornography to the exploitation of women. I'd like to read an extract from one of our major critics, Andrea Dworkin, talking about the position of women in gay porn. She quotes Allen Young of *Gay Community News* who describes 'pictures of a guy jacking off to an issue of *Playboy*; in other words, a guy is looking at a naked woman and jacking off and I as a gay man am supposed to look at the picture and feel more excited looking at the boy because he's straight'. Dworkin comments:

The excitement is supposed to come, in fact, from the visual reminder of male superiority to women in which homosexual men participate. Without that wider frame of reference, masculinity is essentially meaningless. The feminine or references to women in male homosexual pornography clarify for the male that the significance of the penis cannot be compromised ... The evocation of femininity or the presence of women is in itself a part of

the sexual excitement because superiority means power
and in male terms power is sexually exciting. In pornography, the homosexual male, like the heterosexual
male, is encouraged to experience and enjoy his sexual
superiority over women (1981, p. 45).

What are your thoughts?

Dyer: It's probably true to say that power is exciting, for
women as well as men. There are two points I'd make to
begin with. First, the quote suggests people always get off
on a malignant authoritarian power; but power differently
exercised can become a gentle power. Pleasure can come
from feeling powerful or from submitting to power.
Secondly, social relations are always going to have a
bearing on sexuality. It's the case that in this society there's
a power imbalance between men and women. This will
inevitably influence some of the meanings of gay porn.

Wallis: Isn't her argument not that some meanings are
influenced, but that this power imbalance is implicit in and
necessary to all gay porn – it's the very thing which
constitutes it?

Dyer: Because of the stigmatized position both of homosexuality and pornography, discussion of what's going on
in gay porn can't be that straightforward. There are in fact
very few images of women in gay porn. But we can't escape
the fact that sexuality is informed by how gender is
constructed in society at large. For example, I'm turned on
by images of men by themselves. My reaction to these
images oscillates between thinking I'd like to feel that man
and I'd like to be that man. That oscillation is a unique
element of gay porn. Now I think that, when I say I want to
feel or be the man I desire, my reaction is informed by the
notion that 'that image or object is different from women'.
So a sense of gender difference is present, even when there's

no specific reference to women. But the important thing is to ask whether it is merely 'different' or whether the difference always entails an assertion of superiority. Dworkin makes the act of desiring men sound like much German gay writing of the 1920s, which is about bonding with other men, particularly Aryans, in conscious superiority to women. But for me, to acknowledge my desire for another man is *also* to acknowledge I am not a 'real man', that I am not fulfulling a proper role, that I am socially inferior.

Shepherd: Does the response of the gay man to pornography depend on the extent to which he is closeted, or how far he defines himself as gay? Does Dworkin overlook a possible difference: between the out-gay man who is articulate about his desires and the guilty homosexual who wants porn to define his superiority as a male (to offset his supposed inferiority as a queer)?

Dyer: It could equally well be the other way round. There's something stridently male about the contemporary US gay style – yet men wearing this style are also some of the most supportive to women in real life. The closeted gay man may want confirmation of his inferiority, to look at pictures of the wonderful men he is not like.

Wallis: I want to unpick the notion of separate consumers of porn. Certainly as an isolated gay man in this country, you can be situated as if merely a consumer of porn, in the sense that you can go out and buy it. But in doing so you're actually an active part of a social formation, within or supporting its production ... clearly involved.

Dyer: Pornography is the ultimate in capitalist mass media production. It is part of a mass production, but it insistently addresses you as an individual. You buy it and consume it as an individual. That is capitalist cultural production.

Shepherd: Porn as capitalist art-form! Those who oppose it would say it's corrupt because it leads one into a false sense of reality, it dehumanizes those it represents as well as those who consume it. Against this view there are those who say it is liberating and radicalizing. What do you think?

Dyer: There's a range of different reactions. Some people have their unfulfilled desires confirmed, and affirmed, by seeing images in pornography. That is positive (– though one may need to qualify that, by saying it depends which desires . . .). I like porn, but I have misgivings about the kind of porn I like. I like glossy, hi-tech, well-photographed, well-nautilized bodies. I know this is all a construction, but the urgency of the desire it sets in motion is so great that I then find real life, real men, wanting – yet I'm judging them by criteria that I know are ridiculous and even rather repellent.

Wallis: Pornography as an 'incomplete practice'? It offers roles and possibilities which could affirm gay desire, and yet it also idealizes and misrepresents. Is this partly, at least, because we consume pornography as a commodity, gain access to it through the market? Are the alienations in porn connected with, or only similar to, our alienation from the processes of production in general? How could porn, in this sense, become a more complete practice? We haven't talked of the different possibilities for the production of porn – movies, for example, that are produced in a more co-operative way. Is there an erotic practice involving representations which aren't commodities? Representations that aren't reifications?

Dyer: Well, if you look at amateur porn, which is to all intents and purposes produced co-operatively, you don't necessarily see very different imagery. And unfortunately it is not clear to me that if one produced sexual images that were more politically correct, as it were, they would be a turn-on. Porn is about being turned on – I'm very uneasy about the porn/erotica distinction, which, in addition to its class associations, also seems to imply that sex imagery is OK if it doesn't make you come. Some people imply that because porn is a commodity sold for profit, it is a product of capitalism. I would rather say that it is turn-on sex imagery, which, because we live in a patriarchal capitalist society, is inevitably deformed by that.

For instance, there are these images of nautilized bodies, which are body-fascistic, competitive, emphasizing male patriarchal signifiers: one doesn't say despite that, but *because* of that, I'm turned on. But you do get glimpses of something else which turns you on. I like seeing men come. I feel it's a gift. Obviously they're being paid, but in an anthropological sense the come is a gift from one person to another. That's both moving and turning on. I don't imagine living in this society – with all it does to incorporate me, even as a gay man – and not being turned on by things in pornography which are at the same time expressive of all that makes this society rotten. In a better society there would be better pornography. What is not wrong is being made to laugh, or cry, or come when watching a work of art. It is the social relations in which you and in which the art-work are placed which are the problem.

Shepherd: The porn you like seems very different from that which Dworkin talks about. She is so insistent on the sexual pleasures of the male system as antagonism; she focuses on pictures of power relations, not on solo images of desirable bodies. Do we have to talk of different sorts of porn, and of different consumers in different social situations? Much of the writing about porn does not seem to be as sophisticated in its analysis of consumers as it is of the image.

Dyer: Neither the Dworkin line, nor the 'everything goes' line deal with the full contradictions and complexities of response. All art allows us to explore contradictory feelings, why not porn? One of the reasons I like porn is that I fantasize about the picture being taken. It can be quite satisfying to be in porn pictures because it is a validating experience: it suggests you're as good looking as the men you fantasize about. The whole play of the relationship of viewer and being viewed – the excitement from the fact that it is porn – is central to sexual attraction itself – porn can be the occasion of your exploring that. Gay porn especially is often very sophisticated, for instance in the way films or photos show men looking at other films and photos, then at each other, then at the camera and so on.

Shepherd: Discussion of pornography is still the last refuge of moralistic textual critics and of pop sociologists; that's to say, we either read attempts to give porn images a fixed, eternal, moral status, or we hear how it inevitably influences people as does advertising. Both seem crass (and lead Dworkin, for example, into some very disreputable political stances – allied with the FBI and condemning 'deviant' sexuality). I'm interested in how the manufacture of porn changes and develops socially; how it constructs for us ideas about what is desirable or not. For instance, the high valuing of nakedness in porn: does that correspond with general desires (take the fetishism of clothing in so many 'adventure'/sci-fi movies), or is it taught? It's an art-form constructed by the society which produces it; in its turn it helps to construct/reinforce certain types of desirable object. For example, at present, the masculine – and especially American – body.

Dyer: Pornography is normative because of the social relations of pornography in society: if you want to make money you don't want too many different sorts of object. And I wonder whether the dominance of the American image is connected with the relationship of the United

States and Europe, in cultural/social terms. The ideas of freedom, doing what you want to do, being well-fed, well-off, are all suggested by the technically well-produced American porn magazines. And in America there is enough capital available to flood the market. It's a particularly American idea that if you go to the gym you can produce yourself as a desired object, that you can buy your own desirability. This isn't like European thinking, though perhaps Thatcher may want it. What also enters responses to it are the envy and hatred of American power. People who want to buy their desirability, like me, are vulnerable to this porn. Many people are not.

Shepherd: The notion of buying desirability makes that sort of porn very little different from using nice-smelling soap in the shower or wearing a new shirt on a Friday night ...

Dyer: Part of the gay yuppie culture. Tom Waugh (who has done a lot of work on gay porn) pointed out to me how images of working-class men have vanished from North American porn.

Shepherd: We could cut the word 'gay' – the pleasure in dressing nice, wearing perfume ... are all part of a general complicity with capitalism? When I contemplate the porn that is simply an extension of yuppie appetites, I find myself wanting a porn that would be properly bent, really 'dirty'.

Dyer: Have you seen an American magazine called *Straight to Hell*, in which people supposedly send in their 'true-life' experiences, written as *participants*? It sees itself as real and raw, and produces images of the working-class person who likes to be fucked by truckers casually passing through. The magazine is edited by a man firmly placed within New York gay culture. The problem with ideas of the 'raw' and 'dirty' is that they can falsely imagine a realm where feelings are not socially constructed.

Wallis: Both the 'working-class' and the yuppie scenario assume that the consumer is yuppie. In one case, there's an image of the 'other' which can be consumed or used for fantasy identification. Whereas the yuppie image (for example, in the Zipper store Christmas brochures) offers another sort of identification through an idealized image of the self.

Shepherd: My previous question was asked in relation to an idea that radical gay porn would be full of clean healthy images, but would it? By analogy, pictures of SM dykes out in all their clobber are wonderfully celebratory: they're actually refusing certain sorts of categories and morals. It exists on offending the rules, but it does still contest them. This is the area that moralists and 'respectable' voices on the gay scene get, so to speak, het up about.

Dyer: Porn is pursued with greater urgency than other art, and it always tends to be eventually dissatisfying. Maybe desire is always unruly and dissatisfying. But this doesn't mean it is outside social relations. What is most difficult, but also most important, is to take other people's desires seriously, and not to assume you can quickly and easily label them in terms of social relations. If you do that you are usually just laying an un-thought-out moralism on them and understanding nothing. For instance, I find people in SM gear silly – but then I also find my own fantasies stupid, when I'm not being turned on by them. It would be very easy for me to say humiliation is bad, and that SM gives permission to cruelty and perversion. I have a sentimental, lovey-dovey idea of sexuality. What Dworkin and I miss is that antagonism is part of how people live their lives, and how lives are given meaning. I'm not celebrating cruelty, but to avoid antagonism is to avoid an aspect of life. I could easily slip into Dworkin's moral position because it happens to accord with my desire. I love being frightened at the movies, so why shouldn't other people like humiliation scenarios?

Shepherd: Earlier you talked of porn as a consensual relationship of filmer and filmee – but it isn't always so?

Dyer: There's a major difference from heterosexual porn here. Certainly, if you look at Baron Gloeden's late nineteenth-century photos of boys, you could say it's a rich northerner ripping off the Third World, and hence it expresses global social relations – even if he was personally nice to the boys. Certainly, some of the men in porn magazines are from poorer classes, but by no means all, and from the little contact I've had with the business I'd say the relationship is usually pretty genuinely consensual.

Wallis: Isn't it – as far as gay pornographic production is concerned – as consensual and exploitative as working in a shop? Or is it different because it involves sexuality?

Dyer: I suppose it's like the arguments you can have about prostitution. At one level prostitution is just another way of earning a living, another way of being exploited. Female prostitutes are dreadfully abused, but so too are women in sweated labour. But then sexuality is different, because in our society it is seen as uniquely intimate and expressive. Thus we feel that to exploit sexual labour is different from others.

Wallis: Isn't that idea of intimacy a product of labour itself being alienated in this society? This situation encourages a compensatory idea of a core of 'unalienated' sexuality. And that's not at all to deny the very real system of violence against women.

Shepherd: The more taboo and illegal homosexuality is, the more the employer has a grip over the employee – more blackmail and secrecy, more exploitation. The more illegal the sexuality, the more room for bullying and oppression within the activity of prostitution, the making of porn and indeed the consumption of it.

Dyer: There's a paradox that gay porn is even more taboo than is heterosexual, but it's not necessarily more exploitative. Page 3 of the *Sun* is not taboo, but it's very exploitative.

Shepherd: I would want to suggest polemically that the world which makes homosexuality taboo and illegal doesn't of course remove it, but it does produce a situation in which the practice of homosexuality is prone to the worst features of the dominant and banning society.

Wallis: It's a curious situation in that our 'subculture' is positively defined in terms of its porn production, because it is to do with self-image. News magazines carry sexual imagery, not because we're all sex obsessed, but because we define ourselves positively by it. We're almost obliged to find our positive definitions *there*, as a resistance and response to the dominant's reduction of us to a sexual preference.

Dyer: Yes – I remember a woman friend picking up *Gay Times* or *The Advocate* and thinking it was wonderful because they were so full of pleasure on every page. I hadn't thought of it like that.

Shepherd: To finish, let's remind ourselves of the operations of the law with regard to pornography, and of its significant prejudices. Will you tell us about your arrest for importing 'obscene' materials?

Dyer: Last December I went to the lesbian and gay film festival in Amsterdam. The organizers asked if I could bring with me any of the videos that I had referred to in my article about gay porn in *Jump Cut*, which I did. On the way back I was stopped at Birmingham airport and searched by customs officers looking for drugs (because I'd been to Amsterdam). They found two magazines and a porn video, and asked if I had any more at home. I said yes, feeling I had to be co-operative. So they drove me back home and went through the whole house. They took away every single video of any kind they could find and a number of porn magazines. Back at the airport they formally arrested me on grounds of importing an obscene article. I told them I had taken it out of the country, but they said it was bringing it back in which counted as importing. Then they questioned me.

Did I know it was illegal to import this sort of material? I said I thought it wasn't illegal if it was for your own use, unless it had children and animals in it – I became very English and went on and on about children and animals. How did they know I wasn't going to make copies and sell them? I said I did make copies, as presents for friends. They said, but how could they tell I wasn't doing it for gain, and I said that surely that was part of their job, deciding whether people are telling the truth. Did I realize the content was obscene? I replied that if you can get something in Europe which you can also get in Britain, it's not illegal to take it over national borders. They asked whether you could buy this sort of stuff in Birmingham. I told them you can, but that I didn't because it's not very good. What did I mean, 'good'? I said it didn't have the kind of men I fancy in it and was not technically well-produced. They were a little astonished at this level of consumer choice.

Finally they returned the non-porn video material and gave back nearly all the magazines – though interestingly they kept *Boy Chicks* (which isn't in fact kiddy porn, they're young men) – and also, unpleasantly, they took anything with photos featuring Black and white men together. Although nothing different was going on in these photos, these images were the ones which they instinctively considered really unacceptable. The only tape they asked specific questions about was of SM. I did eventually get everything back (apart from the tape I'd 'imported') after a lawyer had written to say they had no right to take it. I won on the grounds that the material had been legally obtained in Britain. I didn't fight to get the remaining tape back, partly because it's so easy to replace, but also because I couldn't be sure of the political support I would get, since the Left and feminists are divided on the issue. Now, however, I'm writing a book on independent lesbian and gay films and I had an experimental lesbian film sent me from the States. This was seized without me seeing it. I am fighting this, on the grounds of academic freedom. But if we win, it won't be the victory I really want. The real victory would be on the grounds that the material is not obscene.

When I returned from the lesbian and gay studies conference in Amsterdam a year later, I was once again very thoroughly searched and I felt that they knew who I was and were trying to catch me out again.

References

Dworkin, A. (1981), *Pornography* (London: The Women's Press).
Watney, S. (1987), *Policing Desire* (London: Methuen).

CHAPTER TWELVE

Gay sex spy orgy: The state's need for queers

Simon Shepherd

Postwar British society has seen a series of scandals involving homosexual treachery. Their impact has given names to our national mythology. Burgess and Maclean are as well-known as Butler and Macmillan.

What is the attraction of, for example, the trials of Peter Wildeblood and Lord Montagu; the treacheries of Burgess, Maclean, Philby, Vassall and Blunt; the 'revelations' about Elton John and Russell Harty; the arrest of a group of Cyprus servicemen? The stories reinforce some traditional notions about homosexuality. They appeal, perhaps, because they reassure most people of their own 'normality' as members of nation, class and sex.

The argument of this essay is in three sections. The first simply lists the characteristics of homosexuality as defined by the scandals. The second suggests how this definition of their sexuality has affected male homosexuals themselves. The third and longest section argues that the scandals, and the ideas in them, are actually *needed* by a state that is manufacturing a sense of 'national community'.

Why queers are treacherous

It is an appropriate prologue to my list of characteristics to quote from Britain's nearest equivalent of a fascist daily:

greeting the opening of the Cyprus servicemen's trial in 1985 the *Sun* reported 'A spy ring of homosexual servicemen caused "incalculable damage" to British security, the Old Bailey heard yesterday.' As it turned out, the homosexuality charges did not stick. But the important point is not whether these particular servicemen were queer or not: rather it is the fact that, in this society, the assumptions about homo conspiracy are circulating, ready for use, and that the media are looking to employ them. The *Sun*'s headline, 'Gay Orgies of RAF Spies', manages with the usual skill to link homosexuality with promiscuity and treachery.

The major homosexual scandals of the twentieth century have created the image of the queer as 'security risk'. This was particularly forceful in the 1950s, during the witchhunts associated with the US Senator McCarthy. Their objective, in the early days of the Cold War, was to weed out Communists from positions within the state administration. Britain, loyal as a goldfish, followed the example set by its NATO ally. The witch-hunt was, however, also directed at homosexuals on the basis of the claim that homosexuals, because of their illicit sexual desires, could be more easily framed and blackmailed by an enemy power. Homosexuals were seen as 'naturally' inclined to treachery, 'naturally' attracted to enemy ideas such as Communism. Now what was there about this sexuality which inclined it, uniquely, to treachery?

First, homosexuality is seen to be associated with passion, emotional ill-discipline, sexual looseness. These characteristics are supposedly associated with women, and homosexuality, in its earliest 'scientific' definitions by sexologists, was explained as a feminine soul in a male body. Homosexual men were thus men who were less rational and disciplined than other men. Furthermore, because the homosexual man is distinguished from other men mainly by his sexual desires, these desires are highlighted: the homosexual's life, unlike the non-homosexual's, is seen to revolve around sexual desire, since it's only that desire which separates the homo from the het. This sexual definition of homosexuality is shaped by, and depends on, a structure of sexual difference in a society where men expect to have more power than women. It's a definition which fosters ideas of male power.

Second, the homosexual is inclined to treachery because homosexuals supposedly form secret brotherhoods. When she is talking of the Communism and homosexuality of Burgess and Maclean, Rebecca West articulates this suspicion: 'Once a secret society establishes itself within an open society there is no end to the hideous mistrust it must cause' (1984, pp. 283–4). Such groupings are not structured according to the 'proper' orders of society, such as nation, class and profession. Homosexual desire links men who otherwise would not be linked: homosexuals are men who are brought together not by money and property interest but by sex. This fact makes them, apparently, ignore traditional bonds of loyalty, to nation, class, etc. The links are the more dangerous because they are secret (which is caused by the illegality of homosex and its concealment beneath the 'national community'). This negative image of homosexuality derives from a respect for, and depends on, the assumption that property and money are the natural and inevitable forces that order 'human' society (ha).

Both of the above ideas about homosexuality can be seen clearly stated in the Eulenburg scandal in pre-First World War Germany. It is interestingly described by James Steakley (1983), on whom I depend for my references. Briefly, a journalist, Maximilian Harden, was politically motivated to expose the corruption among the associates (and homosexual buddies) of Kaiser Wilhelm II. The central target of his attacks (in 1907) was an influential, and *anti-imperialist*, diplomat called Philipp Eulenburg. There was a general feeling that homosexuality (and pornography) were spreading, that the army and indeed the nation had been weakened by corruption within: homosexuals were aiming 'gradually to emasculate our courageous master race before the nation notices what is happening' (p. 43). Harden quoted one of Wilhelm's associates as saying 'we have formed a ring around the Kaiser that no one can break through' (p. 27).

In the Eulenburg affair, the sexual revelations fuelled the antagonism of a 'morally pure' middle class towards a decadent aristocracy. Some people suggested that centuries of aristocratic intermarriage had resulted in hereditary degeneracy, evidenced, of course, in homosexuality (p. 37). This image of homosexuality as the 'sickness' of a leisured and unproductive social class re-appears in the British scandals. Peter Wildeblood notes how press coverage connected Lord Montagu's name 'with all-male parties and champagne orgies' (1955, p. 67). When Rebecca West speaks of the press's unwillingness to attribute Burgess and Maclean's flight to Communist motives, she notes: 'it would be very irritating if a couple of homosexuals, bronzed and fit after a continental holiday, were able to win enormous damages because an ideological motive had been wrongly ascribed to their expedition' (p. 253). The niggle is in that detail – 'bronzed and fit', able to go abroad, unlike other 'normal' British holiday-makers at that period. A working-class (or petty bourgeois) hostility to 'decadent' wealth and leisure is deliberately mobilized by the *Sun* in its exposés of lives of the gay rich, in particular pop stars. Its manufactured 'voice of the people' assumes that homosexuality has no place in the 'real' working class.

The Burgess–Maclean story linked another grouping with homosexuals – intellectuals. These two men were part of a group educated at Cambridge University. As intellectuals they apparently embraced ideas – such as Communism – which were alien to 'ordinary' people. Such an openness to new (and 'enemy') ideas mirrors, in intellectual terms, the queer's continual openness to, and search for, sexual encounters. To connect the intellectual to homosex is effectively to subvert the work and arguments of anyone whose outlook diverges from, or criticizes, the values of the dominant culture.

Bound into the notion of secret homosexual brotherhoods is an idea I've already mentioned – namely, that homosex leads to a crossing of national and class barriers. Homosexual desire is thus seen as 'disorderly'. Some of the muckiest scandals involved cross-class liaisons. Eulenburg's connections with the French confirmed for the journalist Harden (in 1913) that, in Steakley's words, homosexuals 'constituted an international association in much the same way as the socialists – those "fellows without a fatherland" ' (Steakley, 1983, p. 43). Eulenburg was a threat because he was 'the amoureuse who has toyed with sceptres and thrashed in lustful ecstasy on the sweaty sheets of his coachman' (p. 43) (the vividness of Harden's imagination here is interesting). In Britain much of the opposition to Lord Montagu was caused by his enter- taining social inferiors, and the prosecution in court made much of his 'lavish hospitality' to RAF airmen. This tradi- tional queer crime is respectfully memorialized by tabloid stories connecting media personalities with 'rent boys'. As a variant, the *Star* for 14 December 1987 led with the story of a threat to the entire navy caused by sex between an officer and a rating aboard a nuclear submarine – if only nuclear weapons prompted more such encounters.

Lastly, homosex is associated with foreignness. It's a link which does not even need to be explicit. Underlying Harden's quotation (above) is an implicit connection of homosexuals with Jews (who were without a 'fatherland'). Homosexual 'foreignness' takes many forms. Right-wing Labour councillors on Nottinghamshire County Council have argued that homosex is a product of the city rather than rural areas (rural areas being more 'natural', tradi- tional and innocent); workerist politicians claim it's a middle-class phenomenon unknown in the traditional working-class; certain Muslim fundamentalists argue that it's a sickness of whites unknown among Asians; in the

Eulenburg case anti-semites linked Jews with homosexuality. Those who are different or dissenting in terms of class, religion or race are said to be sexually different, and vice versa: the one confirms the other, and the fear of both together works to unite (forcibly) the group doing the excluding.

On a different scale, there is a commonly perceived scenario, based on racist assumptions about Black people and imperialist notions about the Third World, that traces the invasion of AIDS into Britain through the agency of male homosexuals as the trans-atlantic bearers of a disease that had its origins in Black Africa. More than just foreign, homosexuality imports foreignness which undoes the strength of the nation. In the spy scandals, the homosexual is the weak point in the body of the nation, for through the queer traitor British secrets flow out to the foreign agent.

Homosexuality is indeed like a disease when it is seen as a foreign body *within* the body politic. Discussing the Burgess–Maclean affair, Rebecca West remarks:

> An open society has been unable to defend itself against a secret society which has formed within itself. That, when it happens to the cells of our body, is called a case of cancer, and the results were cancerous in their corrupting painfulness. The United States had reason to think ill of its ally, Great Britain, and what was even worse, Great Britain had reason to think ill of itself. (p. 283)

The image of the queer traitor confirms the 'unnaturalness' of the sexuality that refuses the national family, the effeminacy that is the weak link in a *father*land.

By way of conclusion to this section, let's look at some of the characteristics coming together in one text, a *Radio Times* feature promoting the BBC film about Anthony Blunt (shown 11 January 1987). This is just one among many re-tellings of the treachery story which the dominant culture in Britain continually needs to re-tell to itself, in order to reconfirm its notions about sex and society. The article begins by listing Blunt's intellectual and professional distinctions, his high place in the academy. It then notes how he was protected by 'the closing of ranks by an establishment that had guaranteed him, unlike such spies as Geoffrey Prime [who was a lesser civil servant], total immunity from prosecution': the upper-class conspiracy. One of the hypotheses invented in the film is that 'the fact that Burgess defected with Maclean left Blunt emotionally devastated as well as professionally betrayed as a spy': this 'hypothesis' simply draws on the traditional expectation that queer scandals will involve some sort of messy cross-over between excessive emotionalism and politics. Blunt, we hear, exploited Goronwy Rees's 'sense of loyalty to his friends over and above his country': this is the primary ghettoized bond that ignores 'proper' (national) loyalty. In the film itself, Rees was seen as non-homosexual and married; thus, the friendship with Blunt constituted a threat to his marriage. By contrast with Blunt, Rees's wife was seen as loyal: this sets up an antagonism between queers and women and marriage, all within the context of nationalism.

When Burgess and Maclean were revealed to be in Moscow (in 1956), Rees was principal of the University College of Wales at Aberystwyth: he, like Blunt, was an 'intellectual'. Blunt had 'a deep psychological problem ... His patrician background was a kind of actor's mask he retreated behind': the whole story is that of a model double life, the queer close to the Royal Household. It is worth remembering that taboos against homosexuality, particularly in powerful positions, force gays into secrecy and ghetto networks. That enforced double life is then in its turn said to be a symptom of what is wrong with homosexuals: create outsiders, then define them as natural outsiders. Thus David Owen could record that he was 'dismayed and dejected' that Sir Maurice Oldfield could have lied about his private life, which blames the queer for having the capacity to lie rather than blaming the society which forces the queer to lie.

Homosexual patriots

The suggestion that homosexuality is naturally connected with disloyalty and disorderliness has its effect on the way queers think about their sexuality. While they may not altogether accept the connection, they view it as something to be countered rather than disputed. They demonstrate their loyalty and in doing so do not question – conveniently – whether nationalism itself is a good thing. This section looks at ways of being homosexual 'good guys'.

When he was accused in court of infringing Paragraph 175 of the penal code (the bit forbidding homosexual acts), Eulenburg knowingly perjured himself. At the time of the Montagu trial, Peter Wildeblood noted 'every pansy in London was telling "Montagu stories" in a feverish attempt to divert suspicion from himself' (1955, p. 49). Homosexual scandals, particularly witch-hunts and press 'hysteria', produce – and are designed to produce – disavowals of homosexuality. The disavowal works not only to closet the individual but to create barriers, non-recognition, between homosexuals. There are numerous accounts of homosexuals arrested in the 1950s and 1960s who were forced by the police to reveal the names of friends and contacts. Thus, for a gay man all homosexual contacts were potentially self-destructive. In the States in 1952 lectures were given to WAVE (female Navy) recruits that encouraged the women to inform on one another on suspicion of lesbian activity (Berubé and D'Emilio, 1984, p. 762). In general, any climate of oppression, surveillance and 'exposure' produces a self-censorship among those who are already nervous about their sexuality. The climate of the 50s in the US led the homosexual group, the

Mattachine Society, to develop an image of compliant respectability and to abandon organized law-reform campaigns 'because they would only serve to prejudice the position of the [Mattachine] Society' (D'Emilio, 1983, p. 83). Homosexual reactions to GLF marches condemned those who were shouting about gay pride because it gave homosexuals a bad name. There are regular letters to *Gay Times* or *Capital Gay*, often at election times, which warn of rocking the boat.

The defence of homosexuality is couched in terms which reproduce the values and ideas which have themselves oppressed homosexuals. The charge of deviancy is countered by nationalist affirmation. Eulenburg defended himself: 'This is a slam at German friendship, it's a poison that's being trickled into friendship, no one is safe; that is a betrayal of Germany!' (Steakley, 1983, p. 43). In their campaigns as homosexual law-reformers, Peter Wildeblood and 'Douglas Plummer' (in *Queer People*, 1964) referred proudly to their records of war service. This gesture, like that of Mattachine in the 1950s, was intended to demonstrate that homosexuals could be loyal servants of the state and good citizens in a public capacity. Simultaneously this marginalized them as homosexuals. Their sexual orientation was said to be private and thus irrelevant to their public duty. Law-reformers thus opposed those gays who publicly flaunted their sexuality, since such behaviour apparently confirmed the dominant idea that homosexuals conflated private with public. Out of this atmosphere in postwar Britain there appeared several novels which centred on homosexuals who were in the services or in responsible jobs, such as doctors and managers. The political backwardness of Larry Kramer's *The Normal Heart* may be seen, twenty years later, in its profferring of a Green Beret and bank manager as role models. The good 1960s queer could be as nationalist and capitalist as the next little shit.

A third effect of the connection of homosexuality and

treachery is seen at a less conscious level, in the shaping of desire and sexual pleasure. In Martyn Goff's novel, *The Youngest Director* (1961), the central figure – a sympathetic homosexual businessman – celebrates the fact that his working-class boyfriend 'had one of those open, English faces that look so well on recruiting posters' (p. 16). There is pleasure in the Englishness, rather than the foreignness, of the respectable homosexual's partner. My suggestion is that the racism which is bred into all white British is given reinforcement by the desire for homosexual sex objects that conform to acceptable and normal types of manhood. Partly, this selection of sex objects is also motivated by a desire for 'real men', or men who pass as straight (see Jamie Gough's essay). Fashions for homosexual sex objects change within history, but I'd like to observe the following: the currency of soldier as sex object in early twentieth-century Germany; the repeated focus on the guardsman in accounts of gay sex in 1950s London; the preponderance of white males in photographs in *Him* in the late 1970s (where Blacks appear, they are frequently cast in 'acceptable' roles – boxer, commando – which sustain a racist connection between Blacks and violence; see *Ten.8*, no. 22 and Sunil Gupta's essay); the numbers of contact ads that feel it is important to their sexual project to state that they are 'ex-army' or 'ex-police'.

The stories of queer treachery have the effect of creating in homosexuals a desire for a primary identification with nation, race and class. This takes precedence over a positive attitude to their sexuality, which would be 'treacherous'. Those who know themselves to be already 'deviant' are offered a way of being loyal. The price for admission under the umbrella of comforting tolerance is agreement to the very idea that sustains the oppression, that homosexuality is naturally alien.

Why the state needs its queers

Homosexual treachery stories tend to surface in conditions of national 'pride' and reconstruction. This final section explores the general appeal of these stories, and suggests why they may be useful to a state that is occupied in constructing a sense of national community.

The appeal of the stories derives from their ability to spell out the distinction between acceptable and unacceptable behaviour. This is accompanied by an explanation that what is unacceptable results from a 'naturally' unstable sexuality, which is confined to a small and essentially alien group. Those who are non-homosexual are thus reassured of their non-problematic membership of class or sex. For example, in the trial of Lord Montagu and Peter Wildeblood, the press invited sympathy with the young RAF lads who had been led astray (ha, ha) by the corrupt aristocrat. Only the homosexual spends his wealth in a way that crosses and betrays class boundaries. A proper upper-class position, available to those who are 'normal', keeps its wealth to its own class. The story also constructs an idea of the decent working class, which is sexually innocent and which knows its own place. The picture reappears in press coverage of the Cyprus spy trial, when it was clear that the honest young lads had been set up or bullied by military police. The discovery of queer behaviour in a working-class youth constitutes a form of treachery to the class. Thus the recent details of army 'initiation rites' tend to condemn the perverted (though working-class) NCO who subjects innocent recruits to his violence. The homosexual violence of the initiation is seen to be unacceptable, whereas war games and military discipline are, by contrast, natural and acceptable violence.

Lord Montagu's dealings with RAF lads tampered not only with their class but with their masculinity (lower-class female sex objects are acceptable). Homosexual desire is, as it were, unacceptable, whereas an admiration of the power of tough masculinity is supposedly natural and acceptable. In states with imperialist or militarist ambitions, the costuming of the military tends to make erotic the masculinity of the fighting man, to advertise the tough trained body underneath, to show off the individual body that keeps the body politic sturdy. This was observed by a witness in one of the trials involving the journalist Harden in 1907: 'The hushed courtroom was fascinated by Bollhardt's [himself a soldier] report on the powerful sex appeal of the white pants and kneehigh boots of the cuirassier's uniform: any guardsman who ventured to wear it in public was virtually certain to be approached by men soliciting homosexual intercourse' (Steakley, 1983, p. 29). The eroticizing of the military man, and the fetishizing of his accessories, presumably play their part in shaping the masculine identities of all men in society, and thus in reproducing the existence of a tough masculine community. Stories that suggest it is only an alien homosexual minority which abuses the communal rules offer in turn to the non-homosexual a secure sense of their place in this community. In periods of aggressive foreign policy – prewar Germany, Cold War Britain, 1980s Britain and the United States – military chic often appears in civilian fashions; at the same time, there are scandals around soldiers as homo sex objects. The limits of an acceptable and unacceptable mystique of masculinity are demarcated.

In addition to offering confirmation of class and sex positions, treachery stories explicitly spell out loyalty. Thus when a young man employed at GCHQ (Government Communications Head-Quarters) comes out as gay, on the basis that only closeted gays can be blackmailed, he has to be dismissed – as a 'security threat'. Similarly, gay police are pressurized or split from their partners. In neither GCHQ nor the police force are there trades unions. The emphasis is on a supreme loyalty to the state. Out-gay sexuality is as much of a breach of this loyalty as are unions, because it 'implies' an allegiance to one's sexuality. Dis-

cussing Sir Maurice Oldfield, David Owen said 'People
who take jobs like this are going to have to have their civil
liberties interfered with more than other people' (*Today*,
Radio 4, 24 April 1987).

The 'normal' employee of GCHQ is conceived of as one
who accepts the ban on unions and homosexuality. Indeed,
the readiness to accept these limits marks the person's
'normality'. Only a homosexual, or militant, would need to
question the limits; one's safe membership of a loyal
majority is obtained by agreeing to rules that homosexuals
would break. Similarly, on a wider scale, by agreeing to the
fixed rules of class and gender status, one can be assured of
one's secure place in the 'national community'; it's a
contradiction specifically concealed here that the community depends upon maintained divisions and power
imbalances. Indeed the very idea of 'nation' in which we all
pull together is a concept fostered by the state in order to
conceal the divisions of wealth and acts of oppression
which actually make up the state's power.

Stories of queer treachery, comprising as they do alle-
giances to class, gender system and race, are powerful
devices for maintaining a majority of people's consent to
the fabricated idea of nation. But homosexuality is not only
defined by the state, and is not only held at arm's length as
something essentially foreign. Its presence within the family
life of the nation is deeply disorderly, for when homosexuality becomes explicit it has to be dealt with by, and
thus reveals, the structures of oppression which normally
are concealed. The 'illogic' of sacking an out-gay man at
GCHQ shows, as much as the banning of unions, the extent
of state coercion. The scandal of army initiation rites shows
the extent of incorporated 'acceptable' violence within
military training.

The attempts to deal with disloyal homosexuality are
part of, and reveal, the state's oppressive machinery,
dressed up as 'national interest'. A good example of this
was the 'issue' of homosexuality in the McCarthy witch-

hunts. First, it was said that 'sex perversion weakens the moral fibre of the individual', that homosexuals were vulnerable to blackmail and hence espionage agents (my information comes from D'Emilio, 1983, pp. 42–6). This idea suggests that those who are weak and 'perverted' embrace Communism; that Communism is not capable of converting people simply because it is more rational and more moral as a belief, but is an infection of the already weak. The definition of homosexuality as sick and treacherous, then the association of homosexuality with Communism, is a strategy for neutralizing any positive charge in Communism without having to argue directly with it (and thus give its ideas damaging circulation). Second, if you define homosexuals as immature and unstable you have to deal with them in ways which differ from those available for dealing with criminals; that it's a 'personal' problem rather than a criminal offence requires new structures of control which bypass (conveniently) the established, but irrelevant, official procedures. D'Emilio records that

> the armed services employed methods for dealing with gay men and women that seriously circumscribed the rights of its personnel. The military generally bypassed the court martial proceedings required for a dishonourable discharge and instead used administrative mechanisms that terminated members as 'undesirable'. (p. 45)

Dealing with homosexuality 'justifies' the invention of an administrative machinery that is less democratic and public than, say, courts where a defendant can argue back. Wartime conditions had produced a high valuing of democratic rights (as part of the propaganda against fascism); this in turn led to democratic practices and a real commitment on the part of many to individual rights. After the war, corporate business and its politicians needed once again to strengthen their control. One way of doing this was by creating a restrengthened administrative and state management structure which bypassed the traditional rights of individuals in democratic procedures. 'A commander who advised her squadron of its rights under military law was relieved of her post' (D'Emilio, 1983, p. 45). It is not hard to see how the 'issue' of homosexuality, which as a 'personal' problem requires new modes of management, provided the state with an excuse to introduce a structure (aided by an atmosphere of fear) which quashed the democratic practices it no longer required.

Fears of homosexual villainy accompany, establish the mental framework for, and as it were 'justify', the deployment of anti-democratic powers by the state. For instance, in the year after the Wolfenden Committee was convened, to look into homosexual law reform, a series of books appeared which characterized homosexuality as a disease. Thus they pre-empted the results of a possible relaxation of the law against homosexuality by pushing homosex into a new area of secure policing not affected by the courts – medicine and psychiatry (and, incidentally, the show-piece trial of Lord Montagu took place in 1954, the year Wolfenden was convened). Again, it's common knowledge that law reform in 1967 was followed by increased numbers of arrests for indecency, etc. The activities of the elected representatives in the state were thus deliberately shown to be limited and framed by the activities of a non-elected state police force – clarifying the precise limits of the 'swinging' sixties.

The general attempt by the state to centralize and strengthen its power produces a concern with queer traitors. For example, it was only in the context of the development of an aggressive foreign policy that the homosexuality of the anti-imperialist Eulenburg became a scandal: the homosexuality and the anti-imperialism tainted each other. Closer to home (if we may call it that), there were the attacks on sodomy in general, and on homosexuality in the church, at the Church of England Synod in December 1987.

The inference constructed was that the 'liberalism' of the Archbishop of Canterbury had permitted homosexuality to thrive in the church. An attack on homosexuality was part of, and justification for, an attack on liberals by a government engineering a right-wing take-over of the church hierarchy. The church had challenged the authority of the Tory state by, for instance, its refusal to celebrate the Malvinas/Falklands 'victory' and its 'Marxist', i.e., critical, report on inner cities: the combination of national disloyalty and 'Marxist' intellectualism begs for the emergence – in this model – of the 'explanatory key', homosexuality.

As I noted earlier, the convenient thing about sexuality is that it is a 'private' matter, which means not that governments leave it alone but that they can use 'appropriate' administrative or moral, rather than legal, structures to deal with it. In recent years, especially in the States, it has become the target of moral and religious groups (whose real links with big business and far-right politicians are undeclared, because it's all 'private' anyway). In October 1987 Margaret Thatcher gave an interview to *Woman's Own* in which she encouraged the churches to be more outspoken about AIDS (and homosexuality): 'Parliament isn't the great institution of life; churches are your great institutions, as are your great voluntary associations. And you're entitled to look to them and say "Look, there are certain standards, and if you undermine fundamentally these standards you'll be changing our way of life"' (report in *Capital Gay*, 30 October 1987). The choice of magazine shows she is talking only about 'private' personal matters, and therefore it seems appropriate that she can use the interview to downgrade the authority of the major elected body of the land. In place of its mandated legislation, she encourages the voice – and presumably actions – of those non-elected, 'pro-family' moral and religious groups whose stance and membership embody some of the more reactionary thoughts of the Tory Party. Thatcher's formulation apparently conceals the real increase in state intervention in people's lives; but it yet again uses the threat of homosexuality to persuade people to volunteer for limits (in the form of 'standards'). The interview asks for family-life vigilantes to preserve the greatness of the nation: 'A nation of free people will only continue to be great if family life continues and the structure of that nation is a family one'. Reaching well back beyond Rebecca West and her cancerous secret society within an open society, Thatcher's sentiment echoes Harden's appeal to moral vigilantism when he said homosexuals were seeking to 'emasculate our courageous master race before the nation notices what is happening'.

Finally we come to the infamous Clause 28 which was added by two Tory MPs to the Local Government Bill in December 1987. This Clause acts on, and pretends to deal with, a scare about councils with pro-homosexual policies. The features of a good queer villain scandal are present: we already have an association between homosexuality and disease (supplied by AIDS, and promoted by the tabloid press and its government). Then we have homosexuals (or homosexual sympathizers) with some (limited) power (local councils), who have got there by campaigning with the Left (intellectuals, foreign ideas, conspiracy). And the 'victims' are all those decent honest rate-paying folk, and, of course, their children, who wouldn't dream of giving house-room to a poof. The Clause is, of course, part of a Bill which makes a major overall assault on local democracy. The Bill is part of the bid to centralize state power and to silence opposition. The particular function of Clause 28 is to articulate/construct panic around homosexual threats and in doing so to show the links between 'extreme' (i.e., opposition) policies and the alien treacheries of homosexuality. It follows that the passing into law of the means by which a government can ban 'promotion' of any grouping it dislikes is a 'justified' consolidation of powers that may be used against many more than lesbians and gays. In Prime Minister's Question Time on 19 January 1988, Tory MP Anne Winterton suggested raising money for the

National Health Service by diverting funds away from the Commission for Racial Equality, the Equal Opportunities Commission and college courses for trades unionists.

The Eulenburg scandal contributed to an increased militarism and aggressive foreign policy which finally resulted in the First World War. The McCarthy witch-hunts, and the Burgess–Maclean scandal, were part of the West's escalation into Cold War. The current scandal about the villainy of homosexuals coincides with the increased military aggressiveness of Britain and the United States in the 1980s (indeed the wording of Clause 28 imitates that of similar, previous initiatives in the States). The attack on queers focuses unthinking attention on to the demand for a sturdy masculine nation. It thus sustains the mentality which might have faded with the memory of the Malvinas/Falklands conflict. The new stage in the campaign against homosexuals has 'justified' a step nearer a form of totalitarian government. The image of the queer traitor is necessary to the state that wants to strengthen its authoritarian control. Campaigns to deal with queer villains gain the assent of the populace to measures which harm the populace, in the name of national community.

References

Adam, B. (1978), *The Survival of Domination* (New York: Elsevier).

Adam, B. (1987), *The Rise of a Gay and Lesbian Movement* (Boston, Mass.: Twayne).

Altman, D. (1981), 'The state and the new homosexual', *Coming Out in the Seventies* (Boston: Alyson Publications).

Berubé, A. and D'Emilio, J. (1984), 'The military and lesbians during the McCarthy years', *Signs*, vol. 9.

D'Emilio, J. (1983), *Sexual Politics, Sexual Communities* (Chicago: Chicago University Press).

Steakley, J. (1983), 'Iconography of a scandal', *Studies in Visual Communications*, vol. 9.

West, R. (1949, 1965), *The Meaning of Treason* (London: Virago, 1984).

Wildeblood, P. (1955), *Against the Law* (Harmondsworth: Penguin).

CHAPTER THIRTEEN

Gays and the press

Terry Sanderson

It was Francis Williams who said: 'Newspapers indicate more plainly than anything else the climates of the societies to which they belong.' Perhaps these days this should read: 'Newspapers indicate more plainly than anything else the opinions of the Tory Government.'

It is because the majority of the press have a liking for all things Conservative that the gay community has had to endure a sustained and relentless attack over the past five years. Day after day lesbians and gay men have to put up with a constant flow of misrepresentation, ridicule and insult in the pages of newspapers. Ironically, at the beginning of the gay liberation movement, activists complained that their existence was ignored by the media. In those days, unless we were involved in court proceedings or were suffering some other 'disgrace' because of our sexuality, we were simply invisible as far as the mass media were concerned. This gradually changed as gays became more confident and shouted louder. Only a few short years ago it was possible to see our national press being at least neutral on the subject of homosexuality; for example, when an MP was entrapped by police in a Soho gay club there was unanimous agreement from the Fourth Estate that police time should be put to better use. But now such unbiased reporting of the gay community in the popular press is just about unthinkable.

So why have the tabloids become so virulently anti-gay? Are these papers simply reflecting the existing opinions of their readers or are they, as some would say, engaged in the more sinister business of trying to create a new 'morality' which would sustain the Right in power indefinitely?

An obvious element in the sudden upsurge in anti-gay reporting is, of course, AIDS. But it is more than just a reaction to Acquired Immune Deficiency Syndrome that has driven the tabloids to their present level of anti-homosexual hysteria. The right-wing of the political establishment has realized what a potent force homophobia is, and is exploiting it for its own advantage. With the majority of the press in their pocket, the Tories have become masters of propaganda. Gays, among others, are prime targets in this campaign.

This is particularly apparent when elections are in the offing. While television is bound by law to remain impartial, newspapers are traditionally expected to adopt a partisan stance. However, the 1987 General Election resulted in a press campaign of unprecedented bias and scurrility. By endless misrepresentation of opposition parties and disgraceful scandal-mongering, the tabloids ensured that there could be no rational or fair debate about the important issues. In effect, the newspapers starved their readers of real information and instead provided them with a daily diet of prurience and propaganda.

Mr Murdoch's smear machine was particularly active during this period, and the gay community and gay individuals were targeted for special attention. The Tories and their faithful press corps were quick to realize the potential of stirring up the anti-gay feeling which had lain mostly dormant for a decade in Britain. The right-wing had found themselves a potent weapon.

It has been argued that this weapon was handed to them by elements of the Labour Party who, in their enthusiasm to promote gay rights, had not taken into account that there is a lot of education still to be done before such radical changes could become generally acceptable. But this does not excuse the Tory press's ruthless exploitation of the lives of gay men and women. To incite hatred against an already embattled minority, as they did and continue to do, was irresponsible and socially divisive. In the light of the AIDS situation it is also counter-productive.

But the tabloids had been given the go-ahead for their hate campaign when Norman Tebbit put the establishment seal of approval on it by saying:

> Legislation on capital punishment, homosexuality, abortion, censorship and divorce – some of it good, some of it bad – but all of it applauded as 'progressive' was ushered in in quick succession, leaving an overwhelming impression that there were not only going to be no legal constraints, but that there were no need for constraints at all. Tolerance of sexual deviation generated a demand for deviance itself to be treated as the norm.

The Tory Party's 'moral revival' was officially under way, and the hypocrites of the press took on a new mantle as guardians of the sexual morals of the nation.

Leading the way, the *News of the World* splashed the details of the private life of a gay Labour Party official over two pages in the week before the election. Elsewhere, Ken Livingstone's pro-gay opinions were presented as being really those of Neil Kinnock. When the Labour leadership realized what a field day the press were having with the gay angle there was a panic reaction and a rapid attempt to make the issue less prominent. But the press would not let go of it. The coverage became more and more extreme. Words like 'Poofter', 'Woofter', 'Perverts' and 'Queers' began to make their appearance in headlines relating to gay people.

The same techniques were employed during the local authority elections in the same years. 'Vile Book in School – pupils see pictures of gay lovers' screamed the front page of the *Sun* on the day before elections for the Labour-controlled Inner London Education Authority (ILEA) were to take place. The report was a classic piece of *Sun* propaganda, homing in on a little book called *Jenny Lives with Eric and Martin* and totally misrepresenting it. The book concerned a little girl who lived with her father and his gay lover. Its intention was to be supportive and helpful to children who might find themselves in the same situation as Jenny. The *Sun* inferred that the ILEA was making the book generally available in its schools, which wasn't true. There was no coincidence in the timing of that story, either. It was not that the *Sun* had just discovered the book and were anxious that their readers should know about it as soon as possible. *Jenny Lives with Eric and Martin* had been in the bookshops for two years by then, and had already been 'exposed' the previous year by the *Sun*'s sister paper, the *News of the World*. The Jenny and Martin affair illustrated how easily the press can now dictate the political agenda – ILEA has now given in to the totally unjustified pressure and withdrawn the book from its libraries. And although the furore over *Jenny* cannot be said to have been responsible for the government's decision to abolish ILEA, I'm sure it didn't help.

Labour-controlled councils (mainly in London) who were trying to carry out the Labour Party's agreed policy of eliminating discrimination against gays were subjected to a tirade of abuse and distortion. ('Labour picks rent boy as school boss' – *News of the World*; 'A gay day or two away on the rates' – *London Evening Standard*; 'Cash crisis council backs gay festival!' – *London Evening Standard*; 'A gay way to jump the housing queue' – *Daily Mail*, etc.)

Subsequent independent research has indicated that blatant invention and lying took place in the newspapers' efforts to discredit these councils, which they had dubbed 'Loony Left'. Myths about gays being given preferential treatment in housing, adoption and other services were invented and endlessly repeated until they became accepted as 'fact'.

The Greater London Council (GLC) was in the forefront of promoting the rights of the gay community. It paid dearly for its efforts. The propaganda campaign during the period of abolition concentrated its fire upon these modest policies. Newspapers like the *London Evening Standard* continually sought to give the impression that almost all the GLC's rate precept was being spent on gay rights. Every time a gay issue was mentioned in the GLC it was splashed across the front pages, while most other achievements of the council were studiously ignored.

The misrepresentation of Labour Party policy towards gays had become so hysterical that it provided the government with the opportunity to introduce legislation which, only a few short years ago, would have been thought inconceivable. The now notorious 'no promotion of homosexuality in schools' clause was craftily sneaked into the Local Government Bill at the eleventh hour, leaving precious little time for rational debate. The Clause was a direct response to attempts by a few Labour local authorities to introduce 'positive images' of lesbians and gay men in schools.

The parliamentary debates on the subject rested almost entirely on 'evidence' culled from newspaper reports whose authenticity had been challenged over and over again. Once more *Jenny Lives with Eric and Martin* was wheeled out as 'proof' that the legislation was needed. What was lost in the barrage of hysterical anti-gay rhetoric was the fact that the book had never been available in any school in the land. This legislation was the direct result of the press campaign which had been waged against the Labour Party over the preceding three years.

However, the Local Government Bill clause achieved one aim and that was to open the debate on homosexuality once again in the serious papers. The way they came down was predictable. The 'liberal' end of the market, the *Guardian*,

Independent and *Observer*, were fierce in their opposition to the Clause. *The Times* and *Telegraph* supported the government, while allowing dissenting voices into their pages.

Typically, the tabloids were unanimous in their support of the proposed new legislation. After all, after a long and bitter gestation period this was, in fact, their baby. The deliberate perversion of truth, the panic-mongering and the bogus moral outrage generated by the Clause were summed up in a *Daily Express* editorial:

> To tell a captive audience of other people's children that homosexuality is as normal and acceptable as hetero-sexuality can do no other than promote it – as those who broadcast this message know perfectly well. No one has a right to foist such deceit on children. It can lead to great emotional turmoil – and worse. As we know too well, the AIDS virus has turned homosexuality from a so-called lifestyle into a deathstyle ... Clause 28 comes not a moment too soon (January, 1988).

This illustrates the way that newspapers had marginalized and alienated homosexuals to the extent that we now seemed to be some kind of undesirable aliens from another planet rather than an integral part of the society which these moral paragons seek to 'protect'.

There is a third element at work in the press attitude to gays, and this is the vicious circulation war in which the papers are engaged. Over the past decade readership of the tabloids has increased by 2 millions. This lucrative audience is being desperately fought for by the barons who control the press. Someone who has discovered a formula for obtaining and keeping a mass readership is Rupert Murdoch. The day he appeared on the newspaper scene was a sad one for Britain. Single-handedly this man has dragged the standards of British journalism into the gutter. His down-market approach, with its concentration on

'scandal', trivia, soft porn and royalty, overlaid with a
sinister right-wing slant, has ensured that the other tabloids
have had to adopt the same values in order to survive in a
ruthless market. The technique has been aptly described by
Jeremy Seabrook as 'pandering to the mob mentality'
(*New Society*, March 1986). A prurient and hypocritical
approach to sex is another essential ingredient. While
reporting rape cases in slavering detail, the tabloids feed
their readers a diet of naked and semi-naked women. While
poring in great detail over the sex lives of the rich and
famous, they rant in their editorials about falling moral
standards. They seem to have an unquenchable appetite for
details about the sex lives of gay men and women in the
public eye, while despising and abusing gay people in
general. Elton John, Kenny Everett, Martina Navratilova,
Russell Harty, and many others have all been through this
process.

But surely the most disgraceful aspect of this lust for
'scandal' has been the tabloids' treatment of the AIDS
crisis. Instead of seeing the terrible consequences of AIDS
upon the lives of real people with real feelings, the tabloids
treated AIDS as just another sensation with which to
titillate their readers. Under the guise of responsible reporting of the disease, they spread misinformation and fear.
They had the opportunity to nip the public hysteria in the
bud by being calm, sensible and rational. Instead they chose
to encourage it with inaccurate and fear-mongering report-
age. At the height of the first wave of fear the *Sun* led on one
front page with a story about the disease featuring a
prominent quote from a Liverpool publican saying: 'AIDS
is a real threat to the fabric of society. A lot of ordinary
people are going to catch something from beer glasses. We
don't want gays on the premises. Let's face it, they're the
ones that caused it' (5 February 1985). This was at a time
when the medical authorities were desperately trying to
assure people that AIDS could not be contracted from
ordinary social contact. There was nothing in the *Sun* story

to contradict what the publican had said. Indeed, a few days later the unrepentant *Sun* was headlining: 'Cough can spread AIDS' (February 1985).

The death of Rock Hudson provoked the next wave of hysteria from the newspapers. It had all the elements that the tabloids thrive upon: AIDS, homosexuality, profligate sex and an opportunity to knock the famous from their pedestal. Mr Hudson's life was presented as one of un-bridled promiscuity. Hundreds of unnamed 'friends', 'con-fidantes', 'insiders', 'eye-witnesses' and so on were reported, each with something more terrible than the last to say about the deceased. The connection between gays and dangerous, irresponsible promiscuity was firmly estab-lished.

The *Sun*, in the meantime, was still providing its readers with 'expert' comment on the situation – like US psycholo-gist Paul Cameron who was given space to say: 'All homo-sexuals should be exterminated to stop the spread of AIDS. We ought to stop pussy-footing around' (March 1985).

With 'information' on this level is there any wonder that, in the public mind, AIDS took on the characteristics of some kind of medieval plague sent to punish the wicked?

Newspaper commentators like George Gale, Paul Johnson, George Gordon, Jean Rook, Ray Mills, John Junor and many others were quick to jump on the blame-the-gays bandwagon. Vituperative and quite unforgiveable tirades were directed at the gay community by these people. George Gale, writing in the *Sunday Mirror*, said that gay men were 'killers' because they had infected 'innocent' (i.e., nongay) men, women and children. John Junor in his *Sunday Express* column vilified gay people in the most extreme terms week after week. Calls have been made by many of these Fleet Street 'opinion-formers' for the repeal of the 1967 Sexual Offences Act. This relentless call to hatred resulted in public opinion, which had gradually been turning in favour of gays, taking a lurch in the opposite direction.

Readers' letters to the national press (which are, of course, carefully selected to echo the extremist editorial opinions) were almost wholly anti-gay. Repeatedly they called for 'tougher action' to be taken against homosexuals, for people with AIDS to be banished to an island, to be branded, imprisoned or, in one case, in the *Daily Express*: 'Burning is too good for them. Bury them in a pit and pour on quick lime' (13 December 1987). Opposing points of view are either screened out of correspondence columns completely or tacked on to the end as a minority after-thought.

All these elements, when taken together, spell bad news for gay people. The homophobia which had been valiantly beaten back since 1967 has now once again been given 'respectability' by the press and government. After all, if those readers who are already violently antipathetic towards homosexuals see gay people described in de-humanizing terms in newspapers, why should they not put their hostility into action? As when Ray Mills wrote in the *Star*:

Insidiously, almost imperceptibly, the perverts have got the heterosexual majority with their backs against the wall (the safest place, actually ...). The freaks proclaim their twisted morality almost nightly on TV ... where will it end? Where it may end, of course, is by natural causes. The woofters have had a dreadful plague visited upon them, which we call AIDS, and which threatens to decimate their ranks. Since the perverts offend the laws of God and nature, is it fanciful to suppose that one or both is striking back? ... Little queers or big queers, Mills has had enough of them all — the lesbians, bisexuals and transsexuals, the hermaphrodites and the catamites and the gender benders who brazenly flaunt their sexual failings to the disgust and grave offence of the silent majority. A blight on them all says Mills. (9 September 1986)

Gay monitoring groups have reported a significant increase in violence against homosexuals. Is there any wonder when our national press appears to encourage such activities? From the verbal queer-bashing of Ray Mills, George Gale and John Junor, it is only a small step to the physical variety which many gay men know so well. And there seems to be no one who is prepared to speak up for our interests in a sustained and sympathetic way. Our voices – with rare exceptions – are denied access to the mainstream press.

We were promised that the 'new technology' would make the production of newspapers cheaper and, therefore, lead to a more diversified press. The trail was blazed by Eddie Shah and his *Today*. For a while it seemed that Britain at last had a politically left-of-centre tabloid – albeit brought to fruition by the virtual destruction of the print unions. Within eighteen months the Sunday edition of *Today* had died and the daily edition had fallen into the clutches of Rupert Murdoch. In London Robert Maxwell tried to challenge the stranglehold of the right-wing *London Evening Standard* with a liberal alternative, the *London Daily News*. Within five months it, too, was closed, leaving its proprietor millions of pounds poorer. A left-wing alternative to the Sunday scandal-sheets, the *News on Sunday*, staggered from one crisis to another, until it, too, fell by the wayside.

And just when one would have thought it impossible for tabloid newspapers to sink any further into the mire of sexism, trivia and the glorification of macho values, the *Star* had a brief flirtation with the pornographic *Sunday Sport* and reached a level of filth that would have been unthinkable for a national newspaper a few short years ago. But, it seems, the tabloid-buying public was reaching saturation point and as the new-style *Star* lost readers hand over fist, Express Newspapers pulled it back and severed the alliance with the porn market.

On the credit side, the *Guardian, Observer, Independent*

and *Daily Mirror* seem to be secure and provide just about the only non-Tory voices in the whole of Britain's national press.

This concentration of the press in the hands of ruthless tycoons is bad news for democracy. It is particularly bad news for gays whose voices will continue to be stifled while lies about us are piled high for political gain.

Most European countries have some kind of right-of-reply mechanism or right-to-privacy legislation, and it seems to work well. Britain has only the ineffective and oft-derided Press Council which is funded by the newspapers themselves. Like most 'self-regulating bodies', the Press Council frequently falls foul of its paymasters' anger. Often its findings are ignored or ridiculed. Several unsuccessful attempts have been made to bring in legislation to control the excesses of the press. However, the tabloid press in this country has become notorious for its lies, distortions and merciless harryings of private individuals and has never been lower in public esteem. Unless it learns self-restraint it will eventually find itself the subject of dangerous legislation. The newspaper barons must then take the blame for yet another serious disservice to the democratic process.

CHAPTER FOURTEEN
Westminster barbarism
Andrew Lumsden

There are two – no, I think in a moment I shall list three – wonderfully well-kept secrets about the affections and momentary physical exchanges which the Hungarian Benkert taught us from 1869 to call homosexuality. Political secrets. Thanks to a British government's efforts between 1986 and 1988 to prevent publication anywhere in the world of the Peter Wright memoir *Spycatcher*, the world now knows that of all democracies Britain is the land of the desperately hidden *official secret*. It will surprise no one to hear that if we rootle about in the Palace of Westminster we can uncover mysteries about the homosexual *eros*, and the hatred of it, which are never admitted to the British people – and because never to us, never to anyone.

I could be referring, if I chose, to personal scandals within the Houses of Lords or Commons. There is the fact, for which in itself I am as sad as any of us is about any premature decline and death, that in 1985 Lord Avon, a junior minister in one of Mrs Thatcher's administrations and the son and heir of Sir Anthony Eden, Conservative Prime Minister in succession to Sir Winston Churchill in the 1950s, became one of the earlier gay men in Britain to die exhibiting the debilities of AIDS. This one human tragedy, in all the catalogue of AIDS-related tragedies among all kinds and races of people, was not itself successfully kept

secret at the time, but *has been made a secret since*. In all the
moralizing about 'traditional values' and 'conservative
values' which has poured from Conservatism in Britain, as
from the Right elsewhere, since AIDS came to be heard of
and feared, the recollection of Lord Avon has been des-
patched to oblivion. He did not, he does not, fit a preferred
belief in the petty party-politics of Britain in the 1980s that
Left 'extremism' is somehow 'responsible' for AIDS,
somehow inseparable from what are actually the millennial
claims to a New Deal, in place of the old Raw Deal, by
those of us who now call ourselves, retrospectively in
history no less than while still alive, lesbians or gay men.

   Or I could be referring to the circumstantial evidence that
has slowly come to light, but *not* to be popularly appreciated, that Lord Rosebery, the Liberal Prime Minister of
1895–6 (in succession to Gladstone), who died in the
1920s, was deliberately saved from ruinous homosexual
scandal by the deflection of public attention to Wilde. The
Douglas (Marquesses of Queensberry) family remember
Rosebery as having been enamoured in the 1880s–90s of
the young Francis Douglas, elder brother of Lord Alfred
Douglas, Oscar Wilde's lover. Francis killed himself in
1894 'in the shadow of a suppressed homosexual scandal in
which the Prime Minister Lord Rosebery was implicated'
(Montgomery Hyde, 1984).

   Francis's death drew a nervous and wishing-to-retreat
Wilde back into the agonized inner tensions and feuds of
the Douglas family, whose nearly deranged head, the
Marquess of the 'Queensberry Rules' of boxing, threatened
exposure of Rosebery no less than of Wilde himself. When
Wilde refused in 1895 to flee to France from the coming
government prosecution for consenting adult homosexual
acts, the law officers of the Crown set themselves, as
documented evidence proves (Ellman, 1987), to make such
an example of him in court and in his prison punishment
(from whose effects Wilde died, as Reading Gaol's gover-
nor predicted he would, in 1900) that the press would be

deluded into thinking that no energy, *and no person*, was being spared in the effort to expose homosexual 'vice'. Dare I say that the Rothschilds too, into whose family Rosebery had married, and whose English branch were then the acknowledged world leaders of the tremendous fight to moderate nineteenth-century European and Russian anti-semitism, were spared a huge embarrassment by the state deflection of power against Wilde? That today's Chief Rabbi of Britain and the Commonwealth, Sir Immanuel Jakobovits, might pause, and be more modest, and recall a sacrifice the gay writer Wilde involuntarily made for Israel, before he calls for homosexuality to 'be brought [back] within the penal code', as he did in the London *Independent* newspaper in November 1987?[1] Sir Immanuel became Lord Immanuel in early 1988, openly raised to be an upper house legislator of the UK as reward for his advocacy of Inquisitorial approaches to sexuality.

But instructive and absorbing as these fragments of the under-publicized homosexual history of Westminster are, illuminations of how the known can so efficaciously be rendered unknown, it is some far more sweeping political secrets, particularly of Britain, but also of the West as a whole, that I want to touch on. Here they are in chrono-logical order. I'm sorry they are so assertive, which is not only for reasons of compression, though I will hope to do *some* amplifying, but also because the long politics of Western homophobia are not easily or often reviewed in short order, in one place. I should forewarn also that these are the assessments of a political journalist, true to history as I hope, but proceeding out of commonplace observation that few who exercise, or ever have exercised, power care to have motives or consequences pitilessly described.

●   It is to the thirteenth–fourteenth-century despair of the Papacy and its apologists over the Western church's finances, temporal authority, and 'belief', that the Christian 'hard line' on marriage and on the 'blasphemy' of male homosexuality can most helpfully be traced; not to *Leviticus* and/or St Paul, those fainter antecedents forever dusted down before us by both reformers and traditionalists in Christianity and Judaism. A church on the run, before Islam and before the self-interest of monarchs – and in the face of economies booming before the Black Death, wealth-creation in which it had little share – could and did desperately go 'extremist' in its theological definitions of 'heresy', sexual and otherwise, and in prosecuting its claim to have sole voice in the giving and dissolving of marriage contracts (a most profitable monopoly, sheerly in money as well as obviously, as Henry VIII would testify, in influence over the high and the low born). Even if attention to the extraordinary 'racking-up' of sexual doctrine in the century when 'the Holy Land' was lost by Western Europe and which ended, almost incredibly, with the Papacy's loss of Rome itself, is stressed only as a corrective to what people suppose to be the key precipitating moments of institutionalized Western homophobia, that corrective is essential to and yet largely missing from all modern discussion of why the world should be in such a pickle about ... 'GAYS!'

● I don't ignore that homophobic attitudes and practices (like, it should be said, countervailing homophiliac attitudes) are to be found or inferred at periods, or in cultures beyond the reach of those aboriginally Near Eastern evolutions, 'the Religions of the Book', but I repeat that the weird terms of debate in the modern First World – and by cultural/economic impact, almost everywhere – are dominated by unstated premises that were most critically formulated and insisted upon during a superlative and hysterical crisis, not a settled regimen, of Western Christendom, some seven centuries ago.

The principal transmitting agent of what was, and ought to have remained, the aberrant slough of Khomeini-style thirteenth-century clerical xenophobia and would-be sexual totalitarianism – aberration of a tin-pot Atlantic-fringe culture which was simultaneously frightening itself to death over 'the Jews', and 'the Saracens', and (with justice) 'the Mongols' (all three linked to cultures of higher learning), and which soon would be frightening itself to death over 'witchcraft' – was Britain. Here we reach the great British political secret concerning homosexuality, the fact so plain that like the nose on the face, it can't be seen, unless by the nationals of other countries (the 'cold' English, the 'English sexual hypocrisy'); the fact which politically speaking most profoundly underlies the 'English-style politicized gay-bashing' by press and politicians in Britain in the 1980s. (The phrase I quote was used by heterosexual British reporter Denis MacShane in August 1987 when he was following the French Front National leader, Jean-Marie Le Pen, on the campaign trail in Brittany, and saw how even the most enthusiastic of the right-wing politician's Breton audiences became 'embarrassed' when Le Pen tried rabble-rousing against *pédés*, i.e. gays).[2]

For some four centuries, through the sixteenth to the twentieth centuries, England (subsequently Great Britain) shipped criminal proscription of gays across the globe. To put it constitutionally, Westminster, originally as the English monarch with *ad hoc* advisers in Parliament, later as sovereign body with direct rule over the British Isles and dependent territories overseas, sent out statute law, sent out British police chiefs, and sent out British-trained judges to dominate sentencing policy. Through successive maritime empires, from the earliest American settlements up to maximum territorial expansion by 1939, England furthered and entrenched medieval canonical extremism on the subject of male homosexuality into legal systems affecting what had become, by the lifetimes of our parents or grandparents, a quarter of the populations of the globe.

Neither France, nor Spain, nor Holland, nor Italy – and certainly not Germany, the horrors of whose Third Reich 'pink triangle' concentration camp deaths are coming to be a cover-up and distraction from Britain's record – acquired such planetary power within modern recollection. None had so much muscle with which to be civilized or to be barbaric. Even before the Victorian age, the *Code Napoléon* in France detached the 'moral' reproofs still levelled against homosexual affections from actual law enforcement. There is no anachronism, even though there is of course no helping what was done, in suggesting that *if institutionalized and state-backed homophobia is no less a human rights crime than institutionalized misogyny, xenophobia or racism*, then to the British Empire falls an equivalent of the burden the Germanies shoulder about anti-semitism. In terms of world leadership, in terms of exported attitudes, 'freedom-loving Englishmen', Britons in general, have done more to press for a Solution to the 'homosexual problem' than the inhabitants of any other European state.

There is no complete hiding of truth, however strenuously every eye may be averted. Can anyone wonder that *before* AIDS, no less than during it, the *soi-disant* 'moral' opinion-formers of media and politics in contemporary British public life so notoriously denounced again and again some aspect of 'the gays' and 'the lesbians'? Psychopathologically, it is a picking at guilts they cannot endure to face, cannot shed; just as the white racists of the Deep South could never forego more talk and more tales about 'the niggers'. Culturally, it is the quasi-conscious perpetuation of something that they could quite literally and accurately, however shamefully, call a patriotic tradition, a particularly British *pride*. (The language almost revolts against printing 'pride', but no matter how vast the shame that lurks beneath exultant 'queer-baiting', and is forever hinted at in Britain by the fascination that Oscar Wilde exerts over right-wing, not left-wing, writers, the unceasing note struck by British 'critics' of liberation homosexuality *is* one of pride, pride in sustaining the 'Anglo-Saxon' attitude.)

Irony of historical ironies: from the English Reformation, when Henry VIII threw off the medieval Papacy's pretensions to regulate all marriage, but absorbed intact into the Crown Courts, in 1533, that same Papacy's pretension to punish detected male homosexual acts, it was 'no Popery' England which grew to be the principal European secular vengeance upon, secular Inquisition into, homosexuality. The nearest lands to be permanently affected were the colonies of Wales (direct rule by 'Westminster' since the thirteenth century), Scotland (eighteenth century), and Ireland (eleventh century, but most particularly from early nineteenth century). Further afield, the United States in their English colonial form pre-1776 were made a recipient of the *psychopathia sexualis* of the Middle Ages (Georgia's state law against sodomy was upheld as recently as 1986 by the US Supreme Court, which quoted English precedent to support itself). So was Canada, so was Australasia (New Zealand shaking off the inheritance, repealing criminalization of adult gays only in 1986). So were parts of Africa (South Africa is still arraigning, most appallingly, Black gay men). So were parts of Asia (consenting gay adults were still jailed there in 1987). So were parts of the Middle East: most notably Israel, whose criminal statute against male homosexuality was an import from Britain, during the British Mandate over Palestine in the 1930s, and was not, as most Israelis might suppose, a direct re-imposition by the Knesset of the sexual *mores* apparently codified when rabbis were first devised during the Israelis' 'Babylonish exile' some 2500 years ago. The Knesset at last threw out the English law on homosexuality in March 1988.

• And lastly, and most briefly, my third 'political secret' about homosexuality. No one will ever know, but it is a question whether the gay and lesbian liberation movements as they re-formed and were retriggered in New York in summer 1969, to be disseminated across the continental USA and abroad – to Britain by late 1970 – could have taken the shape and language they now did, or had their particular impetus, if it had not been for former British imperial pressure. The pressure which had led, on the one hand, and famously, to a constitutional separation of church and state in the USA, following as every high school kid is taught, a revolt against England; and which led, on the other hand, infamously, to American police persecution of homosexuals in the name, at root, of religious law, in conformity to the old colonizer's custom.

Jewish culture, despite *Leviticus*, does have its haunting story of an admired affection between men, one that many generations have read as homoerotic: the relationship of Jonathan and David. Greek culture in the space of just a few synchronous years of the sixth-century BCE produced (besides all that came later or was to be supposed in Homer before) the revered lesbian poetry of Sappho (nearly all lost) and the true Athenian tale of the male lovers Harmodias and Aristogeiton, tyrannicides recalled for centuries as heroes of the state. On British culture rests, quite uniquely so far as I am aware, the obloquy of having produced, across a span of 600 years, not just the principal native Western European tale of the dire fate which may all-too-probably (*sub-text*: deservedly) await those who 'give in' to homosexual desires – not just the *principal* tale, that of King Edward II, but the *two* principal tales, the second, of course, being Wilde's. And without any significant compensating 'positive image' (like those of Sappho, of David and Jonathan, of Harmodias and Aristogeiton).

I imagine sometimes that, perhaps as a sibling enterprise to the European Court of Human Rights in Strasbourg, professional historians might organize a press. It would create, in plural translation, histories for the European classroom, to redress the balance of those narrowly nationalist ones through which the past is generally conveyed (so far as it is conveyed at all) to the older pupil. Let us call it 'The Frank–Wallenberg Press', in memory of the Swede (Raoul Wallenberg) who in the 1940s saved thousands of

Jewish people from the Nazis in Budapest, though they were not his co-religionists, and who disappeared into the Soviet *gulag* in 1945 after Stalin had overrun Hungary. And of Anne Frank, of the *Diaries*, who it seems increasingly to be conceded was growing up lesbian when the betrayal of her Jewish family's hiding-place among gentiles in Amsterdam put her on to the death-trains.

'Transnational histories': I see volumes named not after countries and dynasties, nor after revolutions or epochs, but after those essentials that have been in common. *The Horse*, say: on whose back after all, in an illustrated text, any of us may travel together from the Dorian Greeks to the agrarian and industrial revolutions, via feudatories and chivalry, not forgetting the postal service from the Mongol network to the Pony Express, the 'horsepower' of the motor car. *Marriage*, through whose variegating laws and customs, at least from Republican Rome, the young of both sexes might watch the changing fortunes of women, of ideas of childhood, of inheritance and dynastic greeds, and altering meanings of 'the family'. And, the most daring volume, if any dared do it, *Homosexuality*.

All that I have already sketchily tried to propose in this essay, and what I am about to say of the odiously British tales of Edward II and Oscar Wilde, could be draft notes to Strasbourg for the assistance of my imaginary editors of my imaginary Frank–Wallenberg Press's imaginary European volume on *Homosexuality*. Pellucid, calm, fully-sourced prose would replace, of course, the present speediness and, I fear, evident anger at my own country's unselfknowingness. Good! To the historian the calm, to the oppressed – at any rate, to the political journalist condemned to witness daily suffering – the outrage. There is so thick a public carapace of ignorance laid over the instruments and causative moments of European homophobia, this distinctive homophobia which is so like (and so intrinsically connected to) the now derided horror of witches and witchcraft, that even the loudest bangings and shoutings from beneath the shell emerge still only as faint murmurs, ghostly knockings, *séance* rappings.

The downfall of the English King Edward II (1284–?1327), and the downfall of Oscar Wilde (1854–1900) are more alike than can be to the credit of any country, given that over half a millennium separated the men in life; given that the one lived in a society whose maps showed Jerusalem as the centre of a small known world, while the other could have met the boy Einstein, and knew London as the globe's 'capital'. Before turning to the minatory force of their legends, the *Strewelpeter*-like power that each story had, at the height, to terrorize with a 'negative image' of homosexuality, notice (for all the natural dissimilarities) the uncanny points of resemblance between the 'stars' of the two evil stories *in life*.[3] I draw, for Edward, on the marvellous archival work of formal historians over the past century or so.[4]

The Plantagenet Edward, of mingled Norman–Hispanic descent, and the Irish Protestant Ascendancy Oscar, were both impressively big men in the eyes of their short-statured contemporaries. Both were humorous (to put it mildly, about Wilde). Both physically courageous. Both largely indifferent to the stereotypical masculine pursuits of their day (Wilde's jokes against exercise, Edward's lazy disinclination for the hunt, the war, the tournament). Both were fascinated by the stage (if we are to believe, in Edward's case, the furious comments on his actor friends). Both – and here we seem to touch on the profoundest resemblance, so great that Edward II's and Wilde's could almost be one tale told in two instalments, unobserved though this appears to have been in all the vast literature about Wilde – *both* were married men, each the father of two sons. In *both* cases, in the end, the wives removed the sons from the father.[5] The two Thames-side scandals both occurred at high-water marks of pan-European 'concern' about homosexuality. And it may be remarked, whether it is to be held of interest, or neither here nor there, that

Wilde after prison felt himself, and called himself, a 'king' in exile.

I have spoken of the concealed Westminster connection of the Oscar Wilde tragedy, how his capture (and captivation) by the quarrelling Queensberry family were brutally used by our country's parliamentarians in order to shield one of their own. An inquiry at Westminster in the 1330s, presided over by Edward II's son Edward III, 'failed' to find out quite what had become of the deposed Edward II at his last-known 1327 place of imprisonment, Berkeley Castle. I put the apostrophes round 'failed' for then certainly, and now commonly, so sensitive an inquiry comes up with the answers most desired by the head of government. Edward II was buried in the presence of the royal family, after lying in state with the face exposed, in Gloucester Abbey (now Cathedral) in 1327. Everyone supposed him to have been murdered in the Berkeley dungeon (still shown to visitors today), and yet one of the men named in rumour, from that day till now, as an assassin sent to Berkeley by the temporary regency, a certain Maltravers, placidly took a seat in Parliament in the 1340s, where Edward III could see him daily from the throne.[6]

An odd document was found in France in the nineteenth century. It purported to be a letter to Edward III by Fieschi, an historically authenticated early fourteenth-century secretary to the Papacy (then resident in Avignon, not Rome), informing the king of the recent death of his father Edward II in Italy c. 1335. Edward II's escape from Berkeley Castle in 1327, subsequent wanderings, and eventual quiet retirement under Papal protection, are described. Legends of miracle escape accrete time and again around celebrity deaths, from Charlemagne to Hitler. But to the best of my knowledge professional medievalists remain perplexed about this one, not knowing whether to trust the Fieschi letter or the flatly contradictory Berkeley murder tradition. Definitely, authentically, one of Edward II's younger half-brothers, the Earl of Kent, believed his brother to have survived. We know, because Kent was killed for wandering the country, seeking Edward.[7]

Another cover-up? Not only the most recent, but *both* the most ringing British 'gay scandals' so expertly tampered with in their years of origin that in the modern, Wildean, instance the hair's-breadth escape of a Victorian Prime Minister stays largely unacknowledged, and in the other, medieval Edwardian, instance *the real chance that there was no truth whatever in the story of Edward II's homosexuality* remains unexamined?[8] It's possible. I've already spoken of Wilde and Rosebery. Wilde, so great, so familiar, a figure, occludes the older scandal, previously the best known in English history and the English language. Let's glance further, very briefly, at Edward II. He may not have died at Berkeley (the exposed face on the bier would, I take it, have been shrouded with linen, like an old face with toothache, so it's not inconceivable that the 'royals' could have got away with a 'ringer').[9] He may not have been assassinated at the age of 43 by the insertion 'of a heated soldering-iron in the fundament', as the tale dating back at least to the 1340s has it. And — I will have to ask the reader to take my word for it — there is *nothing* in the record of his undoubted vast promotions of Piers Gaveston and Hugh le Despenser, and undoubted vast affection for the former, which destroys a hypothesis that they were all three 'smeared' ('negative image' of homosexuality) as sodomites, the king especially as a 'passive' one (that death by anal rape, social vengeance, at Berkeley).[10]

Edward II was a poor ruler, though conceivably an unusually amiable one until his last years. His defeat by Robert the Bruce, the King of Scots, at Bannockburn in 1314 was a greater loss of English face, and loss to English aristocratic pockets (ransoms), than anything in living memory.[11] We shouldn't be surprised if, knowing his incompetent father to be alive, the youthful Edward III would have held a murder inquiry (a son could do no less), 'found' nothing conclusive, 'let' the death-story thrive, evaded hideous revenges. He could have known, as moderns and as the Tudors who were riveted by Edward's story (not only Marlowe, who wrote the tragedy of *Edward II, c.* 1592) could not, or at any rate show they *do* not, that the whole attack on Edward II's relationship as king with Piers Gaveston coincided precisely (1307–12) with the first great pan-European consequence of the new Papal hard-line on gays as heretics: the destruction of the international Order of Knights Templar on charges including ritualized homosexual practices.[12]

What do we learn? That 'virile', big, philoprogenitive, married men are at the centre of both the major English homosexual tales, even though one is as likely to have been heterosexual as the other certainly was homosexual, using both terms broadly. That imputed 'effeminacies' (derelictions from *beau idéal* imperatives laid upon 'real men') are common to both. That something in the 'collective cultural unconscious' of medieval Europe fomented, and of unreconstructed 'Anglo-Saxonry' prolongs, a refusal to examine either story fully in history. And – I suggest – that a habit of lying, politically-purposive lying, flowing from Westminster out, perhaps for as much as seven centuries, is our nation's peculiar gift to the world *koine* (culture, sorority, fraternity) of lesbians and gay men.

Those who carefully watched the 1987–8 passage into law at Westminster of the Clause 28 amendment to the Local Government Bill, prohibiting 'promotion' of homosexuality by elected officials though they are answerable to local electorates, and allowing *no* exemption for civil libertarian attempts to protect homosexuals from 'traditional' inculcated animosities, saw politically-purposive lying about homosexuals once more at full flood in the 'heart' of English democracy. Nearly all the evidence supposed to justify the amendment had been discredited, and was known to have been discredited, before either the upper or the lower house debated and finally approved the

Clause. The *idea* of the Clause was imported from a Republican initiative in the US Congress – an instance of English cultural homophobia exported long ago, absorbed, and now re-imported. The British government refused to back a first 'backbench' attempt at the amendment in late 1986, then supported it in late 1987. Why? Because the Conservative administration could be 'seen to be doing something', even though – as almost always in English political procedures in reference to homosexuality – about a fiction.

Notes

1 *Independent*, 24 November 1987. Besides Rosebery's seeming emotional involvement with Francis Douglas, his Rothschild marriage brought him into contact with the Aston Clinton mid Victorian country household where there was a 'gay squire', Cyril Flower, also married to one of the Rothschild girls (see Miriam Rothschild (1983), *Dear Lord Rothschild*, London: Hutchinson).

2 *New Statesman*, 28 August 1987.

3 *Strewelpeter*: nineteenth-century illustrated German book of tales for children, inculcating good and/or safe behaviour with horrendous examples of disobedient children.

4 English-language historians only, I fear. The reign of Edward II, as a 'backwater' perhaps or apparently lamentable lapse in the 'virile' procession of Edwards I and III, has been something of a speciality of women historians in the twentieth century.

5 Constance Wilde had two sons by Oscar; Isabella of France two by Edward (and a daughter; Edward II also had an illegitimate son, I have been informed by another amateur – lesbian – student of the period, though I have not seen that authoritatively stated for myself). Constance changed the surnames of her sons to Holland, had custody after Oscar's imprisonment, and in the end did not let him see them. Isabella took the future Edward III to France against her husband's orders, and returned with an invasion force which deposed him.

6 'Everyone supposed': the most circumstantial account, which the author claimed to have had first-hand from a murderer, appeared in a work by Baker of Swynebroke in the 1340s–50s.

7 Perhaps there is an echo of Kent's hapless wanderings in *King Lear*. Shakespeare could have known of them, though he could not, any

more than Christopher Marlowe, have known about Fieschi's letter, whether the latter is to be relied upon, or will ever be shown to be a forgery of one period or another.

8 The openly gay and openly Christian Yale professor John Boswell (*Christian Attitudes, Social Tolerance, and Homosexuality* (Chicago: Chicago University Press, 1980), though he gives no extended consideration to the Edward II story, finds the tradition that Edward II was homosexual likely to be correct. It must at once be admitted that Boswell is incomparably better-equipped than the present writer to indicate a sensible view, but he doesn't contemplate the advantages to Edward's domestic opponents of a homosexual 'slur' and the fact that the 'slur' was being used across Europe, above all so that the Templars might be robbed of their 200-year-old accumulation of properties and the proceeds of having been bankers to the monarchies. Archbishops, even popes, were being labelled 'sodomites', with and without specifically homosexual overtones, in the same years. Boswell has been the pioneer of inquiry into formulaic medieval evolutions about marriage and homosexuality.

9 If there are remains within the Gloucester tomb, modern forensics might determine whether they consort well or ill with what is known of Edward II in life, and said of his manner of death.

10 Too much detail would be required even in a note to support this claim. I'll mention only that Gaveston's and Despenser's fathers were both 'royal servants' of Edward I, and the sons were trained up by Edward I to be equally loyal servitors to his heir, essentially in the 'fending off' of baronial pretensions to be 'about the king's person'.

11 A similar disaster (Courtrai) befell French 'chivalry' in the same period when facing 'inferiors'. The feudal levy did tend to fiasco when on 'away ground' dealing with desperate people. See Vietnam lately.

12 The Templars were destroyed at the instigation of Edward II's father-in-law, Philip IV of France, a sovereign bankrupt. The trials, examinations (tortures), and 'defamation' persisted from 1307 until the Papacy at last consented to dismemberment in 1312. Edward II succeeded Edward I in 1307 and his 'favourite' Gaveston was murdered by a group of nobles (after a highway kidnap) in 1312. The only time in English history when, under certain restraints, the Inquisition was allowed to operate in England was in those years.

References

Ellman, R. (1987), *Oscar Wilde* (London: Hamish Hamilton).

Montgomery Hyde, H. (1984), *Lord Alfred Douglas* (London: Methuen).

CHAPTER FIFTEEN
Gays and Marxism
Bill Marshall

Whether expressed in election victories by right-wing parties, or in a general ideological shift within the consensus in favour of the liberal market economy, Marxism in Western Europe seems to be in dramatic retreat as a political and intellectual reference point. In addition, in Britain in June 1987, the code expression 'Loony Left' and the political polarizations it implies indicate a breakdown in the potential unity of groups – including sexual minorities as well as the different sections of the working class – hostile to Thatcherism. An understanding of what has gone wrong since, for example, the 1960s, requires an *historical* investigation of the nature of the emergence of a gay political movement. What I propose to begin to do in this essay is to investigate that generation and particularly the theories and assumptions concerning sexual politics that were available to it; but also to address the relationship between (politically engaged) *intellectuals* and the rest of society.

In the 1960s in Britain, higher education became available (or rather, the development of capitalist production allowed it to become available) to relatively large numbers of people for the first time, with a large influx of students from the lower middle classes, as well as a proportion of working-class origin. The aftermath of the Stonewall riots of 1969, with the development of a gay political movement in many Western countries, was both a reaction to, and made possible by, the social changes and political activities of earlier in the decade: in general, a hostility among the students of 1968 towards traditional parties of the Left, be they Harold Wilson's Labour Party or those groups, Stalinist or Trotskyist, which proclaimed a Marxist heritage; a 'sexual revolution' that had made sex more visible and discussed, but which at the same time had been limited to a greater availability of partners for heterosexual men; the struggle against the Vietnam War or for Black civil rights, which was both a lesson in politics for a whole generation and also an experience that underlined the silence surrounding 'gay rights', in that awareness of what a gay politics might be was non-existent.

By the early 1970s, certain strands of gay political activity had emerged: an emphasis on the struggle for 'rights' of 'gays' as an identified sexual (analogous with racial) minority within the status quo of property relations; an emphasis on the fundamentally revolutionary/dissident position of being gay; an emphasis on personal liberation with wider political pretensions – 'the personal is political'. These positions, sometimes distinct, sometimes interlinked, are clearly inimical to Marxism. They lack a *global* project, whether political (the transformation of class society) or intellectual (a theory of historical development, and within it, the oppression of gays); and they eschew a call to arms against capitalism. What is relevant for our purpose is to examine the positions and arguments of the group that did attempt to set up a dialogue with the Marxist tradition, and that is *Gay Left*. Indeed, it is worth recalling that the foundation of *Gay Left* in 1975, as expressed in its first editorial, was an attempt to move away from the limitations of both personalist and consciousness-raising groups, as well as, of course, the capitalist values of the commercial scene and press. The Collective's theoretical language, attempting as it did 'to draw the links between the family, the oppression of women and gay people, and the class structure of society' (*Gay Left*, vol. 1 (autumn 1975), p. 1), displays certain consistencies in its understanding of Marxism across individual contributions. Its preoccupations centre around the relationship between base and superstructure within Marxist theory; that is, between the economic and material activities society needs to survive, and the domain of beliefs, prejudices, 'common sense', and general culture:

> The sum total of these relations of production constitutes the economic structure of society, the real foundation, on which rises a legal and political superstructure and to which correspond definite forms of social consciousness. The mode of production of material life conditions the social, political and intellectual life process in general. (Marx, 1969, p. 503)

If this is so, how can we explain superstructural phenomena such as 'sexism' or homophobia? How did the category 'homosexual' arise at a particular stage in the development of capitalist society? Despite its awareness of the material reality of the familial institution, *Gay Left*'s major theoretical concern is with ideology, and it deploys its analyses across five guiding notions which seek to break with previous 'Marxisms':

1   Hostility to a 'functionalist' view of the problem, that is, one which assumes 'a simple functional fit between the needs of capitalism and the organisation of sexuality' and also 'a one-to-one fit between intention and actual effect' (Weeks, 1980, p. 14). The policing of 'homosexuals' under capitalism must not be seen as an 'intentional' result of a 'conspiracy' perpetrated by the ruling class.
2   Hostility to 'economism'. In a collective statement, this is decisively rejected for its mechanistic view of history, its passivity and reformism, for the way in

which it conceives political struggle entirely in
economic terms, and for its neglect of the highly
political domains of ideology and culture. At the
heart of economism 'is a too narrow interpretation of
the "economic base", and a subordination of a full
scientific understanding to what is essentially a topo-
graphical metaphor – "the base/superstructure"'.
The statement owes much to the work on ideology
and the superstructures undertaken by the French
Marxist philosopher Louis Althusser:

> Societies are not pieces of clockwork but are multi-
> layered formations in which the *economic* is
> mediated through complex *social* relations, *ideo-*
> *logical* forms, and *political* practices ... This is
> relevant to the struggles of feminists and for gay
> liberation because it is at the ideological level that
> most of our oppression as gays is expressed, and
> not on the economic level. (*Gay Left*, vol. 5 (winter
> 1977), p. 2)

3 An uneasy relationship with the original Marxist
   texts, and in particular the text which might offer gay
   Marxists some specific guidance: Engels's *The Origin
   of the Family, Private Property and the State.* Jeffrey
   Weeks (1975) criticizes this for assuming the
   'natural' biological basis of social roles such as child-
   care, for its bias towards heterosexuality, and for its
   assumption

> that the 'personal' is natural and given, and that
> once the constraints of a society dominated by the
> pursuit of profit are removed private life would
> spontaneously adjust itself to a higher stage of
> civilisation ... There is no concept, that is, of the
> need for conscious struggle to transform inter-
> personal relations as part of the transformations

necessary for the construction of a socialist society.

4   An uneasy relationship with the Soviet Union: not
    only that of Stalin, but also of Lenin. In the article on
    Engels, for example, Jeffrey Weeks quotes Lenin's
    famous remark to Clara Zetkin expressing his incred-
    ulity at German socialist women's groups spending
    their evenings discussing 'sex and marriage prob-
    lems'; similarly, it is pointed out that the Bolsheviks'
    early reforms included little positively to encourage
    homosexuality.
5   The relationship with non-Stalinist non-reformist
    Marxist parties, in particular with the International
    Marxist Group and Socialist Workers' Party who
    eventually did attempt to address the gay issue, was a
    fraught one.

It is possible with hindsight to understand the historically
constructed, indeed generational nature of *Gay Left*'s
agenda.
1 and 2   For example, 'functionalism' and 'economism'
come to be conflated within the *Gay Left* argument; and the
result is that the materialist baby is thrown out with the
reductivist ('capitalism creates homophobia') bath water.
There is a felt need for materialist analysis of gay oppression, but also a need to resist the pull of the previous
orthodoxy. The result is much talk of the economy and
sexuality being 'in articulation' 'in a complex way', and this
can be confusing. Thus, in the introduction to *Homosexuality: Power and Politics* (Gay Left Collective, 1980,
p. 8), the 'economistic' form of Marxism to be resisted saw
'homosexual oppression as a *necessary* effect of the capitalist organisation of patriarchy and the family'; but the
following essay speaks, in all its subtleties, of concern 'with
the life (and especially the sexual life) of the individual' as a
'*necessary* concomitant of the emergence of bourgeois
society' (p. 17).

Of course, the heritage of Stalinism is profoundly undialectical, with no understanding of the dynamic inter-action of processes, for it had proposed a crudely reflective model of base and superstructure, unacceptable to intel-lectuals, often disastrous politically. But Marxism was never an economism. To say that the vital material pro-duction of society itself, its forces and relations, are the ultimate determinant of human existence, society creating consciousness which creates society and so on, is not economism. What is absent from much *Gay Left* writing is an interest in the economy itelf; and indeed the logic of the Althusserian notion of the relative autonomy of the ideo-logical, particularly for isolated intellectuals, is to see ideology as the main oppression. This assumes that 'gays' can only be understood as 'gays' and not as gay coal-miners, gay teachers, gay unemployed, gay capitalists; indeed, it neglects the way in which class oppression intersects with the oppression of gays (for example, poverty restricting access to the commercial scene, or to resources which might facilitate dealings with the oppressive police apparatus; material constraints contributing to the pain of coming out, through fear of loss of job or accommodation.)

This is not to say that the oppression of homosexuality does not have its own complex and specific history which cannot simply be explained by capitalism. But it is the attention to *concrete material conditions*, and to the possi-bility of their transformation, that is the hallmark of the Marxist, however subtle and fascinating the mediations between base and superstructure may be. The anxiety about 'intentionality' suggests the assumption that only something with conscious intent can affect history; again, this suppresses the dialectical relationship of social being and consciousness.

The complexities of struggles should not disguise the fact that the realm of ideology requires certain material con-ditions to prevail. All things being equal, those elements in capitalist society survive that, at the very least, do not threaten its own survival. Thus, pre-capitalist ideologies and economies of gender are worked upon, modified, reinforced in a way which is broadly enabling of capitalist development: the role of unpaid domestic labour in weakening and dividing the working class, the role of the policing of alternative sexualities in the universalization of the nuclear family unit, and so on.[1] Such developments of course contain contradictions which might threaten the existing relations of production: capitalism is both eminently adaptable and eminently unstable. Post 1968 politics of gender have wavered between the possibilities of appropriation or destabilization.

3   Whatever Marx and Engels thought about homosexuality is beside the point; what matters is whether their own 'heterosexism', as we would now call it, structures and limits their analysis of the relationship between the history of production and gender roles. Jeffrey Weeks himself concedes the point that Engels, writing in the early 1880s, could not have done otherwise but to assume a heterosexual norm. However, another look at the text does not bear out the criticism that Engels is blind to the historical construction of his own analyses of the 'personal' (including his famous and rather endearing rhapsodies on 'individual sex-love').

Developing the analyses of Lewis Morgan's *Ancient Society* of 1877, Engels seeks to explain the material historical forces that have shaped the modern monogamous (bourgeois patriarchal) family, and, as the title of his work suggests, links its development to the emergence of private property, when the patrilineal system replaced mother right in order that the owners of wealth – the men – could pass that wealth on to their offspring and be sure of their paternity: this marked 'the world-historical defeat of the female sex' (Engels, 1940, p. 59). The question is, why was it the men who owned property (cattle, tools, hunting instruments)? The answer clearly lies in a division of labour between the sexes. Engels is extremely vague about the origins of this, but his pronouncement remains within an historical rather than a biological viewpoint: 'According to the division of labour within the family *at that time*, it was the man's part to obtain food and the instruments of labour necessary for that purpose' (p. 57; my emphasis). He devalues sexual relations between men (p. 68). However, he is not so transfixed by 'individual sex-love' that he does not see its varied durability, and thus he puts forward the basic socialist demand of easy dissolubility of marriage (p. 89). And, moreover, he shows himself aware of the construction of his own sexual preferences when speculating about future generations: 'When these people are in the world, they will care precious little what anybody today thinks they ought to do; they will make their own practice and their corresponding public opinion about the practice of each individual and that will be the end of it'; and, quoting Morgan, 'Should the monogamian family in the distant future fail to answer the requirements of society ... it is impossible to predict the nature of its successor' (p. 90).

To my mind, where Engels's argument is flawed is in his view of the proletarian family, where, because of the lack of property and the growing participation of the woman in the paid labour force, 'no basis for any male supremacy is left ... except, perhaps, for something of the brutality towards women that has spread since the introduction of monogamy' (p. 77). This is a big exception, and the phrase underestimates the power and persistence of ideological forces, such as assumptions concerning the 'naturalness' of motherhood or female passivity, as well as the specificities of women's oppression. Engels is in fact contradicting himself, for he none the less believes that present arrangements for both bourgeoisie and proletariat are founded on the 'open or concealed domestic slavery of the wife' (p. 79), and that the 'social revolution' will create 'the first condition for the liberation of the wife', which is 'to bring the whole female sex back into public industry [which] in turn demands the abolition of the monogamous family as the economic unit of society'.[2]

4   This brings us immediately to the view of the Soviet Union. The complaint in *Gay Left* (Weeks, 1975) is that the transformation of interpersonal relations is *equivalent* to other changes and struggles necessary for the construction of socialism. Engels's programme – to bring women fully into paid social labour – began to be realized in the early years of the Bolshevik regime. At the same time, all the oppressive Tsarist legislation on abortion, on the legal status of women, and on homosexuality, was swept away. Dr Grigorii Baktis, Director of the Moscow Institute of Social Hygiene, wrote in 1923:

> Concerning homosexuality, sodomy, and various other forms of sexual gratification, which are set down in European legislation as offences against public morality – Soviet legislation treats these exactly the same as so-called 'natural' intercourse. All forms of sexual intercourse are private matters. (Quoted in Lauritsen and Thorstad, 1974, p. 64)

Attempts were made to socialize child-care with free nursery facilities, as well as laundries at the workplace, and communal dining-rooms. However, Lenin did not underestimate the difficulties, nor the 'personal' nature, of this whole issue: 'This struggle will be a long one, and it demands a radical reconstruction both of social technique and of morals' (1973, p. 43). Trotsky, by this time already being edged into opposition, in 1925 addresses thus the All-Union Conference for the Protection of Mothers and Children:

> The human psyche does not develop evenly in all its parts. We are living in a political age, a revolutionary age, when working men and women are developing themselves in a struggle, forming themselves above all in a

revolutionary political way. And those cells of consciousness where family views and traditions reside, and the
attitude of one man to another, to woman, to child, and
so on – these cells often remain in the old form. The
revolution has not yet worked upon them ... And
therefore we shall go on for a long time observing that we
are constructing a new industry, a new society, but in the
field of personal relations much still remains from the
Middle Ages. (1973, pp. 42–3)

He is talking about sexism. He knows very well that
material interventions do not remove sexism overnight. But
unlike much of the post 1960s Left, he realized that the
establishment of certain minimum material conditions was
necessary for interpersonal relations to be able to be
transformed *for everyone*. This reminder of the hierarchy in
Marxism between the material and the ideological is
brought forcefully home when we consider the overriding
struggle fought by the early USSR.

The revolution in the 1920s was fighting for its life
against, first, foreign intervention and civil war, and then
for the vital oxygen that a revolution in the West, and
particularly Germany, would provide for the war-torn,
economically backward Soviet state. This had to be the top
priority: in the case of homosexual rights, the destruction
of the revolution would have meant the erasure of the gains
of 1917. Of course, the battle was lost, or suffered a
colossal setback, with the consolidation of the Soviet
bureaucracy later in the decade. In 1934 a penal law against
homosexual relations was introduced. At the same time,
highly conservative family policies were enacted, including
the illegalization of abortion. It is not our brief here to
dwell on the nature of Stalinism, but clearly the identification of reactionary sexual legislation with 'Communism'
was a major historical factor which influenced the post
1960s Left's attitude to Marxism and the history of revolution in the twentieth century. Since the early 1960s, a

Third-worldist fascination with Cuba gave way to a wholesale withdrawal of support by certain Western radicals because of the homophobic nature of the regime. The parallel with the early Soviet Union, even in its degraded Stalinist form, is a reminder that a gay Marxist might find himself/herself in the position of defending a Cuba or USSR against US imperialism and militarism *despite* those anti-gay policies.[3]

5 The most significant contribution of the post-Stonewall gay movement, and particularly of a group like Gay Left, was to put the issue of 'gay rights', 'sexual minorities' or whatever, visibly on the agenda of left-wing politics. The established parties had to respond, even if inadequately.[4]

The theories pertaining to 'homosexuality' and gender politics which entered departments of literature, film and sociology in British higher education in the early 1970s were very often French: Althusserian Marxism, with its notion of the 'relative autonomy' of ideological practices; Lacanian psychoanalysis, which contributed a theory of the construction of the subject to the emphasis on ideology; the historical analyses of Foucault, which investigate the deployment of power in medical, juridical, and sexual discourses, operating partly within Marxist frameworks (the emergence of bourgeois society, in fact the minimum material condition for the discursive phenomena Foucault describes), but rejecting global causalities in favour of an intricate local understanding of the workings of 'power'. These theoretical sophistications marked a reaction both to a previous Marxist orthodoxy, but also to the apparently non-revolutionary character of the working class.

However, a brief excursion into recent French history demonstrates the genesis, and indeed final results, of this shift in a concrete political context. Althusserianism, for example, whose success as a version of Marxist thought is largely due to its willingness to engage with the dominant intellectual preoccupations of the structuralist decade of the 1960s, has to be understood as both a justification to the (concentrated Parisian) world of intellectuals of the centrality of *theoretical* practice, and, with its removal of active human agents from history, as a way of dealing with the French Communist Party's (PCF's) fraught relationship with Stalinism.

In May 1968 in France, the baby-boom generation of university students, politicized by the Vietnam War and the confrontation with the rigid conservatism of Gaullism both in their place of study and in society at large, shook the regime to its foundations. The crisis was all the more acute in that the French working class staged the largest general strike in European history. However, the two movements did not in fact come together. The traditional left-wing parties were either completely bypassed, or, as with the PCF, struggled to defuse the situation and not to be overtaken on its Left. The crisis is thus also an ideological one, in which the Stalinist party, which dominated the culture of the French working class, was exposed and rejected. New demands for autonomy, decentralization and participation were put on the agenda of the Left. In the years following, these were joined by demands concerning feminist and gay politics, demands that were fundamentally libertarian, individualist and middle class in origin and aspiration. The new Socialist Party under Mitterrand eventually became the vehicle in the 1970s for that new agenda, and so the 'revolution' of May 1968 was easily appropriated to the reformism of the 1981–6 Socialist government. The working class, though absent from much of these debates, emerged from its PCF ghetto, and its political expression diversified. May 1968 can be seen in one sense as the end of socialism in France, and Mitterrand's historical function as the removal of socialism from the political agenda. The lack of a materialist understanding of the working class, or a truly dialectical theory of ideology, or of a link between intellectuals and workers which a Marxist party might have formed, has led to the current situation: total consensus in political debate around French nationalism (including nuclear testing) and the demands of the market; the PCF with less than 10 per cent of the vote compared with over 20 per cent in 1968, with the gains of the period 1981–3 under serious threat.

This is precisely the trajectory of gay politics. Characteristically, its first expression in France acquired a revolutionary title and project – FHAR (Front Homosexuel d'Action Révolutionnaire): the tactic was theatrical direct action rather than a project for power (indeed it possessed no structure at all). Homosexuals were presented as outsiders in history and thus revolutionary (FHAR, 1971, p. 69), or heterosexuals were seen as the oppressors (p. 76). This is all understandable spontaneity and euphoria, if we recall the context. But FHAR's main contribution was to that medium-term ideological restructuring of the French Left I have described, first in its dialogue with the Trotskyist groups Lutte ouvrière and the Ligue communiste révolutionnaire (see Nicolas, 1977), and then more widely until even the moral/workerist PCF pronounced itself, at the end of the 1970s, in favour of the end to discrimination against homosexuals.[5] The Socialist government's reforms – including equality with heterosexual relations of the age of consent at 15 – make us envious in Britain, but arguably do little for the isolated gay man on a working-class housing estate. They have in fact provoked a demobilization of gay militancy, and a consolidation of gay consumerism.

Of course, if you are convinced that you are the revolutionary party, then life is simpler. From this point of view, it is illuminating to contrast, for example, the theories of *Gay Left* with the practices of one of the few revolutionary groups to have consistently defended gays, since the late 1960s at least. From being a tiny propaganda group at that time which sought to keep alive a Trotskyist analysis of society and revolution, the Spartacist League in the USA responded to the post 1968 agenda of New Left politics, including feminism and gay liberation, by addressing political groups founded in that context and attempting to win them over to Bolshevism. Thus a leftward-leaning Los Angeles gay liberation group, the Red Flag Union (formerly Lavender Red Union) fused with the SL in 1977.[6] In addition, the SL has consistently defended the gay community against aggression, whether it be from the state on questions of lesbian child custody,[7] or police harassment in the wake of the AIDS epidemic in San Francisco,[8] or the resurgent far Right: thus it sought to mobilize not just gays, but trades unionists, Blacks, Jews and Hispanics to defend the Gay Pride march in Chicago on 27 June 1982 against attack from the American Nazi Party.[9] The SL despises the New Left for its supposed limitation of liberation to that of a few middle-class lifestylists, which is particularly ineffective on a political level anyway, given Reagan's presidential victories. However, it has to deal with the agenda set in the late 1960s, especially since it is campaigning in a country with an enormous middle class and a politically backward labour movement. Thus it rejects a politics of symbols and representations in favour of a linking of the defence of 'specially oppressed groups' to 'the social power of the working class'.[10] Its programme, then, is one which, in the manner of the Bolsheviks of 1917, seeks as a priority to establish certain minimum material conditions for 'liberation' to take place for all in society. Sex is thus a private matter, neither to be legislated upon, nor to be pushed to the foreground of a political campaign as one inherently progressive lifestyle.

It has not been the purpose of this essay to pinpoint a specific organization as the way forward, nor even to address the vexed questions of reform versus revolution. I have sought to show that a politics of gay liberation needs to think its way towards a recognition of the following: global factors, endemic in a capitalist economy, which are obstacles to a sexuality that is plural and governed by choice; the material nature of oppression; the need for unity with other groups, but via the working class which still exists and which is still the largest and most powerful group dispossessed by the status quo; the need for intellectuals to recognize the historically-constructed character of their outlook, priorities, and class position. Theoretical work, and the potential for intellectuals to exaggerate its role, is less urgent now.

An acknowledgement of these points might mean, for example, that a housing policy for single gays or couples has to demonstrate to working-class people in general that it is being campaigned for, not against *them*, but against the policies of the Thatcher government and the people it represents. It might mean that our ire at the homophobia of the *Sun* needs to confront patterns of *ownership* in the media rather than the text itself. There is much that is inadequate in the analysis of the US Spartacist League. For those engaged in intellectual work, it is insufficient to speak as they do of cultural forms 'reflecting' or 'flowing from' the structures of capitalism; we know the mediations are more complex. Moreover, we know that the agonies for many of coming out are generated by private internalized meanings as much as material considerations. Nevertheless, in the political impasse of Britain in the late 1980s, it is salutary I think to reaffirm the notion of class against the con-trick of Thatcherite individualism, and to place material change back in the centre of a political project. It is through these global ambitions that we might avoid, through an historically understood humility, the twin pitfalls of self-effacement or the view of gay history as a unique martyrdom.

Notes

1 See, for example, the debates on domestic labour in 1970s socialist feminism, e.g. M. Barrett (1980), *Women's Oppression Today* (London: Verso).

2 Engels, 1940, p. 80. For another discussion of this text, see Lise
   Vogel (1983), 'Engels: a defective formulation', in *Marxism and the
   Oppression of Women: Towards a Unitary Theory* (London: Pluto
   Press, pp. 73–92).
3 *Gay Left* published a very balanced article on Cuba in its first issue:
   K. Birch (1975), 'Gays in Cuba', *Gay Left*, vol. 1 (autumn), pp. 8–9.
4 P. Derbyshire (1980), 'Sects and sexuality: Trotskyism and the
   politics of homosexuality', in Gay Left Collective, pp. 104–15;
   L. Starling (1979), 'Glad to be gay: the gay movement and the Left',
   Socialist Review, vol. 12 (May–June), pp. 23–4. I do not wish to
   enter here into polemics concerning particular parties. The theoretical disagreements I have with Philip Derbyshire's article are
   expressed in my discussion of the USSR.
5 For much fuller discussions of gay politics in France, see: Eric
   Darier (1987), 'The gay movement and French society since 1945',
   Modern & Contemporary France, vol. 29 (March), pp. 10–19;
   Jacques Girard (1981), *Le Mouvement homosexuel en France
   1945–1980* (Paris: Syros).
6 See *Women and Revolution*, vol. 16 (winter 1977–8).
7 'Lesbianism on trial in Texas: Defend Mary Jo Risher', *Women and
   Revolution*, no. 11 (spring 1976), p. 5.
8 'Feinstein: Anti-gay "Sex Cops" to make S. F. safe for the Demo-
   crats: Government out of the baths', *Workers Vanguard*, no. 354
   (11 May 1984), p. 9.
9 '3000 stop Nazis in Chicago, June 27: Labor must defend the rights
   of gays', *Women & Revolution*, no. 25 (winter 1982–3), pp. 8–11.
10 ibid., p. 9.

References

Engels, F. (1940), *The Origin of the Family, Private Property and the
   State* (London: Lawrence & Wishart).
FHAR (1971), *Rapport contre la normalité* (Paris: Champ Libre).
Gay Left Collective (1980), *Homosexuality: Power and Politics*
   (London: Allison & Busby).
Lauritsen, J. and Thorstad, D. (1974), *The Early Homosexual Rights
   Movement (1864–1935)* (New York: Times Change Press).
Lenin, V. (1973), *On Women's Role in Society* (Moscow: Novosti).
Marx, K. (1969), Preface to *A Contribution to the Critique of Political
   Economy*, in *Selected Works*, Vol. 1 (Moscow: Progress Publishers).
Nicolas, J. (1977), 'La Question homosexuelle', *Critique communiste*
   (January), pp. 86–134.

Trotsky, L. (1973), *Women and the Family* (New York: Pathfinder).

Weeks, J. (1973), 'Where Engels feared to tread', *Gay Left*, vol. 1 (autumn), p. 3.

Weeks, J. (1980), 'Capitalism and the organisation of sex', in Gay Left Collective, *op. cit.*

CHAPTER SIXTEEN

A conversation about rock, politics, and gays

with *Tom Robinson*

Shepherd: What work are you doing now?

Robinson: I'm continuing to make records – I've just released my tenth album, over a fifteen-year period. Aside from a mainstream career as a singer-songwriter, you can do individual projects. The one I'm working on at the moment is the theme and incidental music for a TV show. I'm trying my hand at that so I can see what area I can move into with dignity in the coming years. It's composing music that's useful to people rather than music that's to your own greater good.

Shepherd: The great attraction of songs is precisely that you can put your own text into them. Making incidental music you literally silence the voice.

Robinson: Only in order to heighten and support the voice of the narrative. A well-made film with music has a very powerful voice ...

Wallis: Why did you start doing openly gay songs?

Robinson: In 1973 I moved to London and came out that year at the age of 23. I joined a band called Café Society which was not gay, and did quite a lot of voluntary work (such as Gay Switchboard) which was. I joined the Campaign for Homosexual Equality because the Gay Liberation Front by then didn't have the same campaigning activities – and I thought it would be possible to change CHE from within. On the side from Café Society I assembled a set of songs to perform at benefits. These were rather self-consciously gay, making an issue of homosexuality itself – a bit like James Brown's 'Say it Loud I'm Black and I'm Proud'.

Around 1976 it began to occur to me that I could achieve more as a lone wolf, concentrating on my musical career as a gay performer, rather than by working in a mainstream organization like CHE or answering the phones at Gay Switchboard. Mind you, without a number of lucky breaks and a hit record in 1977 it's debatable whether that would have been the right decision. I'd been inspired by a number of earlier gay singer-songwriters who hadn't hit a wider commercial market – people like Chris Robison in the States, who made an album called *I'm looking for a boy tonight*. Steven Grossman (not to be confused with Stephan) also did an album of slightly wimpy acoustic guitar ballads on Mercury called *Caravan Tonight* – the first gay record I heard of on a major label in the early 1970s. It was followed in Britain by an LP on Decca from Robert Campbell, who wrote the music for Gay Sweatshop's play *Stone*. Robert had some first-rate gay songs, but Decca buried the album with poor promotion – he might as well not have written them.

Shepherd: Did Decca bury it because of his sexuality?

Robinson: Absolutely not ... merely through incompetence. They were quite happy to have a track called 'Dreamboy' opening the album. For me, being labelled 'the first openly gay singer-songwriter' (as opposed to bisexual Bowie) has proved both an accolade and a curse. But in fact it's simply untrue. I was merely the first one to get a record in the Top 20.

Wallis: What was it about for you? Was it self-expression or creating an environment that could give a positive image for other gay people? You've talked of other gay singer-songwriters that you could latch on to.

Robinson: It was really important to hear those other people. I have Peter Burton to thank for that – he wrote a well-researched article on gay rock'n'roll for *Gay News*. He also sent me an LP by Lewis Furey, which included songs like 'The Hustler's Tango': 'You say you want to rape me, rape me b-b-baby . . . First you know you've gotta gotta pay pay . . .' Fantastic. Those songs showed me you could do it any number of ways.

   It's useful to have started out with a song like 'Glad to be Gay' because it stated 'This is where I stand'. Having said it, there was no need to keep re-stating it – 'Son of Glad to be Gay' or 'Glad to be Gay Strikes Back'. I originally wrote it for the 1976 Gay Pride rally, strictly for internal consumption. But once I'd founded the (modestly named) Tom Robinson Band, the song found its way into our set almost by accident. We tried it out at one or two pub gigs, and straight audiences loved it. It's sort of stuck ever since.

Shepherd: When the breaks came, was there a problem about the sexuality in the songs or did they happen because of the sexuality? Did your breaks bear any relation to your singing out-gay songs?

Robinson: If it hadn't been for the punk movement I'd probably still be working on Gay Switchboard and singing in folk bars in the evenings. Up to 1976, big record companies were able to dictate what would become successful. When punk happened it shook their foundations and they had no idea what would happen next. So they listened to Elvis Costello and Ian Dury, who'd been dismissed earlier as a has-been. Musicians like myself, who were practically ten years older than the punks, got a listen. At that point just being gay was grist to the mill. I can't say the gimmick didn't help.

Shepherd: Did you then experience being trapped as *the* out-gay singer-songwriter ?

Robinson: Yes, but I'm not sure it's related to one's sexuality. Julie Andrews has got trapped into being Mary Poppins. Although it's become patently apparent there's a serious actress in there trying to get out, the public won't let her be anything but Mary Poppins. I have at times felt like a gay Mary Poppins.

Shepherd: Does that pressure come from the record industry, record buyers or the gay scene?

Robinson: The first two certainly, but on the whole I've found the established gay scene to be more or less indifferent to my music. Basically you follow your taste in music rather than the sexual preferences of the performer. I might go *once* to the Coliseum to see an opera based on a gay theme, but I wouldn't keep going because I don't like the music. As a group, gays don't like rock 'n' roll. It's rock'n'roll fans who have bought my records.

Wallis: Is it a generational problem, in the sense that the gays who are most out tend to be the younger post-rock generation?

Robinson: Ten years ago it was the other way round. TRB's audience was mostly young, but even then there wasn't a huge gay presence at our gigs in the way there was at, say, Bette Midler concerts. She could crack jokes with gay references and get ripples of laughter in the audience. I've never had that kind of mass gay following.

Wallis: What about the sorts of images that the post-punk pop industry presents? Have you got views on the ways sexuality and homosexuality figure?

Robinson: It seems that implication is preferable to out-right statement. You can cross-dress, you can sing really sleazy lyrics, but don't state openly what that's all about. It's got to be tongue-in-cheek — but that was always so. Liberace got away with it for years because he never said he was gay. People loved him because he was fantastically camp.

Shepherd: Image can be chic and exciting without being political. As long as it remains just image, it's tolerable. Things like Depeche Mode playing around with their master–servant stuff. Who knows what they're really into.

Robinson: Whether a direct political statement is necessarily *better* is open to debate.

Wallis: The imagery can be merely naturalized, which would be good.

Robinson: The more liberation you can spread further, the better. The Redskins have a really solid message, but that limits them in terms of being heard on North American radio or the Italian charts. David Bowie waters the message down and gets heard from one end of the earth to the other. When Bowie came up with *Hunky Dory* fifteen years ago, I knew what he was talking about and it affected my life in an enormous way. Had that message been stronger, and not broadcast on the radio, I'd never have heard it.

Shepherd: One's caught between singing something which is flexible enough to be interpreted in different ways, on one hand, and, on the other, making it so direct there's no two ways about it. Like all the fuss about Frankie Goes to Hollywood's 'Relax'.

Robinson: That was a remarkable song.

Shepherd: But they went on to deny being gay.

Robinson: Same as the Village People. It's the standard pattern. Even the Pet Shop Boys ...

Wallis: Presumably pressure to deny comes from anxiety about career in the industry.

Robinson: It's a common syndrome. What made Frankie attractive at the start was that they didn't give a fuck. Their mimed live show at Heaven was outrage, pure and simple. Or on *The Tube* with motorcycles, chains, women in bondage. 'Ideologically sound' – bollocks! 'Good taste' – bollocks! And that was what was appealing about them. There was a sense of liberation in the fuck-you attitude. The record managed to encapsulate that – it was *the* definitive sex record. Then megabucks beckoned, they were invited over to the States and told to drop all the gay crap. And the three members of the band who weren't gay suddenly got choosy. They didn't respect what it was that people liked about them. They thought people bought the record because they were great musicians. The most exciting thing in pop music is when risks are taken, which is why the Sex Pistols were more important than Barry Manilow. If I had to criticize my own career in recent years it would be for a lack of risk taking.

Shepherd: Where does the stopping taking risks come from? Do you get complacent, or stop realizing which risks to take, or do you experience pressure?

Robinson: You can take the wrong risks. When TRB fell apart under the pressure, I formed a band called Sector 27. Paradoxically, the safe route would have been to carry on doing songs about – I don't know, Nicaragua, Stalinism,

Gay Oppression ... At that time there was clearly a market for more of the same, so the natural career move was to continue. But I took a risk and ditched the whole thing – refused to play any more political songs during those few years. It didn't pay off.

Shepherd: Why did you decide not to sing political songs?

Robinson: With TRB I'd been accused of exploiting politics to bolster an otherwise pedestrian musical talent. Sector 27 was an attempt to work back up from scratch on purely musical merits. But people had fixed expectations, good or bad: it proved impossible to start afresh as a new and exciting band when the singer had only recently been famous for something different.

It was only after a few years of pop oblivion that 'War Baby' finally re-established my career. That song entailed a different kind of risk: certainly if I'd been consciously trying to write a comeback single it wouldn't have been as personal as that. Luckily it was successful. It's hard to keep taking on challenges. Most performers seem to gradually clean up their act and get tamer over the years – Iggy Pop, Lou Reed, Bowie, etc. One exception is John Lydon, who has never cleaned up or cashed in: the Sex Pistols would have been bigger (and blander) than Genesis by now if they'd stayed together.

Shepherd: Can risks still be taken about where you perform and who you perform to? Is it possible to develop a different sort of audience, different expectations, depending on where you choose to perform? You recently did a concert at Riverside Studios (in London). That potentially positions you as a certain sort of performer.

Robinson: The frame you put around the picture affects the nature of the performance. A couple of days before I performed at Riverside I did a ghastly Radio 1 disco at

Uxbridge – miming. It's the lowest form of crowd-pleasing. But it's not often you can afford to pick and choose where you play. One of my projects alongside my main career is to do cabaret shows at the Edinburgh Festival Fringe. The Riverside gig was a descendant of that. It's what *The Independent* was pleased to call 'after-dinner entertainment' – badinage and story-telling, not relying on the bombast of a rock group. You can make more subtle points, like doing an AIDS song after Noel Coward's 'Marvellous Party' juxtaposed with Martin Amis's quote about the party being over for gays.

Wallis: When 'Glad to be Gay' was out it was important simply to be out-gay. Now there's a distinct reaction happening. One of the important things is the connection between different liberation groups in terms of an analysis of the state and the way it works. Do you see your rock production having a distinctive role there?

Robinson: I've never analysed it in those terms. It's always difficult using your career as a political instrument because it's also your bread and butter. You get an offer to play a May Ball at Reading University: the fact that you're being paid £2,000 for a night's work and you haven't been paid anything for the last month will affect your decision. Whether or not doing that gig at that time in that place to that audience will have a political effect tends not to get thought about. But it might do. It might be that Gay Soc. at Reading University is besieged at the time, or that it is the dominant voice. When you arrive, you can have little idea what the atmosphere is. A little incident may happen during the performance – someone may shout 'fucking poof' – and if you challenge them, that becomes part of the point. In New York I stopped the show and turned the spotlight on a heckler. If you can unite an audience to cheer against a heckler, you've done something for them – they've had a chance to unite in a voice. That stuff the heckler mouths is in their collective unconscious. If you challenge it you can highlight what you're talking about far more effectively than you can in a song.

Shepherd: What do you think of political initiatives like Red Wedge? What was it like being on the tour? Was it useful or supportive? Or were you getting the same old audiences?

Robinson: It was useful in two ways. First, that Top 40 performers, people not noted for political commitment, stood up to be counted. The shows were reported, people noticed the bands who were playing, and it made them think about where they stood. That was useful to some extent. Second, the main function of Red Wedge concerts in my view is not to convert but to make an act of solidarity. Local supporters and socialists, feeling ground down by years of Tory rule, find themselves with 2,000 other people who feel exactly the same. The performers act as a parabolic mirror to focus that energy back at the crowd. People come out of the show with a sense of uplift, and the real good is done by them arguing the case on a one-to-one basis in the town for weeks afterwards.

Wallis: Do you think there'll have to be a Red Wedge tour for lesbians and gays? Would you ever get the bands to do it?

Robinson: I doubt we'll ever be that popular a minority. Homosexuality still stirs up all kinds of dark irrational fears and taboos, and for some people 'lesbians' and 'gays' will always reside in their category of bogeymen ... bogeypersons. We've barely achieved tolerance for our existence – let alone the wider goals of equality and liberation. Local councils attempting measures to ban heterosexism in schools seems like sending an expeditionary force to blow up a few bridges in Berlin before you've even got off the beaches at Normandy.

Wallis: Did you think it was tactically mistaken?

Robinson: It's just so far in advance of the main body of opinion. A premature strike on the enemy heartland by a handful of saboteurs would only alert Hitler to our main forces crawling ashore in France. Which is precisely what's happened: the opposition are massing their battalions to push us back into the fucking sea. That's the trouble with ghetto consciousness. When you only work within your own group—and I've done this myself—you breathe a rarefied kind of oxygen. It doesn't necessarily relate to the reality outside.

Wallis: Can we relate that to Red Wedge – to what extent were you required, silently or directly, not to be too obviously out?

Robinson: Not in the least. It's funny how the issues of racism and homosexuality do tie up. Junior Giscombe got some racist shit off a Billy Bragg supporter in Liverpool. Junior stopped and confronted the bloke. Subsequent performers who went out were all a bit more on edge. I went out and did 'Glad to be Gay' solo, with acoustic guitar. I held it in place by sheer will-power. The other performers said they were really glad I did that song.

Shepherd: And the response of the audience?

Robinson: They went crazy, loved it. Because they knew somebody earlier had been pushed into saying 'Hey look, I live – don't deny me my right to be who I am.' So the crowd was right for 'Glad to be Gay'. Red Wedge was right-on as far as that goes.

Wallis: You can win that battle with Red Wedge: but it's difficult to win the same one in the Labour Party?

Robinson: Absolutely. Each time a senior Labour politician endorses gay rights loudly and unequivocally, they lose some votes. It's a fact. You want the Labour Party to

come into power because if there's another Tory government after this one we've all had it. You want Labour to
come into power by any means, yet you want gay rights. Do
you shut up till they're in power, or do you ensure it gets
into the manifesto, and risk them never coming to power?
Ken Livingstone is great because he's clear about this. He's
been smeared with his support for gay rights, yet he gets ten
to one letters from people offering their support as a result.

Shepherd: That's the argument for speaking out clearly.

Robinson: But it's not clear-cut. I'm appalled when
right-on lesbians and gays refuse to vote Labour simply
because they disagree with Kinnock. That's another
example of the rarefied atmosphere.

Wallis: It's possible to get demoralized. We're feeling
exhausted because of the lack of support from the leadership – we've been queer-bashed by the leadership.

Robinson: But not in the same sense that the present
government is queer-bashing us. Lack of support from
Labour versus active persecution under the Tories is the
real issue. There's more at stake than gay pride: what about
pensioners, hospitals, schools, the unemployed ... For
God's sake let's just get that bloody woman out.

Wallis: Rather than council initiatives, would it have
been more useful if lesbian and gay performers had started
coming out?

Robinson: Well, the media can help a lot by showing
people who simply happen to be lesbian or gay – whose
homosexuality is merely incidental. The more mundane it
becomes, the better. In that sense an episode of *Brookside*,
however stereotyped, may achieve as much as a hundred
meetings of Haringey Council – though, of course, those

are crucial as well. The important thing is: if we disagree with the way others on our own side are fighting, it's up to us to do something better rather than waste energy attacking them. In-fighting is so destructive: all that energy needs directing outwards, against our real enemies. There's no shortage of them at the moment.

CHAPTER SEVENTEEN

Gramsci-the-goalie: Reflections in the bath on gays, the Labour Party and socialism

Mick Wallis

Voices on steam radio

January 1988. Clause 28 is being debated on the radio. A media presenter chairs a discussion between someone from the Arts Council and a sponsor of the Clause. The fear is that the arts will be censored – no more Orton, *Normal Heart* and (who knows) *Edward II*. The ministerial assurance is that mere *presentation* of homosexuality is of course allowable; only its *promotion* is not. Neither presenter nor arts bureaucrat asks, 'why *not* promotion?'

The answer to the unasked question is, of course, that homosexuality is 'against public policy'. It would not be put that way in such an interview. It is simply stated that rate-payers have a right to see their money spent decently. The question 'why *not* promotion?' is not asked because the response is foreseen. To untangle the knot so tightly tied between consumer choice and the policy of rulers would distract from the immediate issue. To the presenter and the bureaucrat the knot maybe doesn't even appear.

The question is unasked. The goal posts have been

moved. 'Public policy' is to be further enshrined in law. There is to be an official consensus that homosexual people are less valuable (though in certain circumstances mentionable) human beings than heterosexual ones. Seemingly (on the evidence of steam radio) without protest. Why?

Tactics, of course. The Arts Lobby and other organizations are working for the best result in the given circumstances. We have the most reactionary British government in most living memories, with a thumping majority of parliamentary seats and – so the tabloids tell us – a popular mandate. To stand out against the Clause wholesale would be to risk everything. So for the time being, at least, don't ask the question – though maybe you can hint at it.

You hint by warning that something more than merely *preventing promotion* lurks behind the Clause. You warningly detect a whiff of the Third Reich. It seems to imply that homosexual people themselves are to be assaulted. If this is not the direct purpose of the Clause, then it is so imprecisely worded as to be interpretable in such a way. At least tighten the wording, then, so that the rights of homosexual people will be protected. And in return, we will not ask the question (here), 'why *not* promotion?' Our right to remain an inferior subspecies in private is valuable to us, you see.

... Which is partly (but only partly) to misrepresent the tactics. Lesbians' and gays' very social, cultural and political organizations are under threat. The Tories want to wipe out the institutions we have sweated blood for years to build for our protection, just as they are trying to break the trades unions, even to stifle any residual press freedom. Most people opposing the Clause knew what it was they were defending – the future means to fight back for our freedoms. The campaign literature geared to the lesbian and gay communities and the labour movement was clear on this. But elsewhere the goal-posts had been moved –

what follows is to rehearse a little of what most of us also
know – the how, and the why of their moving.

Tactics done with. Now for betrayal.

If I use the term 'steam radio' it is partly to indicate the
apparent marginality of the medium to the culture of the
1980s. Especially since by 'radio' I mean Radio 4. But as
one who aspires to the creative arts, I am also attempting a
figure of speech. I listen to the radio in the bath. Perhaps it
(the figure of speech) is a synecdoche? I doubt it.

Listening in the bath in the provinces, where reception is
not always at its best, sometimes *forces* you (one) to listen
to programmes you (one) would rather give a miss. *Any
Questions* is one (one) of them.

The panel on this day in January 1988 includes Junior
Health Minister Currie and a Labour MP. This week, some
nurses have taken token strike action in defence of the
NHS, and a recorder (judge) has resigned after the *Sun* –
with the help of a blackmailer – has exposed him as a
homosexual. There is a question about each of these.

Currie is against striking nurses, obviously. The Labour
politician supports the nurses, obviously. But support the
strike? Ah, well now ... The Labour parliamentarian
cannot bring herself to argue for the nurses' right to strike.
She argues very properly that any blame in the matter
should attach to those responsible for the state of the NHS
the nurses are struggling to cope with. But her argument is
predicated on the assumption that, in general, *nurses
should not strike*. The goal-posts have been moved.

There is in fact some consensus in the matter of the judge.
All are pretty much agreed that it is *unfair* for him to be
forced in this way to consider resigning. Currie, of course,
manages to bring in AIDS, and the Labour politician tells
her off for saying (for the umpteenth time) that it is a
'homosexual' disease (mostly heterosexuals are affected in
Africa). I top up with hot water the better to wallow in my
feeling of reassurance.

And then the Labour speaker develops her thesis. She urges that we all know that things we disapprove of, or wouldn't do ourselves, go on. It would be hypocritical to pretend otherwise. There *is* a problem, though, when these things are thrust before the public in such a way. Perhaps the unfortunate man has been put in an impossible position, robbed of the public's trust. *Private* lives should be protected from such scrutiny.

So the assumption that homosexuality should be private, that it is and will be distasteful to 'the public' goes unchallenged. It is not even a question. The *Sun* and other blackmailers can carry on. The goal-posts have been moved. Two betrayals in two questions.

... But no, not betrayal. That's unfair. Probably shrill. The word I am grasping for is not 'betrayal' – it is *Gramsci*. No, not an Italian footballer – but the Communist that Mussolini threw into jail to 'stop that brain working for twenty years'. Him. The Labour Party have discovered Gramsci.

The way it goes is this. Gramsci pointed out that rulers rule not only by direct power but also by assent. Coming to, and staying in, power requires that you also win the minds of the people. This is especially relevant when what you want to do doesn't seem automatically to appeal to large sectors of the population. You have to create a climate of progressive opinion that will favour the changes you want to make, which while benefiting specific groups of people in the short term, will thereby transform the whole system to the general benefit of future generations. Damned simple, isn't it?

Well, it *was* simple. What Gramsci had in mind (wasn't it?) was the problem of a division of interests between regional and occupational groups of Italians that was forestalling their union against a common system of oppression. Also, a little differently, the use the Bolsheviks made of non-proletarian progressives in winning power for a small and infant Russian working class.

The Labour Party are a little aware of having lost the

ideological initiative to the Tories. This means they have to persuade the 'haves' (as they have it) that it would be jolly good to help out the 'have nots' (who indeed haven't, have they?). The best way to do this, of course, is to find out what people are thinking these days, and start from there. One of the ways to do this, apparently, is to tour the country listening to people. 'Labour Listens', as the campaigning cry was in January 1988.

Ah! A slight problem. If rulers rule partly by assent and all that, won't 'people' largely be thinking in a sort of, um, *ruled* way? Might it just be worth arguing for fresh ideas rather than passively responding to things as they are? Setting an agenda rather than reading somebody else's? (Funnily enough Labour conferences have come up with some jolly good ideas in recent years.) And, anyway, are you sure you know who you're listening *to*? You see, the problem with the existing 'public' agenda is that the oppressed (to use a quaint and embarrassingly old-fashioned term) don't appear on it – except as extremists, that is, when it's planned to scrap unions in the NHS and elsewhere, beat down the conditions of the unemployed still further, restrict women's rights to control their own bodies, legalize queer-bashing...

I'm getting us into a terrible muddle, and (yes I know) it's because I started off making things far too simple. I should have admitted at the start that there are in fact *two* Gramscis. One was an Italian Communist who wanted radically to transform Italy (and the world), to liberate the oppressed and expropriate the expropriators. The other one is a goal-keeper. Only the posts keep moving.

It's funny to reflect that after the 1985 and 1986 National Labour Party Conference votes in favour of action (action) on lesbian and gay rights, various organized queers in the party tried to get Labour to Listen to them (by 'Labour' I mean, of course, the leader's machine). Only Labour didn't. It refused even to meet the queers, until the queers got shrill (as queers do) around election time.

Naughty old queers. They were spoiling the game for Gramsci-the-goalie.

An everyday tale of Nottinghamshire folk

At the start of 1986, both Nottingham City and Nottinghamshire County Councils were Labour-controlled. Both had made manifesto promises on lesbian and gay rights. Promises, promises. A manifesto (written more or less democratically by the local party) was one thing. What councillors would do with it was another.

In October 1986, 700 people marched through some appallingly wet and windy Nottingham backstreets (we accepted the police's route: some suspected them of arranging the weather too) against Nottinghamshire's *discriminatory* 'equal opportunities' provision. It had had to be wrung from them in the first place. It was drastically underfunded. And it specifically *excluded* lesbians and gays.

There were two main responses from the majority of the Labour councillors who resisted our demands for a Lesbian and Gay Working Group. One was that homosexuals did not suffer discrimination, were not oppressed. The other was that they indulged in filthy and corrupting habits and children should be protected from them. Frequently, these two responses issued from the same lips in the same breath. And there was, of course, the occasional 'friendly' voice that regretted that 'the public' was not yet ready for such licence.

The reasons for the county's refusal to set up a working group were clearly complex, contradictory and commonplace. There was the fear of a closeted but powerful man at County Hall that he might be 'exposed' and so lose respect and thus power. There was straightforward homophobia: plenty of it. And also, of course, there was that genuine perception that prevailing 'public' attitudes run counter to lesbian/gay rights: Gramsci-the-goalie again. Many even of the sympathetic minority could not (or rather, would not) see that public attitudes are constructed and so capable of political transformation.

The county's refusal also resulted from institutional racism. One Asian councillor was prominent in his four-square opposition to lesbian and gay representation: all the more prominent because he was himself powerfully inserted into the 'equal opportunities' machinery. He said homosexuality was offensive to his community – though he didn't say what the lesbians and gays in his community thought about it.

The man is not racist. He is racism's obedient product. The white male politicians who run the county – fondly known as 'the Mansfield mafia' – would never prioritize Black rights. It would be unpopular with many of the racists they depend on for their power. The money squeezed out of them for 'minority development' was miniscule, and would have to be fought over – so long as nobody fought for more. Aslam (the councillor) fought his corner. Projects he favoured grew, others did not: his power and influence grew, as did *competition* between ethnic groups. In Notts as elsewhere, the whites continue to divide and to rule.

I'm being parochial, I know. But what goes for our parish has gone on in many more. And you may not be gay, dear reader, or not be used to labourism's frustrations. Or you may be either or both and a glutton for punishment. So read on if you will.

Besides, this is not *all* parish news. Councillor Aslam's fame soon spread much wider. Sharon Atkin, the Black socialist chosen by Nottingham East Constituency Labour Party to win their seat for Labour in the general election of June 1987 committed an indiscretion. She let slip the fact that racism is as ingrained in the Labour Party as in every other nook and cranny of this country's institutions. And she supported Black Sections. Labour's National Executive, the leader's machine, got shot of her and imposed their own candidate. And who better to step into her shoes than a divisive and homophobic careerist?

To complain of this at election time, especially as a queer, was to stand accused of being petty, sectional and immature. We were spoiling Labour's chances by talking about small issues or about extremist ones. No, no Mr Kinnock. We were talking about the safety of our lives.

What could be said of Nottinghamshire in the mid 1980s could be said of so many Labour councils across the country – including Nottingham City. Things didn't develop so badly there – at first. In April 1985 a Lesbian and Gay subcommittee was indeed set up. Activists stirred enthusiasm, and precious hours, days, months were devoted to devising plans, preparing papers . . . to minimum effect.

The naffs in power were terrified of managing the 'monster' socialists had brought into being. Open hostility from monopoly press, organized far-right, and non-socialists in the Labour group encouraged the leadership to bend to public prejudice and private fear. Basic papers on victimless crimes and non-oppressive working environments were blocked before they reached the agenda. The lesbian demand for a separate subcommittee outraged councillors who thought they had given the queers enough rope. The council couldn't even provide swimming sessions without drowning in confusion.

Bets were, in pessimistic quarters, that a new Labour administration would scrap the subcommittees. Labour lost the May election, so the Tories did it for them. The anti-union *Nottingham Evening Post* carped that 'moderate' Nottingham had had enough of 'London' politics. The paper that sought Sharon Atkin's demise had also heralded the advent of the Moderate Labour Party in January by bannering 'BACKLASH!' and printing their manifesto in full. The MLP set out to become a national alternative to the Labour Party, standing against their candidates. The

Post promised that in their Nottingham home, they would 'sweep the board in May . . .'.

As it happens, they didn't win a single seat. They *did* scrape up enough votes to convert a few Labour marginals into Tory ones. What the press claimed as evidence for the end of the Notts Left in fact signalled its gathering strength. Left candidates in Nottingham's Park Ward came to within three votes of unseating a safe Tory. Socialists in Mansfield could still claim the bulk of the 'traditional' Labour vote while attracting new support. If damage was being done, it was by the routed Right.

The MLP met its demise in its proposed heartland – UDM country. The 'Union of Democratic Mineworkers' had set itself up as an alternative to the National Union of Mineworkers during the long strike of 1984–5. Collaborating with Coal Board bosses in defeating the strike and dismantling the industry, it has since learnt the logical result of its actions: the closure of Mansfield colliery, its organizational hub, hitherto supposed to be safe from cuts in return for the UDM's compliant attitude.

The MLP was to be the 'political wing' of the UDM. It was the unsuccessful project of ex-Labour right-wingers to find a fresh political base after deselection. Its politics were inane. But its right-ward march set the agenda for too many Labour authorities, and was able to while the logic of Gramsci-the-goalie persisted.

The MLP spoke with the voice of the *Daily Express* and the new Tory Right. It invented an idea of 'ordinary people' and then claimed to fight for them against 'outsiders'. It put the dove and the rose – value-laden symbols wrenched from other contexts – into the melting pot with the language of fascism.

Clearly, the MLP was not fascist. But it was part of the development of right-wing populism that will usher in something very like fascism unless it is opposed. Its motto was 'All That is Required for Evil to Triumph is That Good People Do Nothing'. Evil was 'the strident militant policies of the Labour Party', now seeking a new base in 'vociferous fringe groups – like the Campaign for Homosexual Equality [CHE], lesbians, and so-called ethnic groups'. 'Dedicated faceless people' would usher in a 'Marxist regime' to rob local people 'who work extremely hard for their living'.

Perhaps the MLP was enough out of touch with the real world to imagine CHE really was running the Labour Party. They certainly were in touch in claiming that Labour nationally had lost contact with the working class, and that local Labour was bureaucratic.

The UDM grew from the soil of state capitalist decline, manured in Notts by decades of a corrupt labourism characterized by personal ambition and a steel grip on the party machine. The MLP and UDM offered the same personnel and politics to *cure* the situation as *created* it.

And hiding their real interests and pasts required the construction of bogeys: faceless people, Scargill, Londoners, Marxists, 'so-called ethnic minorities', lesbians, gays. Real working-class frustrations, suffering and fears, capitalism's characteristic products, gave energy to a deadly fiction about their actual cause. 'Notts people' and 'ordinary people' were offered a retreat into self-protection from a myth, rather than self-organization against the real enemy.

Ordinary Notts lesbians, gays, trade unionists, Blacks and Asians recognized what this meant for them. Their interests would be discarded. They might rock the boat that straight white male careerists had sailed over Notts people for decades. And as one section of the old Labour establishment viciously clung to a position it was being prised from, another shrunk into a no-policies vacuum to protect itself from Right and Left. Queer-bashing suited them both.

Just one of the targets of the UDM was the Haringey Lesbian and Gay Unit. The scab 'union' sent down material support to the religious bigots and vicious reactionaries who were stirring up hatred and confusion. The unit was

promoting the idea that lesbian and gay people suffer
discrimination and should be protected from this. They
were promoting the idea that lesbians and gays should have
equal rights with straight people. They were promoting the
idea that our political administrations (local councils) have
a *duty* to defend the rights of all citizens. Which is to say
they were promoting homosexuality on the rates. The unit
was attacked by the *Sun*, the scab union and the Labour
leadership. And, of course, the same leadership *supported*
Clause 28 in its early stages.

During our Notts campaign, we won the paper support
of many labour movement organizations and individuals.
But, as many commented on the day, that only rarely
included a turn-out with the banner to march with the
queers. Such support would undoubtedly have been much
more forthcoming in January 1988 – partly as a result of
such demonstrations themselves. Unlike the Labour Party
leadership, the rank-and-file of the labour movement,
having seen the support of lesbians and gays for the miners,
for people threatened with deportation like Viraj Mendis,
and for *dozens* of specific struggles up and down the
country – and having seen, too, the unprecedented attacks
being made on us – recognize at last that we have a
common struggle. And thousands more lesbians and gays
recognize this, too.

Promoting AIDS

In January 1988 'Britain' hosted a world health conference
on AIDS. It is supremely ironical that this conference
should be held in the country that has done most to
promote AIDS within its own shores. It needs no rehearsing
that while the HIV virus in Britain was principally confined
to – and rapidly spreading within – the gay population, the
government maintained a screaming silence about the
disease. At that time, too, the loyal opposition did nothing

to challenge that silence. While AIDS killed queers, Latins and Africans it might as well not have existed.

I went to a marvellous party. In the winter of 1985–6. A leather-queens' thrash in a Nottinghamshire village. There I met a man who was at that time typical of *many thousands*. He was too frightened to buy a gay magazine and therefore unable to obtain (by mail order, the only way anonymous enough) condoms suitable for anal sex. So he was keeping his fingers crossed. Not many months previously, he would have had next to no inkling about 'safer sex' whatsoever. (I thrust condoms upon him, and later we had sex, which was fun.)

That man's life was being put at risk by the government. The same government, we remember, that tried to *stifle* the Terrence Higgins Trust and other anti-AIDS organizations that were 'promoting homosexuality'. The Tory government's silence and inaction over AIDS, their assaults on gay organizations, and the Labour opposition's *complicity* in the silence, inaction and assaults, *promoted AIDS*.

AIDS has been the greatest single emergency Western gay men have had to face. It has been a 'natural' catastrophe, taking a heavy toll of lives and producing extensive fear and misery. It has also been the occasion for a redoubled assault on gay men by reactionary individuals, media, political parties and state institutions.

The AIDS emergency has also been a source of strength for some gay men, as they have had to face this double emergency. Many of us have for the first time seen the need for and logic of organization *as gay men*, for mutual care and mutual protection. Many have seen clearly for the first time the logic *for the state* of pushing the urgent needs of gay men to the boundaries of its concerns, while using a disease to mythologize gay sexuality as being itself diseased.

There are two related and interdependent myths. One is that gay men brought AIDS upon themselves. When in

January 1988 Currie said that Clause 28 had been motivated by 'people's fear of AIDS' she was of course being
economical with the truth. Clause 28 had nothing to do
with AIDS. The *use* made of AIDS meanwhile had a lot to
do with what has also motivated Clause 28.

The other myth, accepted by too many gay men, is that
by *promoting homosexuality* we have gone too far, and in
fact brought Clause 28 on our own heads. The notion is
that 'public opinion' was not (and maybe never will be)
ready for such a thing. Maybe more of us need to learn with
confidence that while 'public opinion' is a reality, it is a
reality that can be changed. It would help, of course, if the
Labour Party also thought that way.

Round about the time of the marvellous party I met an old
friend doing AIDS counselling work in Manchester. He
talked about the rapid politicization that was taking place
among formerly 'conservative' gay men (who had felt snug
enough in the ghetto, very properly valued it as one of the
few safe and sociable spaces in their lives). Some white men
were for the first time *recognizing* racism when they saw
what immigration officials were doing to Blacks from parts
of Africa especially affected by AIDS.

The ghetto was changing, dissolving and spreading under
other pressures anyway. Other safe and sociable places
were being found in addition to the few pubs and clubs
(though *not* very rapidly outside the metropolitan centres).
The AIDS crisis and our response to it sped this process.
Our culture and our politics broadened. In January 1988
Clause 28 was sharpening our politics as we defended our
culture and possibly our lives.

As general outcry gathered against the Clause, the
Labour leadership came coyly to the fold, eventually to
denounce it in the most vigorous terms – but mainly in
private, of course. Press releases selectively to the *gay* press
and forthright speeches *within* the immediate context of
labour movement institutions did nothing to promote the

progress of the wider political position. Consenting thus in private, Kinnock and Co. did two things. They revealed how far they were behind those they claim to be leading. And they confirmed their fear of 'public opinion', their subservience to an agenda set by reactionaries.

In both this and the joke of 'Labour Listens', the Kinnock machine revealed their contempt for the actual opinions of many of the oppressed, and their refusal (or inability) to form and promote analyses and programmes that might counter oppression. It was well known, indeed, that the suitable questions to be asked the peripatetic 'Listeners' by the party faithful were themselves carefully defined.

Through our concrete struggles some of our perceptions have changed and new connections been made. Perhaps sentimentally (I am, as you will remember, a Radio 4 listener), it's sometimes possible to feel that our building of practical solidarity and common perspectives with others in struggle – together, that is, with the 'public' promotion of those perspectives – might be one of the many sources of what the Communist Gramsci might have called a new socialist hegemony.

But it will have had nothing to do with Gramsci-the-goalie. He, of course, has secretly been playing for the other side all along.

Index